MW00561809

JOB MOVES

JOB
MOVES

9 STEPS
FOR MAKING PROGRESS
IN YOUR CAREER

ETHAN BERNSTEIN,
MICHAEL B. HORN,
BOB MOESTA

HARPER
BUSINESS
An Imprint of HarperCollins*Publishers*

HarperCollins books may be purchased for educational, business, or sales
promotional use. For information, please email the Special Markets Department
at SPsales@harpercollins.com.

FIRST EDITION

Designed by Bonni Leon-Berman
Illustrations by Luke Newell

Library of Congress Cataloging-in-Publication Data

Names: Bernstein, Ethan, author. | Horn, Michael B., author. |
Moesta, Robert, 1964- author.
Title: Job moves : 9 steps for making progress in your career / Ethan
Bernstein, Michael B. Horn, Bob Moesta.
Description: First edition. | New York, NY : Harper Business,
an imprint of HarperCollins Publishers, [2024] |
Includes bibliographical references and index.
Identifiers: LCCN 2024025103 (print) | LCCN 2024025104 (ebook) |
ISBN 9780063283589 (hardcover) | ISBN 9780063283596 (ebook)
Subjects: LCSH: Career development. | Career changes.
Classification: LCC HF5381 .B3765 2024 (print) | LCC HF5381 (ebook) |
DDC 331.702--dc23/eng/20240710
LC record available at https://lccn.loc.gov/2024025103
LC ebook record available at https://lccn.loc.gov/2024025104

24 25 26 27 28 LBC 5 4 3 2 1

To all the individuals struggling to make progress in their careers, now and in the future, including those in our homes and hearts:

Marty
Mary
Henry
Susie
Kayla
Madison
Covell
*Clayton**

---

* Including both Claytons, small and tall

CONTENTS

Introduction
A NEW APPROACH TO YOUR CAREER

If you're here, you're probably looking to make a job move. So what's holding you back?

Maybe you're feeling frustrated or disengaged in your current role but hesitant to leave what you know. Maybe you've been out of the workforce—by choice or by circumstance—and you're looking to get back in but haven't yet found the right next thing. Maybe you've recently switched jobs but already suspect that where you landed wasn't the best next step—or that making your old role work would've been the better move.

You're not alone.

Every year an estimated 1 billion people switch jobs worldwide. Most regret at least some aspect of the process. Yes, a lucky few stumble seamlessly upon their dream jobs, but this book is for the rest of us—those who are experiencing some career struggle. We originally wanted to call this book "Hire Your Next Job," given that a successful job move isn't just about an organization hiring you to do something. It also involves *you* hiring an organization so you can accomplish things. But that title didn't resonate with others. Rather, employers are typically treated, and tend to behave, as though they hold most of the cards. That's remained true even after the COVID-19 pandemic sparked the Great Resignation and more than 98 million Americans left their jobs over a period of two years, the highest quit rate in US history. Far too many people, nearly 60 percent, remain frozen in jobs they "quietly quit." When individuals do search for their next job, they often feel confused and stuck as they wade through a morass of opaque postings and rejections.

We're here to change that experience. This book teaches the nine steps that we've distilled from our analysis of thousands of job switchers. The steps will help you make the right next move *for you*—just as they've helped those with whom we've worked and tested our process. That will empower you. Because when you decide to work somewhere, *you are hiring your employer*, consciously or not. You are choosing how and where to spend your precious time and what compensation you'll accept for it. You are choosing the work you'll do and with whom you'll do it. If those choices don't line up with the type of progress you're seeking in your life, no one wins. Not your employer—and certainly not you. To be clear, you cannot avoid trade-offs. We are not talking about finding a pot of gold with little to no sacrifice. But you can embrace those trade-offs to make wise choices that set you on a path to progress.

Ironically, most people already know early in life that they will hire their future jobs, but they forget it along the way. When asked what they want to be when they grow up, young children answer playfully and imaginatively. But as people advance in years, the question takes on greater urgency, which constrains their thinking. Once they come up with an answer that seems plausible, they look for the clearest possible route to follow: *If you want to be a _____, then _____ is how to get there someday.* Some subset of people stick with that straight, simple path. This book also isn't for them. We wrote it for those whose paths zig and zag, loop, or stall in whirlpools of discontent.

The data are clear: Quiet quitting notwithstanding, millions of people are going through a job change right now. Over half the world's workers are passively or actively seeking a new job. If you're not one of them, you likely will be soon. In the United States, 30 percent of the workforce switches jobs every year. Individuals change jobs, on average, every 4.1 years. We're living and working in a fluid market—a time when change is the only career constant. So switching jobs isn't necessarily a sign that something went wrong. It's how we make progress. Therefore, the better you become at switching, the more progress you will enjoy.

The Difference Between Progression and Progress

The time is ripe to help you with this process because the job market is undergoing a major transformation. One of the biggest changes has to do with how work is structured—where and when it occurs, how people connect, and the culture in which they operate. Another centers on employment relationships, which are becoming more of a two-way street. Workers have more power now because talent is scarce. The COVID-19 pandemic that spurred the Great Resignation contributed. It reminded us that life is short, so it's worth reassessing our priorities around whether and where to work. Korn Ferry estimates that by 2030, the global talent shortage could exceed 85 million people. Midway through 2021, the ratio of job openings to unemployed individuals in the United States reached its highest level in a generation; it continued to rise through the end of 2022, to nearly two job posts per unemployed worker. This dynamic appears structural and lasting.

At the same time, behavior is shifting given the uncertain future of work. People are nervous and looking for good advice as employers turbocharge their investments in technology, artificial intelligence, and robots. Those investments are tangible, unsettling reminders of McKinsey's 2018 prediction that by 2030 "around

15 percent of the global workforce, or about 400 million workers, could be displaced by automation." The debut of OpenAI's ChatGPT in November 2022 threw fuel on the fire. More than 100 million people—a rate of adoption never seen before—rushed to register and try out this chatbot that demonstrated just how powerful artificial intelligence can be.

All this change is leading people to ask big questions. And rethink what progress means to them.

What's certain is that many individuals have realized that progress in their careers and lives doesn't necessarily track with employers' increasingly antiquated ideas about "career progression." For ages we have talked about how people climb the "ladder" in their organizations—moving from entry-level jobs to managerial ones, for example, or from lower-paying jobs right out of school to higher-paying rungs after they've acquired more experience. It's also often described as moving "up" in one's career. Although this personal trajectory doesn't always mirror the prescribed organizational path, that's how employers still tend to look at it. They engage in what we call "supply-side" thinking—viewing individuals' movement in the labor force through the company's prism of organizational charts, key performance indicators (KPIs), and other management tools.

But these days, careers rarely follow a linear progression as someone else has defined it. Most of us think about growth more holistically—not just within a single company or role or industry but across our entire careers, our health and wellness, our personal and professional relationships, our interests, and our other needs and desires. Many, for instance, are realizing that they want to do more purposeful work. For them, the definition of making progress in their careers is better aligning their work with what *gives their lives meaning*. For others, progress involves better fitting one's job into one's personal life—such as moving to be closer to family or freeing up more time to spend with loved ones outside of work. Today, progress is a phenomenon best understood by assessing your own struggles, circumstances, and goals. It's best achieved by consciously hiring your next role and employer.

Learning to Help You Make Progress

The three of us have been researching how people navigate their careers for well over a decade.

It started when we realized that all the job-hunting, career-advice, and self-help guides out there—from books to coaches—weren't helping people make their best moves. We kept seeing our students, mentees, and consulting clients struggle to do the recommended steps and exercises. Even when they completed all the time-consuming homework, the advice often fell flat. Our recommendations at the time were just as unhelpful as anyone else's. And the immensity of the problem was staring us in the face. Those 1 billion people who switch jobs every year? Hundreds of millions of them don't feel that they're making real progress in their careers.

So we began studying both those who made progress and those who didn't. We weren't aiming to write a book at first. We just wanted to create a useful process to better advise the people who came to us for support. We wanted to build something fit for the current moment, as well as something that had been tested and refined. In short, we wanted to understand and capture the moves of successful job switchers in today's market.

The realization that people hire their jobs and employers fell into our laps. That's because one of us, Bob, had been collaborating with the renowned business thinker Clayton Christensen in the 1990s when they figured out something similar about consumers. Their big aha was that customers don't buy products or services because they fall into a particular demographic. Rather, they *hire* a product to help them make progress during a struggling moment. In other words, people buy quarter-inch drills because they are in situations where they need to make certain kinds of quarter-inch holes. This insight led to the development of the Jobs to Be Done theory, which ushered in a new approach to innovation. Thousands of better products, services, and businesses were created across nearly every industry, including health care, transportation, financial services, consumer packaged goods, food, defense, software, and education.

Ethan soon realized that Bob's underlying theory could also explain why individuals make the job moves they do. If others could see that, then it might help them make better career choices. To explore the possibility, he designed the online Harvard Business School course "Developing Yourself as a Leader." The course gave us a way to work with and learn from thousands of participants worldwide from a range of industries, including high tech, consumer products, agriculture, real estate and construction, professional services, and health care. These individuals tested our emerging advice in their own lives. We learned from their experiences and updated our thinking to reflect what did and didn't work for whom and under what circumstances—and why.

The three of us then doubled down on this work at the outset of the COVID-19 pandemic. We studied more individuals who had recently switched jobs. We coached more people as they navigated a turbulent job market—including entry-level folks, mid- and late-career professionals, gig workers, entrepreneurs, and individuals looking to reenter the workforce after time away. All the while, we continued to refine our process to help people successfully switch jobs.

And then it happened. Those we had advised, coached, and taught began introducing us to a flurry of their friends, colleagues, and loved ones who were struggling with whether and how to make a job move. We couldn't say no because we genuinely wanted to help. But we also couldn't say yes to all these job seekers, at least not one-on-one. So we wrote this book to help them—and now you—make progress.

The Journey to a Better Job

To be clear, we haven't written a guide to hacking the job market and raking in attractive offers. Although we do provide some new advice on how to get the job you want once you've identified it, that's not what's really special here. The most important things you'll get from us are help clarifying what progress looks like for you, what jobs exist or can be created to enable you to achieve it, and what trade-offs you're willing to make in exchange for that progress, given there is no magical, perfect job. Such clarity is no small thing. In our experience, most people don't have it in any of these areas.

We begin by peeling back the mystery of why people switch jobs rather than dive straight into the "how to do it better." That's because the "why" is complex. In most cases, whatever reason someone gives for switching actually has several other, subconscious reasons behind it. Without a deeper understanding, it's hard to know what to optimize for. Across the thousands of careers we've studied, we've seen four consistent patterns at play—what we call **quests for progress**. Although each person's path has its own contours and points of departure from the norm, here are the four primary quests:

1. **Get Out:** When I can't see a way to thrive in my current job or my manager makes it feel like a dead end, I want to escape to a place where I can be supported and challenged.

2. **Regain Control:** When I'm feeling overwhelmed in some aspect of my life, I want to find an employer that gives me a say in how I allocate my time and do my work.

3. **Regain Alignment:** When my current employer does not fully value my experience, knowledge, or credentials, I want to find an environment and a role in which I will be respected, acknowledged, and reengaged by making full use of my skills.

4. **Take the Next Step:** When I have reached a career or life milestone, I want an exciting place to move forward and take on more responsibility.

Chapter One provides more detail about these quests. Because they are multidimensional, it fleshes them out with real-life examples. Many people looking for change can relate to more than one quest. But at any given moment in your career, one will take precedence over the others. Understanding them in depth will allow you to jump into our process to identify your current priorities and the trade-offs you're willing to make to get those outcomes. That will allow you to figure out what the right job move is for you now.

Nine Steps to Making Progress in Your Career

Chapter Two introduces Step 1 in our process. Most of the steps (check out all nine in the figure on p. xvii) contain multiple parts—a set of activities and reflections to help you home in on and seize the progress you desire. In this chapter, you determine which quest you were on the last time you made a switch. "But wait!" you might say. "Why should I care about why I last changed jobs?" The answer is that we're building your pattern recognition. We want you to be able to look at your own life and understand what's been driving you up until now so that you can continually put our process to work in a way that matches your evolving priorities. By looking carefully at your past, you can better navigate the present. To that end, we share the first of many tools, templates, and examples that live at jobmoves.com, a website that we reference throughout the book. That first tool is an assessment we use twice in this chapter: to identify the quest that drove your most recent job move and then to get an early read on what's causing you to consider a move now.

Chapter Three provides the bridge to identifying your current quest. It shows how all the quests relate to one another along two dimensions: the types of experiences that give you energy and your capabilities. Exploring how these factors interact leads into the practical work ahead.

Chapter Four explains Step 2 of our process, which involves using your résumé to reveal which activities brought you energy and which ones depleted it in your past roles. You then identify recurring energy drivers and drains over your career so far, see how your past jobs rank on each, and figure out which of the activities that bring you energy are most critical for your next role.

Chapter Five is where you take Step 3: compiling the skills, credentials, and experiences you've accumulated and accounting for them as career assets and liabilities on a career balance sheet. We use this tool to assess your current capabilities and clarify which skills you want to prioritize in the future.

Chapter Six cross-references the results from the prior two steps with our assessment tool at jobmoves.com to build on the insights you've gained so far and confirm which quest you're currently on in Step 4. That will allow you to better understand the forces driving you forward and the guardrails that can protect you from making a bad move.

Chapter Seven teaches you to build a wide range of "prototypes" for what you might do next. The idea here in Step 5 isn't to find a job. It's to create contrasting visions of your future to expand your sense of what could be a good choice at this point in your career. Here, we teach you a new way of doing an informational interview so you can learn before switching whether a job that looks great on paper is the right move for the progress you desire.

Chapter Eight lines up all your prototypes—and your current job—with your current quest in Step 6 so you can converge on one or two possibilities that will form the basis for a job search. Do people sometimes learn at this point that their current job is better than their imagined alternatives and stay put? You bet. In that way, they avoid making a move they'll soon regret.

Chapter Nine matches your vision with reality. It's where, in Step 7, you check the one or two promising paths from Step 6 with what's actually available on the job market. To do so, we teach you how to unpack real job postings to see how they match with what matters most to you. But knowing what you're trying to achieve isn't enough. You also need to determine what you're ready to give up to make progress so you won't feel blindsided and frustrated by trade-offs later on. Yes, as decision-making expert Annie Duke, the author of *Quit*, observed, "We have this really valuable option, that when we discover new information that things aren't going the way that we had hoped, we can quit." But our research suggests that people who quit their jobs often stumble right back into situations with the very same problems—or new problems they didn't foresee. In those cases, switching hasn't led to progress. Step 7 helps you "try before you buy" to avoid making this mistake.

Chapter Ten walks you through Step 8: telling your career story. Crafting a strong narrative pays dividends across the board, from clarifying your thinking about what you're looking for so you can pursue the right opportunities to getting you to and through your job interviews. Here we draw on techniques from Pixar, one of the best storytellers in the world.

Chapter Eleven is about taking your career story to the marketplace—Step 9 in our process. True, this isn't a book about the nuts and bolts of applying for jobs (like writing cover letters and negotiating compensation packages). But here we offer résumé and job interview tips to improve your odds of getting hired. We also explain how to turn what you've learned in this book into a one-page personal cheat sheet that can give your current and potential employers clear ideas about how you can best contribute.

Chapter Twelve shows how organizations can take advantage of our insights. The good news is that companies, which are under mounting pressure to change their ways, can build better jobs and pathways. We hope that the moment we're in—the Great Resignation, the growth of hybrid and remote work, and other major trends—will spark organizations to change, as similar moments have in the past. Many of the management students and coaching clients who have gotten the most out of this material over the years were not planning a career change of their own. Rather, they wanted to retain good employees by addressing the reasons they might leave. From them, we learned that by viewing *employee development* as *career development* and enabling individuals to live into their definitions of progress, companies can better recruit, manage, and keep the talent they need.

Finally, **Chapter Thirteen** covers how to take what you've learned and pay it forward. This chapter is a guide for mentors, advisers, hiring managers, chief human resource officers, and anyone else who wants to offer meaningful career support to colleagues or friends. It also gives you a nice set of tools and resources to share with and "train" those who are supporting you in your own journey. If you are a mentor, manager, or friend who just wants to know what to do to support those around you as they look to make a job move, these last two chapters cut to the chase. You can start with them and consult the earlier chapters as needed.

This last chapter also underscores what a social endeavor job switching can—and really *should*—be. We've found that when people work through our process with trusted friends and family, mentors, or advisers, the steps become more doable and enjoyable—and outcomes improve. If you invite others in, they won't just hold you accountable. They'll also help you unearth insights about yourself that you would miss on your own. They'll remind you to stay true to the progress you desire at this point in your life and not get caught up in job titles and other trappings of organizational "progression." And, as decades of research show, they can provide another benefit: Those around you—your colleagues and informal connections—hold keys to opportunities about which you would never otherwise know.

Can you read this book by yourself and get value out of it? Sure. The nine steps in our process mostly connect with work you need to do anyway to search for a job, so they don't amount to extra work. They equate to smarter work. But bringing someone along for the ride keeps you honest and might just make the process fun. That means you'll engage more deeply with it, which will boost your odds of a successful job move.

The Power at Your Disposal

As we wrote this book, the labor market grew tighter while other aspects of the economy—inflation, for instance, and threats of recession—grew more volatile. Such shifts are anything but fleeting. Even when things stabilize, it's never for long. That will continue to cause anxiety, uncertainty, and frustration for workers and employers alike. But it also presents prospects for growth.

Regardless of whether the war for talent is hot or just lukewarm at any given moment, people who navigate our process will remain in a position of power. Remember, you're going to hire your next employer and every new one after that. You're even going to hire your next role in your current organization. Factoring in what you care about most, the challenges in your life, and the sacrifices you're willing to make, you get to decide whether you do or don't want to make each move. And wherever you land next won't be the end of your journey. Your career is ultimately a series of successive explorations. Each time you switch jobs, the goal is to move closer to the sweet spot of what you really love and want to do, given your life circumstances. With practice, you'll get better at choosing to do the things that bring you energy and moving away from those that drain it.

So try not to stress too much. We know the stakes are high. But think *progress, not perfection*, to move toward a tomorrow that is better than today. We'll show you how.

PART I

UNDERSTANDING JOB MOVES

If you don't know why you're looking to change jobs, then it's less likely you'll hire the right next one. That's why Chapter One illustrates the four main quests for progress among job switchers.

Even with the benefit of hindsight, people often don't fully recognize why they make the professional moves they do. Chapter Two helps you analyze why you've switched jobs in the past by helping you understand the forces that underlie the quests. It's the forces that cause individuals to change. By understanding them, you can begin to discern what's driving you to look for something new now.

ONE

LEARN WHAT CAUSES PEOPLE TO CHANGE JOBS

As Alex sat at the kitchen table with his wife, he didn't know what to think.* His manager at work had been clear: The company was shutting down his department in Wisconsin and paying every individual to relocate to another state. No one on the team would be allowed to work remotely. No exceptions.

Having agonized over it with his wife and her extended family through countless conversations, Alex was now equally clear: He couldn't pick up and move. Just as he had spent the past fifteen years building his career with this employer, his family had spent that same amount of time building their lives in Wisconsin. And his wife's aging parents needed them nearby to help care for them and drive them to medical appointments. That was a nonnegotiable priority.

Head in hands, Alex felt stuck and resigned to his fate. Yes, he liked what he did as a midcareer professional. Actually, he loved it. Working as a digital project manager who interacted directly with customers was the best job he had ever had. He hadn't been looking for new work. But because he couldn't move locations, he was going to have to move jobs. Even though he hadn't been laid off, it didn't seem all that different.

---

* Names and other details are disguised to preserve anonymity throughout this book.

When Alex asked us for guidance, we asked what he wanted his next job to do for him. He scoffed. Given that his longtime employer had just abruptly announced the move—and if you couldn't go, well, that was tough—he was pretty sure he wouldn't be calling any of the shots in his career. Companies seemed to have all the power.

We pointed out that at least he had the luxury of time. The relocation of his division and the associated logistics would take a while. His manager had told him that he had roughly six months to figure out what he wanted to do next.

Still, he was nervous. He knew the days would pass quickly. What should he do now to get moving?

Our initial advice was to use the time to his advantage—and slow down, just a little. Moving slowly isn't something many people do at this stage. They often frantically scour job boards, amp up their networking with colleagues, fire off résumés—and fall into a suboptimal situation. Easing up a bit was what Alex needed to do. True, he was facing an imminent switch because his company had forced his hand. But he had also made a big decision that we encouraged him to examine more closely: Why had staying close to extended family outweighed moving—or commuting—to keep a job he treasured? We knew that his wife's parents needed them around. But if he had a great job, why did one set of needs outweigh another? Were his own needs evolving? What were the sorts of things he wanted to keep doing—and maybe no longer do—on a day-to-day basis? What might progress look like for him at this point in his life?

You're probably reading this book because, like Alex, you or someone in your life has at least begun to think about making a job move. But do you know why you're in that frame of mind? Do you *really* know what's compelling you to think about making a change?

Career advancement, more money, balance, and flexibility are top-of-mind reasons that people tick off on surveys. But these surface-level explanations capture only some of what's going on. What's more, rarely—if ever—is it just one thing that causes someone to say, "Today's the day to put myself out there. I'm going to switch jobs." Instead, there's an intricate combination of interdependent factors driving that choice. And just as Alex did, people typically struggle to recognize what all those factors are. Even those who have been let go from their job still struggle to sort through what they really want from their next job.

So we've looked for patterns among the thousands of job switchers we've studied, taught, coached, and observed over the years—a racially diverse sample representing a mix of ages, career stages, fields, roles, income levels, educational backgrounds, family situations, and other life circumstances. Critically, we didn't look at people just *considering* a switch. We studied those who actually *made a change*. There's a big difference between the two. Many people think about switching but don't actually do it. They complain, dream about all sorts of better futures, and sit passively. Or they keep a close eye on opportunities but can't work up the confidence to follow through on any of them. None of that will help you make the progress you seek. What you need is a clear, actionable process.

To create one, we analyzed what *causes* people to actually make a move. Later on, in Chapter Two, we isolate these causes as two types of forces—what we call pushes and pulls—and describe them in detail. For now, though, here's the punch line: Although a host of functional, social, and emotional factors can lead individuals to seek a job change *now*, in our data they cluster into four common sets of struggles and corresponding goals that compel people to switch jobs: Get Out, Regain Control, Regain Alignment, and Take the Next Step. Each of these is a **quest for progress**.

What does that mean? For starters, the quests we've identified aren't simple, one-dimensional goals or paths. Each one is a combination of problems to solve, experiences to seek, and outcomes to obtain. They're a particular mix of pushes and pulls that emerged repeatedly across a large number of people in our dataset. Making "progress" amounts to improving one's life—however one defines improvement at that juncture. For some, progress might occur when they take a job that offers more money or status; for others, it might involve taking a job with less money or status in the pursuit of other things. It all depends on the individual's quest and the set of experiences they are seeking to optimize. Understanding someone's quest allows us to transcend surface-level explanations and explain *why* that person takes the actions they do.

Most everyone in our data pool has wrestled with more than one of the four quests over time, often without recognizing them as root causes for their decisions and actions. This isn't unusual. Each quest is likely to matter to you at some point in your life. But at any given time, one will prevail in importance over the others. Which quest you're on now depends on what's most pressing at this moment, in light of your current challenges and priorities.

When job switchers don't understand what's prompting them to move and fail to examine the trade-offs they're making, they often end up just as unhappy wherever they land. Sometimes they repeat unconstructive patterns of behavior. They learn *by* switching rather than learn *before* switching. In many cases, this comes at a cost to their career trajectory and quality of life. It's like buying shoes online only to find that they don't fit well when they arrive. Except it's far more difficult and riskier to "return" a new job than to return a pair of ill-fitting shoes.

This can happen to anyone. When we ask alumni of the Harvard Business School MBA program what is the fastest they've ever gone from taking a job to discovering that it is not the right fit, usually around 30 percent answer less than a month. Another 45 percent say between one month and one year. That means three-quarters of individuals have regretted a job move within a year of making it, even if they suffer through it for a while longer before making another switch.

But our research shows that you *can* learn before switching. If you understand the four quests for progress, then you can navigate yours to make changes consistent with what you're really seeking. That means you will more reliably end up in better roles for you. In short, understanding these quests is not just an academic exercise. It's a practical way to prioritize and play through your career options.

Before we help you begin to identify your quest in Chapter Two, here's a brief overview of each quest for progress—a framework we explore, deepen, and apply throughout the book to help you decide what you should do next.

Quest #1: Get Out

Many people who start looking for something new do so because they feel pushed to flee their current situation at work—a classic fight-or-flight response. Perhaps the way they are being managed is wearing them down. Or they feel stuck in a dead-end job and can't put up with it any longer. Or they're in way over their heads, without the confidence, desire, or organizational support to acquire the skills and knowledge needed for success. Or seemingly unsurmountable obstacles—such as a negative culture, a role that's a bad fit, or an awful commute—are preventing them from putting their capabilities to good use. Or there's an ethical conflict with their boss or colleagues. Individuals who are strongly at odds with their work environment—for whatever reason—tend to feel frustrated, isolated, ignored, and unsupported.

Once they reach their tipping point and decide to switch, their quest is to get out fast. They want to escape to a different place. A place where they'll fit in better and be more supported by their manager and colleagues. A place where they can better learn and grow and do work that is challenging at the right level for them— not too easy, nor too far out of their comfort zone. For these people, the quest is framed almost entirely as the opposite of their current circumstances.

In our research, we've spoken with many professionals who fall into this category, all in their own ways. For example:

> A salesperson who had worked in start-ups his whole career took a position at a large tech firm where he had more administrative support and a much higher base salary than ever before. Almost immediately, though, he felt suffocated by bureaucratic systems, an overly prescriptive sales process, and a lack of say in his performance targets. He was boxed in—and miserable.
> An associate director of admissions at a boarding school who loved her workplace suddenly lost her "seat at the table" when a peer became her boss. As she was assigned more and more dull, thankless work, she became worn out and disheartened, unable to muster the energy to do her core job well or even to seek enrichment through after-hours courses.

Once these situations developed, both individuals left quickly. They decided they couldn't take it a minute longer than necessary. A telltale sign of the Get Out quest is leaping before looking.

Those on this quest are seeking a hard reset and are willing to make dramatic changes to get it—like moving to a different city, switching fields or industries, or changing their kids' schools or childcare arrangements. They are inclined to take risks because they have a sense that anything would be better than their current circumstances. They don't care much about what others think of where they're headed; they aren't doing this to receive validation or to impress others with a promotion. An urgent need for change outweighs all that. They want a new job to rescue them from their current one.

Quest #2: Regain Control

People in this second group often feel over-whelmed—at work, at home, or both. Although they may like what they are doing, their current circumstances make them feel ill-equipped to do it. Having lost control somewhere along the way over how their job makes use of their time or how they do their work, they look to regain it. Even though they may appreciate their work's purpose or impact, they want to be in a job where they can be more intentional about how it uses them and their time.

That sometimes means they want to rebalance their mix of work and everything else in life. To do so, some search for an employer who will trust them enough to make those time-related choices more flexibly, because their current workplace—whether in-person, virtual, or hybrid—makes it harder rather than easier for them to work effectively. Others simply want a workplace that makes the decisions for them but offers more predictability.

Like those on the first quest who feel stuck and above all else must get out, people who look to regain control often feel stretched in ways they don't like to be stretched. That could be because of their bosses, colleagues, customers, or the organization's culture. They also have a nagging sense that their current situation is untenable. Levels of fatigue, stress, uncertainty, or tension are mounting. Another similarity that people wanting to regain control share with those who want to get out is feeling they have "burned out" on the job—like many individuals during the Great Resignation, such as health-care workers and teachers.

Yet there are also key differences between these first two quests. Control seekers aren't searching for the nearest escape hatch. Rather, they're mainly looking for flexibility, freedom, and agency over their work environment and how they do their job, as well as ways to better integrate their work with the rest of their personal life and what's often referred to as the Ds: death, divorce, diapers, diplomas, debt, and so on. They want more time and energy or a more accommodating venue to do the things they care about (and may already be doing at their current job). In short, they want to deliver some or most of what their current job entails, but they don't feel equipped to deliver *all* of it because of the way the job is framed or structured or because of the sacrifices required. And they therefore tend to be cautious and risk averse about switching until they find a job that will make them feel both willing *and* able, whereas many people in the Get Out group are ready to make more trade-offs, accept more unknowns, or even bet the farm to get away.

For example:

> An administrator who had worked in loan collections for many years at various companies found that her latest role was a total grind. She was working from noon to 9 p.m. every weekday, often putting in substantial hours on weekends, and accruing

limited vacation time. She had little room for life outside of work and struggled to maintain her personal relationships as a result. In particular, she desired better hours so she could have the time to repair the growing fissures with her significant other.

> A dev-ops programmer at a tech firm enjoyed her job. But when her company replaced her manager with someone who took credit for her contributions, the atmosphere became toxic. She felt helpless, as she had no control over whether her work received its due recognition. She wondered, Why work hard, be stretched thin, and not see enough of her two kids—and stomach an arduous commute—when she received so little in return? After learning that the company had unceremoniously laid off a colleague while he was on vacation, she decided it was time to make a move. No longer would she be at the mercy of the organization's whims.

Both professionals still liked the work they did but had a strong desire—or experienced strong pressure—to have more control over their time and how they were used. They didn't jump at the very next opportunity that came their way, however. They stayed put as they weighed their options and made intentional choices. The loan collections administrator eventually switched to a company with more predictable hours, and the dev-ops programmer went to an organization run by women who she felt would honor her choices and contributions more.

Overall, control seekers aren't particularly worried—at this point in their lives—about gaining skills to advance in their career, hitting certain milestones, or finding more meaningful work. They're more concerned about imposing order so they can match their investments of time, effort, and skill with their current priorities. To reap that benefit, some are willing to give up prestige or a title or to take a lower salary. But they tend to consider those trade-offs more carefully than those in Quest #1 who want to get out at any cost. That's in part because the problem is not one of unhappiness but rather of unsustainability. They just can't keep doing what they've been doing without giving up things they value as much or more at this stage of their lives.

Quest #3: Regain Alignment

If you feel like belting out Aretha Franklin's R & B anthem "Respect" every time you think about your current job, you can relate to the people on this third quest. Most of them feel a profound lack of respect at work. In contrast to the control seekers, their concern is less about how they are managed than about how they and their skill set are valued. They're often bored in their role and unable to see a place to go or grow in their organization. Because they aren't being engaged, they don't feel present at work.

As a result, they are looking for a job where their skills, experience, and expertise at the core of their work identity will be utilized, appreciated, and acknowledged. Then they believe they'll be able to deliver value in line with what they see as their potential.

Lacking such validation, they tend to have a dark outlook and fixate on the many ways their current job isn't aligned to their skill set. For instance, they may struggle to find meaning in what they do and believe they're having little impact on their organization or on the world beyond it. Or they may think the work is beneath them.

Sometimes misalignment occurs when an organization doesn't sufficiently value the capabilities an individual possesses; perhaps the employer's focus is simply elsewhere at the moment. As a result, the worker may feel unappreciated or even forgotten. In other cases, misalignment happens when the organization is asking the individual to use capabilities for which the employee doesn't wish to be known. This is more common than you might think. Our careers and lives have a funny way of changing direction without anyone noticing, at least at first. People often accept roles, project assignments, interim positions, extra tasks, or even side gigs that look attractive or seem like valuable "stretch" opportunities. Before they know it, their trajectory at work has changed drastically. They feel that their career is careening out of control. Although a radical shift can be serendipitous for some, for others it feels more like hydroplaning on a rain-drenched highway. For example, in a former life as a consultant, one of us—Ethan—reluctantly agreed to work on a restructuring project that would involve layoffs when one of his closest mentors asked him to do so as a favor. Fast-forward a couple of years, and he had been staffed on two more of those projects. He was becoming known as the go-to consultant for layoffs and restructuring. This was a capability that he had never wanted to develop, let alone be known for! When a senior partner introduced him to a potential client as a layoff expert, Ethan was exasperated—and knew it was time to regain alignment.

For those seeking to regain alignment in their jobs, changing their fate seems like an uphill battle from where they are now, so they search for a new opportunity.

For example:

> A highly qualified job trainer spent much of her time driving high school students to volunteer jobs where they could gain work experience. She had taken the role to pay off her student loans with the hope she'd eventually get hired as a social worker in the

same district. Despite strong performance, she wasn't offered that opportunity or any other indication that bigger things were in store for her. Bitter, bored, and feeling disrespected, she took a job farther away to put her education to better use.

> A US Army field artillery specialist had switched to an operations role at a hospital because his family needed him to have a more predictable schedule. The work was manageable yet dull. He eventually asked to move back to a job that would better leverage his skills but was told his time at the hospital wouldn't count toward a promotion in rank. His army career suddenly felt thankless. Where was the recognition for his years of service? Disillusioned, he left the military for an operations job in a private health-care company.

As people look for a place where they can reengage and command respect, they typically gravitate toward work they know they can do well and seek an environment where there's little risk of being underestimated or misunderstood. That may entail finding a new boss who knows how to value and appreciate them. Or switching jobs just to show their old organization or boss their true market value. Or finding a job that draws on the same skills, expertise, and experience but in service of a larger purpose or a more "core" function in the organization. That way others will recognize the importance of what they bring to the table. Because this quest for realignment isn't about acquiring new skills, people are often willing to take an incremental step forward or even a lateral step to feel valued and essential to a team, division, or organization. They usually won't take a step backward, though, or switch career paths entirely, as those desperate to escape might do. Many who seek realignment worry that they'll have to change jobs again soon if they don't get the treatment they deserve once they move.

Quest #4: Take the Next Step

Our final group of job switchers consists of people who have reached a personal or professional milestone—such as completing school, getting married, earning a certification, achieving a performance or development goal, or becoming empty nesters. They're looking to take the next step in their careers. In many cases, that means more professional or management responsibility. Driving these individuals is often a desire to support themselves or others who are depending on them. Sometimes they're no longer sufficiently challenged in their current role and growing a little restless. In other cases, their role or company has shifted away from what they liked doing. They now want a back-to-the-future transition into a job more like the one they had before the shift.

People on this quest—unlike those looking to get out, regain control, or regain alignment—aren't necessarily reacting to a bad situation. They aren't pushed away from their prior job because of a lack of engagement or agency. Rather, they are pulled toward something new because they want even more of both. This quest for progress is more about pursuing growth and less about leaving an unsupportive manager, a stressful or toxic work environment, a struggling company, an unsustainable situation, or some other set of problems. Job switchers in this group want their next move to be a real, positive step forward—in their own eyes and in the eyes of others.

For all those reasons, despite any anxiety they may feel about their skills or capabilities, they are often willing to leap into a stretch role. They may even leave a job they love if they believe a new one will bring the opportunity for growth or increased status.

For example:

> An assistant women's NCAA basketball coach loved his job, but changes in his personal life led him to take stock of his career. When his serious girlfriend took a new job that required her to move states, it prompted him to take a new job himself: a steadier and more stable government role that offered a clear path to opportunities ahead, which would help him feel secure about starting to build a family.
> A lawyer at a large firm knew he'd prefer working in public service, but he had needed his employer's generous paternity leave policy to support his growing family. After his third child was born, he and his wife decided they wouldn't have more kids. That meant it was time to switch to the type of work he was called to do. Most would think of this as a U-turn away from corporate law toward public service. But from his perspective, this was the logical next step for which he had always planned.

Both the coach and the lawyer had reached personal milestones. One was eager to start a family and sought a steadier job with growth potential. The other, having established a family and saved for the future, was ready to swap high pay and great benefits for meaningful work, the next step on his chosen career path. Of course, milestones need not be personal: work milestones—such as seeing a peer get promoted or reaching a work anniversary—can also trigger this quest.

Now What?

When Alex approached us for career guidance, he didn't know what quest he was on. In fact, his first gut response was that he wasn't on any of them—that our quests didn't represent his reality. But that changed as he worked his way through the steps in our process. It takes some time and effort to figure out what kind of progress you want to make at this point in your career. And that can morph as you search because of the things you learn about yourself, the jobs that are available, how your situation changes, and the choices you make as you seek your next job. In other words, you also have some freedom to choose which of these four quests makes the most sense for you now. That kind of agency is a blessing if you have a process to help you make good choices and a curse if you don't.

To get Alex to a place where he could more deeply understand what he wanted and what moves he might make to get it, we introduced him to the underlying forces that compel people to change jobs and dug more into his past and current job choices. You're now in that same place. In the next chapter we discuss those forces and walk you through Step 1 of our process: identifying the quest you were on when you last changed jobs so you can figure out what's prompting you to think about making a job move now.

TWO

STEP 1:
IDENTIFY WHAT JUMP-STARTED
YOUR LATEST QUEST

 Clara, a woman in her late twenties, was in a different place from Alex. Whereas Alex felt thrust into the search for a new job, Clara was antsy in her role as a rehab technician in a physical therapy clinic. She knew she was ready for something new. But she also had a lot of anxiety around switching, which led her to work with us. She had held roles in three organizations over the past six years—and made some dramatic moves along the way. She had worked in different fields and continents. From the outside, she looked restless. And as the pandemic receded, she was struggling to figure out what her next step should be.

Before we started to coach her, we *interviewed* her—not about the present but about her most recent job switch. The goal was for Clara to develop a deeper understanding of the forces within each of the four quests—those *pushing* an individual to make a change and those *pulling* someone toward something new—and to sort out which forces applied to her latest move. That insight would then help her determine what was driving her now.

In this chapter, we take a close look at how the various underlying forces can play out in a job switcher's timeline so that you, too, can understand what's been motivating your career moves and begin to define your current quest. That's the first step of our job-switching process. To guide you through it, we introduce an activity—the interview—and some additional tools. Later in the book, you'll build on this step by developing a much fuller picture of where you are now. That will help you decide whether to actually switch jobs. It will also highlight what may be holding you back, help you avoid mistakes you've made in the past, and home in on the right trade-offs you should make to get the progress you seek.

Following the Job Switcher's Timeline

When people switch jobs, many attribute their new role to luck ("It's who you know!") or a numbers game ("One of those applications was bound to pan out!"). Our research suggests they're giving chance much more credit than it deserves. Switching jobs isn't random or independent from the experiences you've had in the past.

We've actually seen a consistent timeline play out over and over when people are looking for a new job. It's similar to the timeline that they follow when they purchase products and services to make progress in their life. It's generally subconscious, but it's not random.

As Figure 2.1 shows, the switching timeline starts with a **first thought** that something about the present situation isn't as good as it could be. You need to make progress for some reason. The status quo isn't working anymore, or something else appears more desirable.

You then move into a **passive looking** phase, where you're not putting real energy into searching for something new but are noticing options you didn't see previously. That "fluke" conversation with someone who mentioned that their friend had a job opening on her team? You might not have picked up on that detail if you weren't passively looking. But once you are in that phase, you hear and pay attention to those sorts of things with greater frequency.

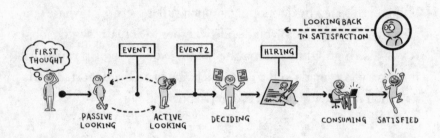

Figure 2.1
The Timeline of a Job Switcher

As you're passively looking, something (**Event 1**) happens that makes you say, "It's time to take action." Maybe your company laid off a bunch of people and handled it poorly. Or someone close to you died and you started to reassess what was important to you. This event tends to be a wake-up call, but it isn't always negative. For instance, you might take a course or attend a conference where you learn about new opportunities.

Now you're in **active looking** mode. Whereas before you simply had your antennae up, now you are spending energy and time on finding something new. You might update your LinkedIn page, quietly let friends know you're on the market, network with former colleagues, search for openings on job sites, and apply for some roles. This phase feels like job shopping. There are endless possibilities with blue skies all around you. You don't feel the need to wrestle with trade-offs yet.

Although this timeline isn't strictly linear—the transition between passive and active looking can be fluid and fuzzy as you might move back and forth several times, for example—what propels you forward is a **second event** that makes you realize the clock is ticking. Perhaps a big life milestone is approaching, or you must decide about a job offer by a certain date. Whatever it is, that event triggers a go or no-go **decision**: to switch or keep looking. If you take a new job (that is, you "**hire**" what the employer has to offer in the marketplace), you then start "**consuming**" it like a product as you begin doing the daily work. At that point, you can't help but look back at your first thought and what you were doing previously to assess whether you are satisfied with your choice.

Of course, you won't necessarily be happier after making a change. Just ask the "nearly three-quarters of workers who quit to take a new job [during the Great Resignation and] said they felt surprise or regret," according to a survey by The Muse, a job-search and career-coaching company. According to the *Wall Street Journal*, which reported on the survey, "nearly half of those workers said they would try to get their old job back. More than 40% said they'd give their current employers two to six more months before switching again."

But here's the good news. You're much less likely to regret your next move if you understand your past journey through the switching timeline and learn to approach job moves more deliberately.

Finding Your Past Pushes and Pulls

With that timeline firmly in mind, let's apply our framework to *your* life to figure out why you made your most recent career move.

To do this most effectively, turn to a trusted mentor, friend, or confidant who is willing to invest time in your development. The ask is for them to interview you about your most recent job change and work with you to interpret your responses (we describe *how* to do both in the activity that follows this section).

This is what we did with Clara. We didn't focus yet on the boredom she was experiencing in her current job or what she was considering next. Instead, we talked about her past move from expat lab manager in Ireland to physical therapy assistant in Colorado. When we started the interview, Clara already knew that she had been motivated to move back to the United States and that she had tired of some of the day-to-day work in Ireland. But until we drilled down, what was less clear to her was that her dissatisfaction stemmed partly from a lack of opportunities to continue learning and growing. After our interview, she came to see her move to Colorado as a "jobcation"—a less onerous stint that allowed her to have more time to explore her interests outside of work (this is a concept we revisit in Chapter Seven).

As we did for Clara, your interviewer will ask you to describe your actions leading up to and during your job switch. It's important to examine *what you did* before reading too much into why. When the interview is done, you'll debrief together to figure out what forces were driving you to switch at the time and what may be driving you this time around.

These forces—what we call pushes and pulls—lurk within any major change in behavior, whether you're switching jobs, going back to school, seeking medical care, or buying a product or service that promises to make life better. Although there are undoubtedly many times at work and in your daily life when you feel frustrated, upset, angry, bored, disgruntled, and more, they usually don't cause you to switch jobs. You persist. Sometimes things get better, and sometimes they don't. But *bitchin' ain't switchin'*. You don't actually make a move until certain forces come together and override the reasons to stay with what you're doing currently. Those pushes and pulls are what you're seeking to identify during the debrief. **Pushes** propel you away from a situation. **Pulls** move you toward something new and exciting.

The pushes can be quite powerful. As research across disciplines has shown, "bad is stronger than good." In other words, negative information, experiences, and interactions have stronger impacts than positive ones. That's why pushes often trigger a job search—even if that search doesn't go anywhere. That said, a push doesn't have to be an entirely "bad" thing. For instance, welcoming a new baby to the family—a wonderful life event for many people—can also create a push, or a struggling moment, in a professional's career. When one of us, Michael, welcomed his newborn twins, he soon realized that he no longer wanted to manage people professionally. The joys of the new babies changed how he wanted to work and led to dissatisfaction in his executive director role at the nonprofit he had cofounded. Roughly a year after their birth, he resigned from his job and joined the gig economy.

Because we've already analyzed thousands of data points across a wide range of situations, demographics, career types, income levels, and more, you and your interviewer don't have to identify all your pushes from scratch. A list of the most common ones is in Figure 2.2.

Figure 2.2 Common Pushes for Job Switchers

> When I don't respect or trust the people I work with
> When I feel that the work I'm doing has little or no impact on the company, the world, or my life
> When the way I'm managed day-to-day is wearing me down
> When my current company is struggling and the end feels near
> When I end up with a new manager and feel like I'm starting over
> When I feel disrespected or not trusted
> When I've reached a personal milestone in my life

> When I've reached a milestone in my job or career
> When my work is dominating my life and I sacrifice myself or my family to get things done
> When a trusted adviser, mentor, or previous boss guides me toward my next step
> When I am challenged beyond my ability, logic, or ethics
> When I don't feel challenged or am bored in my current work
> When I can't see where to go or how to grow in my current organization (or it will take too long or be too hard)
> When I feel that I have been on my own, ignored, and unsupported at work for a long time

Research by Wharton economist Katy Milkman shows that behavioral pushes become even more powerful when there's also an alluring new idea or solution **pulling** people toward change— something they can aspire to when their current situation is not working for them. Here's an example: One of the switchers we studied disliked her job's odd hours and weekend commitments. But she stayed put until an alluring offer that guaranteed a 7 a.m. to 4 p.m. day, with no weekends and reasonable vacation time, compelled her to leave. Another individual, the salesperson from Chapter One who felt micromanaged in his job, was enticed by an offer that would allow him to take control over all aspects of the sales cycle.

When we first met with Clara, there wasn't yet a clear pull to cause her to make a job move. Without something positive pulling us, we tend to just stay on a treadmill. We want and think about change, but we don't act. The new idea or solution needs to be enticing; it must hold some magnetic promise for improving our lives to get us to move. Even when people are pushed hard to make a change—those desperate to get out of an awful situation, for example—some degree of pull must typically exist for them to leave. In that case, it might just be the hope of fitting in, being valued, or doing meaningful work somewhere else.

A list of the most common pulls is in Figure 2.3. In Appendix A, we provide a glossary that defines the pushes and pulls in language that people we've interviewed have used when they experience them.

Figure 2.3 Common Pulls for Job Switchers

> So I can have more time to spend with others outside work
> So my values and beliefs will align with the company and the people I work with
> So my job will fit into my existing personal life
> So I can reset my life and start over
> So I can acquire the skills I need for a future job or career (stepping stone)
> So I can be acknowledged, respected, and trusted to do great work
> So I can find an employer who values my experience and credentials
> So I will feel that my job is a step forward, for me and in the view of others
> So I will have the freedom and flexibility to do my best work
> So I can be recognized for my work's impact on people and the business
> So I will have a supportive boss who guides me and provides constructive feedback
> So I can be part of a tight-knit team or community that I can count on

> So I can be challenged, grow, and learn on the job
> So I will be in a job that I know I can do and not feel at risk
> So I can support my growing personal responsibilities
> So I can have more time for me

Even though we've already identified the most common pushes and pulls, we urge you not to skip the interview and jump straight to selecting which forces applied to your most recent job switch. Doing so will shortchange you of the opportunity to go deep into what caused you to make the change you did. Without the interview, you aren't likely to challenge your up-front assumptions about what caused you to change, and your answers are likely to remain superficial. Don't think too much about the pushes and pulls before you're interviewed. These lists are for afterward, during the debrief.

After the interview, to determine the extent to which each push and pull was a factor ("definitely," "somewhat," "not really," or "definitely not"—see activity for more detail), talk concretely with your interviewer about where and how each force manifested. That will encourage both of you to look for evidence from the interview to support your assertions. Feel free to debate about whether something did or didn't match your situation. If you remain stuck on whether a certain push or pull was a factor, then you can consider it a "not sure yet" so you won't overload your list with things about which you lack conviction. You can revisit your answers later.

Clara's concern about some of the research practices in her lab, her feeling that work was dominating her life, and her growing boredom with her job were pushes that she classified as definitely a factor in her decision to leave. Pushes that were somewhat of a factor included feeling the work had little or no impact on the organization, the world, or her life, and being worn down by the way she was managed day-to-day. The pulls that were definitely a factor in her move to the physical therapy job were having more time for rock climbing and for friends and family, fitting her job into her existing personal life, and having an employer that valued her experience and credentials. A pull that was somewhat of a factor was taking on a low-risk job she knew she could do well.

Activity: Invite a Mentor to Interview You

To set yourself up for a fruitful conversation with your mentor,* schedule roughly two hours together—one to answer the interview questions and one to debrief afterward. Find a comfortable place to talk where you can speak freely and casually, either on the phone or in-person (we actually prefer the phone so we don't get distracted by nonverbal cues and can listen more carefully).

When advising job seekers and mentors alike, we often compare the interview to filming a documentary about a particular career move. You want to capture everything you did when you first started thinking about switching, when you were looking for something new, when you decided to change jobs, and when you made the switch. In other words, the interview should help re-create the job-switching timeline from Figure 2.1.

It's good to just talk uninterrupted for a bit when you begin describing how things unfolded. Provide some personal and professional context, such as where you worked at the time and what you switched to; where you lived at the time and with whom; and any other important background about your life. Then start talking about the first thought you had of switching jobs. Filling that

---

* Here, we assume that you have had at least one job switch in the recent past. If you are relatively new to the workforce, or if you have been in the same role for so long that your memory about your most recent job switch is likely to be unreliable, then you may skip ahead to analyzing your current pushes and pulls with your interviewer.

silence up front allows you to lay out the contours of your story as you naturally recall it. As your interviewer gathers these basics, they'll prompt you to fill in blanks about what was going on in your life at the time and to clarify any actions you've described using vague language.

Provide as much detail as you can, but stick to what happened and avoid conclusions. There's no need to speculate about why you did something or to justify the actions you took. No one's here to judge you. The objective is to understand the story of what happened to you and the actions you took. There are no right or wrong answers. And if you don't remember, don't make it up. Work with the facts you can recall.

YOUR INTERVIEWER'S ROLE

Your interviewer should poke and prod like an investigative journalist to help you discover things you aren't yet seeing on your own. They should also approach the conversation with humility and a beginner's mindset. Yes, they may know you and your situation pretty well. But instead of weaving their assumptions into your story, they will best serve your interests by asking lots of questions, making sure they truly understand your answers, and not taking any detail for granted. They can play back things you've said, in their own words, to confirm they are really getting the sentiment of what you're saying or what led you to take a certain action. Feel free to push back when they don't get the details quite right—as will almost certainly be the case at times. Listening intently and truly understanding everything someone is saying is much harder than people often think it is.

During the interview, your mentor will ferret out clues about what propelled you through the switching timeline: What *caused* you to have a first thought about switching jobs—and how long ago did that occur? What was that first event that shifted your attention from passively looking for a new job to actively looking? What were the forces behind that event? How about the second event—what caused you to move into the deciding phase? What caused you to make the final choice to switch? Throughout the process, what conversations did you have with those close to you? These are the stories you will share during the first hour.

During this conversation, a clearer picture of your switching timeline will emerge. Your interviewer should sketch that out as you talk through the events and forces that propelled you to switch (we provide an example of what this can look like in Appendix B—a set of notes around Clara's job switch from the lab in Ireland to the clinic in Colorado). This is a first draft at documenting what caused you to switch jobs. It therefore should be messy. Your interviewer may have to cross out items that had *seemed* to represent a first thought, for example, when they realize that there was a much earlier moment that caused you to start searching. Or they might circle items to revisit later, list multiple forces that may have caused you to move forward in your search, and add question marks where they don't fully understand something. Then, having captured what you've shared in this rough set of notes, your interviewer can help you unpack the conversation.

It may seem like a rambling conversation, but the timeline will keep it focused. Before your interviewer conducts the conversation, make sure they read Chapter Thirteen. In it, we present a concrete way to structure and manage the conversation.

DEBRIEFING WITH YOUR INTERVIEWER

After a short break, you'll debrief and interpret your narrative. For this follow-up conversation, you need another hour together to identify the forces that propelled you through your most recent job move. What pushed you away from the old job, and what pulled you toward trying something new? See Figures 2.2 and 2.3 for the most common forces that emerged in our research. Those will give you and your interviewer a place to start as you compile your own list.

Pushes take the form of "When I . . ." statements because they refer to forces that acted on you as you did your job. For example, a manager at a fast-growing high-tech company began wondering about the growing bureaucracy around him. "What the [heck] is everyone working on [here]?" he asked himself. "How many [product managers] do we really need?" The pushes that led him to these thoughts could be articulated as "When I feel that the work I'm doing has little or no impact on the company" and "When I can't see where to go or how to grow in my current organization." Another individual was asked to take on a role as a commissioner of a struggling sports league. Even though he felt it was beyond his ability, his manager encouraged him to try it. He was glad he did, because he managed to grow into the role and turn the league around. The push in this case could be articulated as "When a trusted adviser, mentor, or previous boss guides me toward my next step."

Pulls take the form of "So I can . . ." statements because they refer to something you'd like to be able to do in the future. For example, one of our students took a detour from working in education to work in a baseball team's front office because two of his best friends invited him to join them. "I would have worked with them on any company," he said. In that situation, the pull was: "So I can be part of a tight-knit team or community that I can count on."

Next, go through your list and discuss with your interviewer *to what extent* each push and pull factored into your job switch. There are typically three to five pushes that you can easily label "definitely a factor" and another three to five that were "definitely not a factor." The same goes for pulls. Identifying these most- and least-relevant forces is critical to this debrief.

As for the other pushes and pulls, try to discern whether they were "somewhat" or "not really" a factor in your move. Although changing jobs usually occurs as a result of a confluence of factors, if almost all the pushes and pulls seem to qualify as "definitely" or "somewhat," you probably need to process your interview data more carefully. Some factors are always more relevant than others to any particular career move. And if you identify too few, you haven't moved beyond the surface-level story you've been telling yourself and others. While discussing tensions between your perspective and that of your interviewer can be productive, if you find yourselves derailed by how to rate a couple pushes or pulls at this point, it's also okay to agree that you're not yet sure and come back to them later.

Grappling with Obstacles to Change

One mistake some people make is to think of the pushes and pulls as mirror opposites. They aren't. They're propelling you in the same direction—away from the present and toward the future. Their mirror opposites are two formidable forces that do their darnedest to obstruct change. You need your pushes and pulls to overcome them.

One of those opposing forces is **anxiety** about anything new. It's natural to think about all the things that the new job might *not* do for you. Will it fail to deliver on its promises? Where will it fall short? Will it leave you feeling trapped? Where will it create more problems? That anxiety—a fear of the unknown future—creates friction that can thwart movement toward a new role. It is the mirror of your pushes—your reasons to move away from a situation—because it pushes back against that movement. Clara's anxiety about leaving the lab started with big questions about what kind of work she really wanted to do. What if she wasn't qualified for any other type of job without earning another degree? And were there any jobs out there that would really give her the time to pursue her new passion, rock climbing?

The other opposing force is the **habit of the present**. A classic example is when people say, "I don't love this, but at least I know I can keep doing it." The thought of switching to something new can feel overwhelming. Sticking with the devil you know may seem bearable in comparison because of what it enables you to do today. It is the mirror of your pulls because it tugs you back to the status quo, as Clara's neuroscience training did for a while. As research on decision-making has long shown, people are much more motivated to avoid losing something than to take an action that offers a potential gain. As a result, when considering a switch, individuals tend to overweight the things that they may lose at the expense of an even surefire set of things they might acquire.

Those opposing forces are more than strong enough to block progress. They often do—and sometimes should. As shown in Figure 2.4, people make a switch only when their pushes and pulls are so powerful that they can overcome anxiety about the future and familiar habits of the present. Only then do those forces fuel a full-fledged quest.

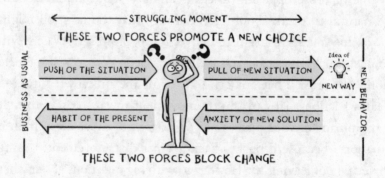

Figure 2.4
The Forces That Push, Pull, and Block Job Switchers

Knowing about your habits and anxieties is important in helping you work through your current quest because it will help you understand what's holding you back. But in analyzing a past switch, you don't need to dig into them (after all, you overcame them to make the move). For now, it's useful just to be aware of how they work.

Zeroing In On Your Past Quest

With the forces identified, you can now consider which quest for progress aligns most closely with your most recent switch. Go to jobmoves.com and use our free assessment. After answering the questions about your pushes and pulls—it takes less than ten minutes—you'll receive a "fit" score for each quest. One or two quests will generally rise above the others. For Clara, regaining control was the closest match when she left the neuroscience lab for the physical therapy clinic. Regaining alignment was a distant second.

One reason the assessment doesn't give you "the answer" is that these quests aren't mutually exclusive (nor are they collectively exhaustive—they're just poles on a map). Each one is fueled by a mix of pushes and pulls, some of which show up in multiple quests. But our tool will take your specific circumstances into account and give you a sense of how you relate to each quest. You are not trying to choose one of four options; instead, you are trying to roughly locate yourself somewhere on a map where the four corners are the "pure" quests and all the space in between represents some combination of them. This is a tool you can use again and again as you explore and iterate on your quest for progress.

Consider the attorney from Chapter One. He had been working long hours at a large law firm for years, but the work had never really resonated with him. When he thought about why he originally went to law school, it wasn't to represent corporations.

He wanted to practice law to focus on making society a safer and more just place. And he wanted to be able to tell his kids that. The money had been nice, but it didn't drive him. When his third child was born, he decided to *take the next step* in a career journey he had long ago decided upon and enter public service as a district attorney prosecuting criminal offenses. He was pleased to be able to tell his children that the work he did helped protect individuals and society from criminal offenders. But the move also had elements of *getting out* of his role at the large law firm, where he was worn down by the long hours and work he didn't enjoy.

That dev-ops programmer we mentioned in Chapter One? She left her job after her new manager began taking credit for her work. She wondered why she was investing so much of herself and sacrificing critical time with her kids for so little in return—all for a company that laid people off while they were on vacation! She was primarily looking to *regain control* by moving to a women-run company that she felt would better honor her time and choices. But in some ways, she was also looking to *regain alignment* by working in a place that would properly acknowledge and respect her contributions and skills.

In each of these cases, although multiple quests were present, one took precedence and ultimately drove the switch.

Improving Your Chances of Being Right

Of course, if this work were simple or obvious, you wouldn't be here with us. People aren't naturally good at surfacing their own pushes and pulls. It's a real challenge for human beings to be coldly analytical about the functional, social, and emotional forces moving them. But we've found that the resources above—the timeline, the interview guide, and the list of pushes and pulls—make it doable, for three reasons.

First, it is easier to identify pushes and pulls from an existing list than to start from a blank slate. We developed the list in this chapter by chronicling and analyzing the experiences of thousands of job switchers and identifying the most critical forces that caused them to make a change. So you're working with a template that is grounded in real-world experience.

Second, it is easier to identify these forces in the rearview mirror than during a job move, when things are in flux. That's why we taught you how to do the same type of interview we did with Clara and asked you to focus on your latest switch before mulling over your current situation. Practicing on the past significantly informs—and improves—the work you will do on the present.

Third, and perhaps most important, it is easier to identify pushes and pulls with help from a trusted mentor, friend, or confidant—someone to interview you, listen to you, and process your words with you. Although it's possible to interview yourself, you won't get the best results that way. When we talk about decisions we made in the past or things we'd like to do in the future, we're all, sadly, unreliable narrators. Despite the desire to better understand ourselves, we rationalize our choices and actions when left to our own devices. Sometimes we rewrite history. Other times we just miss important events and details. Having an interviewer who can ask tough questions about what actions you took keeps you honest and brings new insights to the surface.

Some people we've coached—especially the academics—have worried that these tools might unduly influence them and skew the results. That's possible, but our process has built-in checks for that later. Plus, in our experience, the tools' benefits far outweigh that risk.

Using Insights About the Past to Clarify the Present

Digging into what drove you to switch jobs last time is an exercise in metacognition. You're learning to recognize patterns in what you care about and what motivates you to act, which gives you some clues about what may be driving you now.

To be clear, before you have actually switched jobs, you can't say which forces propelled you to move. That's because your situation is dynamic. Circumstances, options, and priorities can change. New forces can emerge as you make a switch, and others can fade in importance. That, however, doesn't mean we can't identify the forces acting on you now.

Thinking about your current situation, revisit the timeline of the job switcher (Figure 2.1). What prompted your first thoughts about making your next move? What's pushed or pulled you to passively or actively look for a new job?

When Alex, the product development manager in Wisconsin, embarked on this job-switching process with us, all he knew about his quest was that there was a big push coming his way: His team was moving to another state. Although the company had offered to pay relocation expenses, moving wasn't a viable option for Alex, given the demands in his personal life. With that understanding in place, he could look again at the most common pushes and pulls and identify some of the other forces fueling his current quest. If he relocated, his work would dominate his life (a second push) by forcing him to sacrifice nonnegotiable family priorities around caring for his in-laws. For that reason, it was also hard to see where to go or how to grow in his current organization (a third push). Although his company wasn't struggling, his role in Wisconsin was certainly nearing an end.

Like Alex, you can go through the lists in Figures 2.2 and 2.3

and identify an initial set of three to five pushes *or* pulls (not both) that you believe are "definitely a factor" in prompting your quest to this point, as well as another three to five that are "definitely not a factor." Then consider which pushes *or* pulls (not both) might be "somewhat of a factor" or "not really a factor" just to keep an eye on them as you move through the rest of the steps in our process. We recommend focusing on either pushes or pulls to simplify the analysis this early on because the forces you list at this stage may very well change as you work through the job-switching process. Then go back to jobmoves.com and enter these initial forces into the assessment tool to get an early read on what may be driving you to switch. If you don't know whether a given push or pull is present, that's okay. Just mark it as "not yet sure" for now. As you clarify your thinking, you'll revisit this tool in future steps and update the forces.

If you find yourself struggling to figure out which pushes and pulls to choose, or "shopping" for a quest by entering different combinations to see if it seems like you, you're not alone. It's tempting to spin the narrative you want—to reverse engineer our process to get a particular result—rather than face what's really sparked your quest. But there's an easy way to address that issue. Call your interviewer and ask for another interview, this time about your current quest. This interview will be shorter than the previous one, because you haven't made a switch yet and you're focusing only on what's caused you to start thinking about one. Having an outside party work with you will help you more accurately identify these initial forces jump-starting your current quest. Feeling your way toward your quest now will inform how you approach the rest of our process—and improve your chances of making a job move that results in progress.

When Ellen, a senior manager at a manufacturing company,

first approached us, she was just starting to think about what might be next in her career. Maybe she'd move to another employer, or out of manufacturing altogether, or maybe she'd try a new role at her current company. Everything seemed to be on the table. Before wrestling with her present, we took her into her past to examine her most recent job move. During the interview, she identified the main pushes away from her previous job as feeling disrespected and ignored, worn down by the way she was managed, challenged beyond her ability, and unequipped to make an impact. She had been pulled into her current role—launching a new division at a manufacturing company—by the allure of being trusted to do good work, reporting to a supportive boss, learning and growing day-to-day, and knowing that her job was not at risk. As is the case for most individuals, there was no exact match between her list of pushes and pulls and the different quests, but Ellen's closest match was the quest to get out, with elements of regain control and regain alignment. Those insights about the past enabled her to recognize that *different* forces were driving her current curiosity about new roles. She realized that those new forces were pushes: She felt she was at a personal milestone and was growing bored in her current role. There wasn't yet a pull.

A few years back, Michael took a similar approach. Having received a preliminary offer to be the president of a new university, he was excited by the role and the school's mission. The pulls seemed clear. As Bob talked with him, however, about what had caused Michael to enter the gig economy and what might drive him to take on something new after his children were born, Michael had some epiphanies. First, his current priorities were similar to what had led him to change roles most recently. When Michael had last switched, he was looking to regain control. He wanted freedom and flexibility to do his best work and time to devote to his family.

He realized that if he accepted the new offer, much of what he'd gain—a large increase in prestige and responsibilities—would be inconsistent with what he had gained from his last switch. That wasn't a sacrifice he was willing to make. At this point in his life, he wanted to maintain control. The pulls weren't strong enough to overcome his current habits. As a result, he turned down the role without losing much sleep.

At this stage in his process, Alex didn't yet know what specific pulls would lead him to choose what to do next. But unlike Michael, he knew that he had to do something new. And he could say with certainty that having control over his time and where he did his work were table stakes. Although not earth-shattering, these realizations clarified things he knew in his gut. And that made it easier to move through the rest of our process. This is something we've seen time and again. The quests and underlying forces give people the language to name their feelings, which makes their circumstances more concrete. The framework also provides the comfort of knowing that others have been in similar situations.

Recognizing that his status quo wasn't tenable—he needed a new job—Alex felt an urge to rush. He wanted to prepare his résumé and start having conversations about local job opportunities—yesterday. Wasn't that clarity enough? he asked. Why did he need to identify the quest he was most likely on? He wasn't even certain that the forces acting upon him aligned clearly with any of the four quests.

We counseled him to slow down, lest he rush into a job that didn't actually help him make progress. He had been given an opportunity to hire his next job. Why waste it?

We then asked him if he had any sense of what he wanted to do next. It was clear he knew parts of what he *didn't* want. But what motivated and energized him? What capabilities did he want to invest in? Those were tantalizing questions to which Alex didn't yet have answers. But engaging with them would clarify how expansive his job search should be. It would also help him eliminate options that might look great on paper but would turn out to be a step backward in his quest for progress.

Understanding how those two critical questions about energy and capabilities relate to the four quests is the work of the next section, where you'll further flesh out the demand side of your search for a new job: what you really want.

PART II

DISCOVERING WHAT'S
DRIVING YOU NOW

You've developed some early ideas about what's driving your current job search. Now it's time to go deeper—and to start shaping the future. Over the next six chapters, you'll strengthen your insights into the kind of progress you want to make next. Then you'll use that information to brainstorm a wide range of options before converging on one or two "prototypes." This foundational work will guide your job search in a way that's consistent with your quest for progress in your career and life.

THREE

THINK "EXPERIENCES"
BEFORE "FEATURES"

After we finished analyzing Clara's most recent job move, she left with a better understanding of her past motivations—and some useful early clues about her current frame of mind. She had a strong sense of what was *pushing* her to start looking for something new. She was bored, wasn't being challenged, and couldn't see a place to grow at the physical therapy clinic. The mundane repetition in her job was wearing her down.

But without a clear idea of what she was moving toward, her *pulls*—and thus her quest—remained undefined. Without that clarity, how would she know which jobs to explore and which ones to avoid? And how would she know whether any new possibilities would be better than her current role?

Unless you're in the Take the Next Step quest *and* the path ahead is clear, you likely feel similarly. Sure, the deep dive into why people switch jobs may have been interesting—and even illuminating. And yes, it's nice to have concrete language to explain why you're thinking about making a job move now. But how is that information supposed to shape your future?

This chapter is where we begin making that connection. Here, we outline how any quest you may be on relates to two key questions.

Compared with your current role:

1. How do you want your next job to motivate or energize you?
2. And how do you want it to make use of your capabilities?

Although those are not novel questions in the world of career advice, we have found that by answering them in the context of the pushes and pulls, job switchers can make a lot more progress. After explaining that framework here, we help you answer both questions in the following chapters as we walk you through the next steps of our process.

This all requires a major shift in thinking—away from focusing on what you might *be* next to figuring out what you'll actually *do* on a day-to-day basis.

A Shift in Mindset

At least once a week, someone approaching us for career advice comes bearing a list of *features* they want in their work life—like better hours, less travel, higher pay, a worthier title, faster advancement, greater responsibility, and more impact. All those things sound nice. We want them, too. But such lists rarely help job seekers make progress because they fail to ground people in the reasons they're looking for a change—the pushes and pulls driving them to find something new.

As a result, the job search can quickly become an exercise in frustration—much like house hunting or apartment hunting. If you've even glanced at real estate listings out of curiosity, you know that they tout features: open kitchens, granite countertops, natural light, finished basements, and so on. On their own, however, those descriptions—while initially enticing—lack meaning. They all start to blur together after you've been hunting for a while. They can also mislead people and cause them to make poor choices. To envision living somewhere new with any degree of accuracy, you need to dig deeper by considering the day-to-day experiences you have now and those you want to change.

Let's suppose you're a working parent of young children. You might say to yourself: "It's hard to work from home where I'm currently living. My house is cramped and noisy. I need a quiet, comfortable, well-lit area so I can focus. And my kids need a separate space to play so they can run around without disrupting me." If that's your train of thought, then you've shifted away from considering a home's features in a vacuum to identifying what you've been struggling with—the pushes causing you to look for a new house—and what experiences, or pulls, would improve your life. And now you can think about natural light and finished basements *in that context*. You still end the search by considering the features of a house, but that should be grounded in an up-front understanding of the experiences you desire.

Job switchers who make smart moves take a similar tack. They don't contemplate what their job *will be*—its features, such as a better title or more money. Their focus is instead on what they *will experience* on a day-to-day basis and how that will help them progress from their past and current moments of struggle, which helps them avoid the fate of those who quickly regretted their moves during the Great Resignation. That means they must have a clear sense of what their struggles are and have been, what progress looks like in their current situation, and what trade-offs they are willing to make to achieve that progress. When you start with features, it's nearly impossible to make wise trade-offs between them. But when you focus on experiences—the day-to-day and week-to-week of a job and how that lines up with the progress you desire—it's easier to understand which features you value most and why.

With this in mind, look back at the lists of pushes and pulls in Chapter Two. Note how they are all *experiences, not features*, of a job. Even after we asked Clara to do this, she had trouble letting go of the old mindset. She told us that her next job absolutely needed to pay more money. That feeling isn't unusual. We are programmed to believe that progress means moving up—in pay, in rank, in scope, in the numbers of people reporting to you, and the like. But unless you examine the underlying reasons why and consider what's currently happening in your life, simply prioritizing features like income won't help you find the *right* next job. Do you suddenly have new expenses to cover? Are you saving for your kids' college tuition ten or more years out? Are you trying to create a cushion so you can reduce stress or increase your quality of life in the long term? Are you hoping eventually to gain status or respect with greater wealth? All those reasons have different implications for what the right move might be now—and what moves might be inconsistent with these goals. To be more precise, if you have medical needs in your family, perhaps different health insurance is more important than higher income. Or if you have a young child who requires day care, then perhaps you need more money, an employer that provides day care, or more flexibility—which raises another set of considerations to investigate.

Without any context wrapped around it, money is just a feature. It's not the underlying reason to change jobs. That's one reason it doesn't show up as one of the pushes or pulls—or as part of the quests—that cause people to change jobs. If you use features like money or job titles as your criteria, your honeymoon in the new job is likely to be short and your next job hunt near at hand. As soon as you have more of one feature, like money or status, you will be frustrated by not having more of another, like time to do what you want with it. As one Fortune 100 CEO once told us, choosing a new job for its title can have a great return to ego, but the glow will be short-lived.

When we asked Clara why she needed more money, she saw our point and started to rattle off reasons—to afford better rock-climbing gear, get a larger apartment, and travel with her boyfriend, who was originally from Europe. This was just the beginning of identifying her pulls—and charting her quest for progress.

What Motivates You? And How Do You Want to Use Your Capabilities?

Because what you'll do is more important than what you'll be, at this stage it's critical to think about how you want your next job to motivate or energize you each day *and* how you want it to make use of your capabilities. Our analysis suggests that each of the quests can be plotted along these two related dimensions (see Figure 3.1).

What motivates and energizes you can include what you like in your current job, how it makes you feel, and how well the job fits in with what matters in the rest of your life. But it's more than that. You also derive motivation and energy from being excited by aspects of your work and, as psychologist Mihaly Csikszentmihalyi termed it, finding yourself in a state of flow when you do it. Across our dataset, job seekers were either searching for more of the things that drive their motivation and energy in their current role (that is, looking to build on them) or hoping to encounter fewer of the things that tax it (in other words, yearning for a reset). For example, one individual longed for a *reset* from a role at a large multinational company where, in her view, "over-achievers [went] to feel bad about themselves." Her job was sapping her motivation. It was a stark contrast from a prior one-year stint in an organization where the "people were genuinely kind with each other." An individual at a tech company was energized by her team. She wanted her next job to *build* on that feeling of community spirit by fostering a culture where "people stood up for each other."

How a job makes use of your capabilities involves the ways in which it leverages your expertise, experience, and skills. Whether you feel equipped to do your job can change over time. People build careers by proving themselves through stretch assignments that develop their expertise and enhance their credibility. Your track record on one stretch assignment opens the door to others, which further expands your base of expertise. As leadership expert Linda Hill has shown, this iterative process propels you forward on a career path. Although the path can be one of your choosing, it can also be more accidental, based on the opportunities you happen to have had early in your career. It's therefore not surprising that, in our research, many job transitions are defined by a desire either to double down on an individual's "chosen" capabilities or to move away from the "accidental" ones.

One individual who had worked in the global health arena, for example, found herself as the chief of staff to the executive director of a research institute. She loved the organization's mission but quickly realized that the role she had wasn't aligned with her skill set. She wasn't challenged. Nor did she feel that she was having much of an impact. As a result, when she gave birth to her second child, she used her maternity leave as an opportunity to *reset* how work made use of her capabilities by taking a new role within the same organization. When another individual was thinking of leaving the military, a phone call telling her that she was up for a prestigious promotion persuaded her to stay. That's because the new role would allow her to *build* on her current capabilities—something she desired. "It's flattering when you're asked by name to do something," she said. "It was an indicator that they thought I could be [a high-ranking officer] one day."

Putting the two dimensions together (see Figure 3.1) allows us to visualize how the four quests relate to one another. It also sets up the key questions you're going to answer in the next steps of our process so that you can better understand your current priorities and what you want in your next job.

People seeking to "get out" want to completely reset how their work motivates them because their job is draining rather than driving their energy. They *also* want a total reset on what's required of them because they aren't developing the expertise they desire or using it for the purposes and impact they want.

Those seeking to "regain control" want to preserve and build on the skills used in their current job. But they want to reset how they and their time are used because it's demotivating and draining them. That's why so many who are on this quest complain about burnout; they feel overwhelmed and depleted.

Those looking to "regain alignment" are the opposite. They pride themselves on being well equipped to do what their current job demands. But they want a reset on capabilities so that their organization uses, appreciates, and acknowledges the skills they want to use and thus more fully aligns with the purpose and impact they seek.

Finally, those who want to "take the next step" seek more of what is presently motivating them and want to build on the capabilities they have developed so far.

When people worry that knowing these quests ahead of time might create a self-fulfilling prophecy, we remind them that the purpose of the quests isn't to be predictive. They're simply a tool you can use to figure out what you want to prioritize at any given point in your career. What do you want to build upon, and what

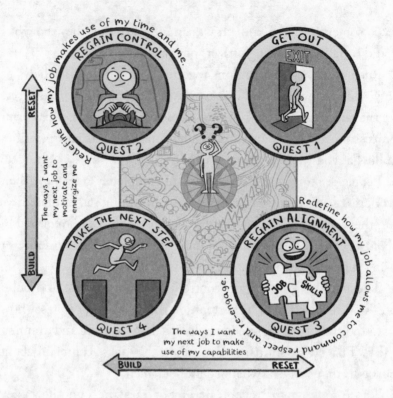

Figure 3.1

Choosing Your Trajectory for Progress: The Map of Quests

---

*   Figure 3.1: If you're coming at this from an academic lens, you're probably trying
    to figure out how to draw bright lines between the quests. In rigorous scholarly
    work, a framework must have what is called "discriminant validity"—one category
    or measure needs to be clearly distinguishable from another. But as we noted in
    Chapter Two, our quests are not mutually exclusive. To identify them in our dataset,
    we induced patterns across the combinations of forces that *cause* people to switch
    jobs, rather than segmenting individuals by demographic. So the areas of overlap
    are a feature, not a bug. Not only do people find themselves in different quests at
    different stages in their careers but they also rarely fit neatly into one quest, because
    it's a set of distinct reasons working together that causes them to make a change. Our
    categories aggregate the predominant underlying reasons we see in each quest. As we
    also shared in Chapter Two, individuals who most identify with one quest will often
    see glimmers of others. Given that "motivation" and "capability" are interrelated (i.e.,
    when you are motivated to do a job, you seek additional capabilities to do it well, and
    when you feel you are more capable of doing a job, you are more motivated to do it),
    it makes sense that you might find yourself in the large white space between quests
    rather than squarely within one of them. That's why this tool is designed to be seen as
    a landscape rather than as four distinct choices or cells.

do you want to reset? Even if the answers to those questions are fluid—depending on your changing circumstances—knowing where you roughly are on each dimension will help you to proactively stake out your quest. It will help you learn before switching, manage your transition, determine what advice is most useful to you, and clarify the trade-offs you should make to get what's most important to you now.

Because we focused on the most prevalent drivers of change when we did this research and haven't captured *every* possible quest, it's unsurprising that some people say they can't identify with any of the quests. In our analysis, these individuals fall into two categories.

First, there are those who have been let go from their jobs—or, less disruptively, those who worked for a rapidly changing organization and woke up one day to discover that the job they loved had morphed into something they no longer recognized. Either way, they typically tell us they want to return to what they were doing. But really, the moment that job went away, they had another big decision to make: Should they embark on a quest to find a new role or stay out of the workforce? And *then*, if they looked for work, what should they seek to do? In other words, their reference point isn't the job they had; it's their present circumstance once the job is gone. When we frame it that way, most of these individuals can then identify at least somewhat with one of the quests. And just about all of them can see value in figuring out whether they are trying to build on or reset what motivates and energizes them and how their capabilities are used.

The second category of job switchers who don't immediately identify with the four quests struggle because they don't see a precise fit for their circumstances. When this is the case, we help them step back. Can they see pieces of a prior job switch in any of the quests, even if there's no clear match? With that prompt, nearly everyone can identify with at least certain aspects of some of the quests. And Figure 3.1 helps people see that their current job does fall *somewhere* on each continuum between building and resetting.

That's an important realization. Our data suggest that a key reason many job switchers fail to make progress in new roles is that they lack a clear understanding of where they fall within this framework. They don't know whether they are looking for more of the same (build) or something different (reset) in how their job uses their capabilities and motivates them *at this juncture* in their life and work. By defining what you want on these two dimensions, you can put a finer point on what progress means to you now and tailor your job search to align with that definition of progress.

That's what Steps 2 and 3 of our process enable you to do. In the next chapter, we first focus on identifying which specific activities have historically motivated you—or brought you energy. Then we sort out which of those activities are most relevant for you today.

FOUR

STEP 2:
KNOW WHAT YOU WANT
DRIVING YOUR ENERGY

 When we began working with Clara, her ideas about what she might do next were all over the map. Having explored health-care roles and landed in one she didn't love, she was wondering if the whole health-care idea had been a big mistake. Or maybe she just hadn't found the right fit. Perhaps what she needed was another degree—in medicine—so she could try something *different* in health care. Suffice to say, she felt lost and directionless.

Because Clara hadn't yet identified any clear pulls, her current quest was still murky, which is what we expect at this stage. To begin figuring out what she did want, we asked her which sorts of activities drove and drained her energy. She couldn't answer that question off the top of her head, which made it hard to place herself along that axis in the map of quests (see Chapter Three). She asked us if that really mattered. We said it did, unless she wanted to fall into another unfulfilling job that didn't feel like progress.

And so we dove into the second step of our process: identifying what drives your energy to understand one dimension of your quest. In this step, you once again analyze your past roles so you can spot patterns across your career, identify recurring energy drivers and drains, and roughly prioritize which drivers are most important to you now. This part of the process provides insight into whether you want your next job to reset or build on what energizes you relative to your current role.

You may be relieved to hear that this won't involve a ton of extra work. Your résumé has a lot of the information you need to get started.

Looking at Your Résumé in a New Way

Listing activities that create and drain energy to define what motivates you isn't a novel idea. Many experts have offered such exercises. For example, Bill Burnett and Dave Evans, educators in Stanford University's Design Program, suggest writing down when you feel bored, restless, or unhappy, as well as when you feel excited and focused every day. As you do so, you also record what you are doing at those times to notice patterns in what engages you and what drains you. Others recommend the simpler act of journaling: writing for thirty minutes a day, for five consecutive days, for example, about anything that comes to mind. If you do, more often than not you start to write about things you enjoy and things you do not enjoy, as well as accomplishments, challenges, and what you have learned along the way. The advantage of a journal is you can admit things in private that you might not want to say aloud.

But for Clara's purposes, we wanted to look at her energy drivers and drains in the context of her career. Rather than think about these experiences at a high level or ask her to do an exercise that she was unlikely to start, let alone complete, we pointed Clara to her résumé. That's something she would have to work on anyway to make a job move.

Most résumés offer a concise list of past positions, skill sets, and accomplishments. On their own, these items don't offer insight into what gives you or drains your energy. Nor do they give clues about what your current pushes or pulls are. If they did, you wouldn't need to read this book because your past would automatically chart a path to your future.

But your future trajectory is anything but automatic. After all, people with similar pasts—and therefore similar résumés—can find themselves in very different places in their career. Consider two lawyers we coached. One was burned out and discouraged by the progression from associate to partner that she was expected to follow. She was going through the motions without real support or passion. The other, a junior associate at the same firm, was energized by the competitive culture and fast pace but insufficiently challenged by the work he was being asked to do by his assigned practice group. These individuals were more or less on the same track in the organization, but their pushes and pulls were quite different.

For our purposes here, it's what's between the lines of your résumé that matters most—what energy drivers and drains truly motivated you to go from one line of your résumé to the next. To flesh that out, you'll use your résumé in a novel way (see activity below). Not only will you jot down the basic details about all the roles you've held but you'll also record what drove and drained your energy. This activity can unlock emotional memories and "transport" you back into remembering what your day-to-day experiences felt like.

Figure 4.1 shows what Clara's table looked like after she filled out her energy drivers and drains for each of her roles.

Activity: Identify Your Energy Drivers and Drains

Start by imagining that you have rotated your résumé 90 degrees to create a timeline table that summarizes your career path to this point. Then at the top of a blank page or a whiteboard (physical or digital), create a column for each role you've held in your career. If you've held multiple roles at one company, list each of those separately. If you've done substantial volunteer work, include those experiences as well.

Under each job, write the location, how long you held the role, and what your responsibilities were. You'll list both tasks and accomplishments, such as:

- Oversaw a team of ten people
- Managed a P&L
- Grew sales of new product by 2x; exceeded targets by 50 percent
- Negotiated contracts with buyers
- Developed an award-winning new product from conception through launch

So far, all the information needed can come directly from your résumé. But as we've discussed, what you *do* at work is more important than what the job "is." Listing tasks and accomplishments captures that. It also jogs your memory about how each job felt, which triggers a visceral response to help you recall details about energy drivers and drains. *Energy drivers* are the things that make you excited to go to work, dive in, and get into the flow of the job. You can think of them as your source of passion for the job. *Energy drains*, on the other hand, are the things that irritate or frustrate you, that diminish your enjoyment of what you do, or that you even dread about the job. You'll list them below your responsibilities under each role you've held.

We've found that this activity works best if you allow thoughts to come to you as you're doing other things. You'll capture richer, more telling details if you don't rush it. You can spend anywhere from a few days to a few weeks jotting down any time you remember feeling energized or drained on the job. Chatting with a few friends about your past roles can prime the pump. And if you want to return to this exercise later on as other memories come to you, that's okay as well.

Remembering Why You Thrived and Struggled

One person we worked with on this activity, Jacob, was a content producer at a media company. He had originally approached us for help because he was struggling to understand why, after just a couple years in each of his roles throughout his career, he kept finding himself bored and disengaged. By the end of his tenure, he would be drifting through his day without purpose. A couple of employers had even laid him off as a result. We asked Jacob to write down the things that drove his energy in his current role. After a couple weeks, he came back to us with the following list:

> Hearing from clients that he was doing a great job
> Finding new ways to be efficient with budgets
> Creating win-win situations for clients
> Knowing that his division was allowing the rest of the company to grow

We also asked about his *energy drains*. This was an easier list for Jacob to create. He rattled off three things he hated in his current role:

> Not receiving proper training on the overall production process
> Needing to constantly ask his coworkers for help
> Struggling to get traction on long-term strategy

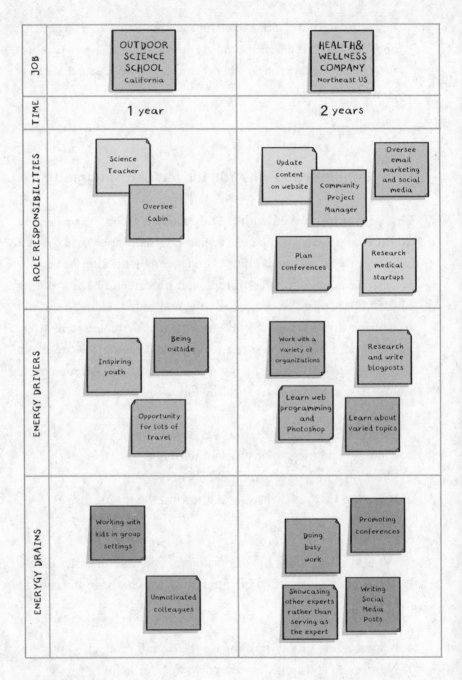

Figure 4.1
The Energy Drivers and Drains in Clara's Career

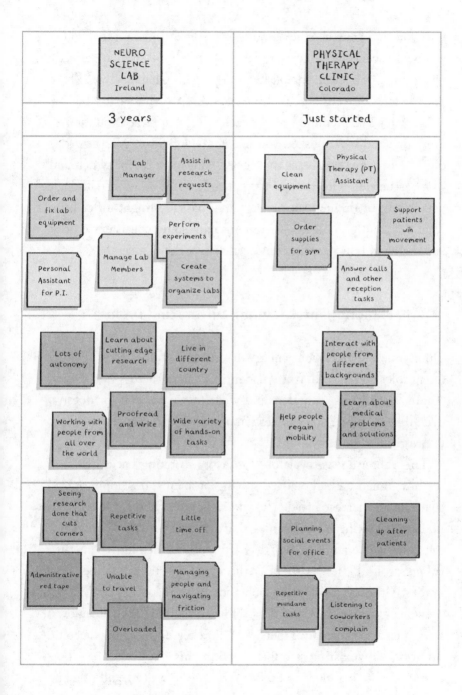

If you find yourself stuck or just want some validation that you've thoroughly captured your energy drivers and drains, we have already given you a crib sheet: the pushes and pulls in Chapter Two. These don't belong on your energy drivers and drains whiteboard, but revisiting them can remind you, for each role, what pulled you to work every day and what pushed you to eagerly anticipate your next day off. Look first at the forces that fueled your most recent switch and those associated with the quest you think you're on now. Although what drove or drained your energy in a past job might differ from what's currently doing so, there is usually some consistency, or at least logic, to how people are motivated over their careers.

Exploring the Recurring Drivers and Drains

Once you've charted your energy drivers and drains across the different roles you've held, you can identify patterns across your career. Again, the idea is to understand what motivates you (or doesn't) overall so that later you can zero in on which experiences you want to prioritize right now.

This exercise was revelatory for Jacob. Looking back, he could see how much he had enjoyed solving problems, developing novel solutions to increase efficiency, and satisfying clients. He realized he loved working at companies that struggled in those areas because he was energized by the hard work of helping them turn things around. But as soon as the situation stabilized, he grew bored. Although this seemed obvious in retrospect, Jacob hadn't previously connected these dots. He also realized that he enjoyed having clear performance metrics and processes on which he could improve using existing resources, working his way up from the bottom, and sticking close to home. Working in a dead-end role and having to bring in resources from the outside drained him.

Clara benefited a great deal from this part of the process as well. It helped her think more deeply about her past experiences and moves so she could more accurately envision and assess future experiences when considering new roles.

When we looked at her drivers and drains (see Figure 4.1), clear patterns emerged. Working with people from different places and cultures energizes her. Managing them and dealing with politics doesn't. Learning new things energizes her. Doing the same things over and over doesn't.

For other people in our dataset, common drivers include security, creativity, freedom to work independently, having impact, helping others, being part of a community, performing at a high level, and creating new things. Common drains include not having control over your own time, pressure to meet unrealistic goals, an overly political work environment, incessant travel away from family, nonstop meetings, a lack of time to think, a lack of meaning in the work, and repetitive work. But here we offer a critical warning: don't fall into the trap of adopting certain energy drivers and drains because you think they are "standard" for "people like you." Some people, like Clara, may not like "dealing with politics," whereas others might instead view that same activity as "getting to influence other people to get things done and make an impact." Similarly, some people find working from home isolating, whereas others find it wonderfully refreshing. There are many other examples of how much energy drivers and drains differ between two people who otherwise seem similar, especially when viewed through their résumés. This is why we don't simply refer to energy drains and drivers as likes and dislikes. They are not features of a job like those granite countertops and natural light that almost everyone finds appealing in a real estate listing but rather experiences you have in the job that drive or drain your motivation to bring your best self to work.

With that in mind, try to identify five to ten recurring energy drivers or drains across your past roles. If you're struggling to do so, this is another place where a mentor can help. Often an outside person can more easily make connections between roles or lift you out of the details to see the bigger picture.

Unpack What the Drivers and Drains Mean to You

Next, define concretely what each driver and drain means to you. For example, "having impact" could mean many things—from making a positive difference on your team to transforming an entire sector of society. What kind of impact are you hoping to have? And how do you want to see that materialize—day-to-day or over the long term?

It helps to think about specific situations and ask yourself "five whys" to really nail what each driver and drain means to you. For instance, to define "having an impact," you might follow this line of inquiry (the responses are examples of how you might answer):

Why did working on that project to support a client have an impact?

It changed how our company operated. The lessons learned on that project held up a mirror to all of our work. We took a hard look at ourselves and thought, "Hey, maybe this is a better way to do things." So we started changing our internal processes.

Why did these changes matter?

People started feeling a spark again. We began to find more meaning in our work.

Why did people find more meaning?

The work wasn't just about going through the motions inside our functional group. The new processes put us in closer touch with colleagues in other groups, which created more camaraderie throughout the company. Imagine an office where the walls disappear and you're suddenly part of something much bigger.

Why was that so meaningful?
We previously felt isolated from others and lacked a sense of community. We were lonely before—whether we were in the office or virtual. All of a sudden, we felt part of an awesome work tribe.

Why do you think a sense of community creates impact at work?
People develop shared identity and purpose, which offers intrinsic value. When you have that sense of belonging, you're not just working for a paycheck. You've got a team behind you and a real purpose that's bringing you all together.

Five whys later, impact in this particular instance appears to be more about building a positive work environment, helping others find meaning at work, and fostering connection among colleagues. It's less, in this case, about things like competitive strategy, customer relationships, and the bottom line.

Asking what each energy driver or drain is "less about" is important, too. It takes advantage of how our brains are wired. Neuroscience research suggests that to facilitate better decisions, for example, eliminating the worst choice is a better first step than picking the best one. That way, you rein in your options and weigh them more accurately. For that reason, it's often easier to figure out what's not relevant to a particular driver or drain than to figure out what you're really prioritizing.

Once Clara identified colleagues as a recurring source of energy, she drilled into what this meant to her. In her case, it was less about socializing and more about being inspired and supported by others, getting the job done together, learning from one another, and trusting one another. And it stood in stark contrast to some of her persistent energy drains—being around unmotivated coworkers, being micromanaged, and having to micromanage others.

Ultimately, Clara took the common drains and reframed them as drivers so that everything on her list was represented as an energy driver. We recommend you do the same. Here's a simplified version of Clara's list:

> Time for hobbies
> Intellectually challenging
> Personal impact
> Learning opportunities
> Variety of tasks
> Autonomy
> Inspire curiosity
> Collaboration
> Time to think
> Physically doing tasks
> Generating new ideas

The next order of business is to determine which items matter most at this point in your life.

Comparing Past Experiences Against Each Energy Driver

It's almost certain that your next job won't deliver every single thing that energizes you, so you'll need to prioritize your energy drivers. But first, for each one, you'll force rank your past jobs on a continuum between "not present at all" and "fully present." This helps you more vividly recall how the drivers have manifested in your work.

We know this exercise can feel difficult or even a bit artificial. Forced ranking deservedly gets a bad rap in other work contexts, such as performance evaluations. It creates a zero-sum race for rewards like bonuses and promotions, which means many worthy contributors are left behind in the dust with feelings of bitterness.

So why use a forced ranking here? When you're assessing career moves rather than human beings, it's a helpful tool to surface insights you might otherwise miss. And there's little risk of unintended consequences. To illustrate what this looks like, Figure 4.2 shows how Clara's past roles compared on just one of the energy drivers of importance to her: learning opportunities.

Clara noted that although her current physical therapy role allowed her to explore areas of interest outside of work, she wasn't learning much in the job itself. That had been okay, maybe even

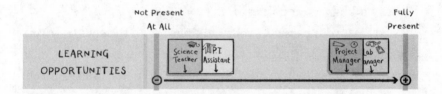

Figure 4.2
How Clara's Past Jobs Rank on One Energy Driver

desirable, when she had first switched jobs. But it was rapidly becoming a source of friction.

This exercise kept her from falling into the Goldilocks trap, in which past experiences look neither too hot nor too cold but just right. By assessing past roles along each energy driver, Clara instead had to tether her memory of each job to something concrete. Doing so helped her avoid romanticizing her past experiences. It also prevented the common Lake Wobegon effect—where everything seems "above average" in every way, which makes it tough to distinguish between experiences and to remember the compromises you made in each case. General, bland assessments won't give you enough information to understand trade-offs you made in past roles and to recognize your priorities—in the past, now, or in the future. That's because they don't force you to grapple with the fact that any given job couldn't possibly be equal across all aspects relative to other jobs you've held. Nor could it be "just right" in all ways. There are difficult parts to all jobs. There are always trade-offs, even in the job you loved the most. We want to make those trade-offs explicit. We want to help you understand your experiences more clearly by showing them in relation to one another across each energy driver and taking advantage of the fact that *contrast helps create meaning.* We want you to recognize that a past job you loved perhaps wasn't as good on a certain energy driver as another job you didn't enjoy quite as much. Forced ranking accomplishes all that.

Next, cast your eyes over your rankings for all the energy drivers (see Figure 4.3). This allows you to see the value of your past roles in multiple areas, which provides a more complete and concrete picture of each experience.

By comparing jobs across recurring energy drivers, you deepen and enrich your understanding of what matters most to you. It's not the precise location of one job versus another on each energy driver that will help you find your next job, but rather the larger trends you observe, and where you observe them, over time.

The relative importance of your energy drivers will also shift over time, which can be surprising. People often discover that jobs they vaguely remember loving actually rank quite low on energy drivers that became more important to them in their most recent roles. That happened to Clara. As a teacher at a science camp for high schoolers, she had loved working with young aspiring scientists and finding ways to inspire them. But when plotting this job across the

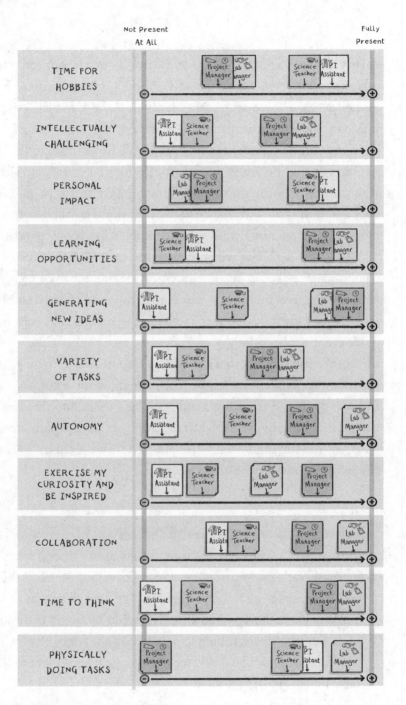

Figure 4.3
How Clara's Jobs Ranked Across Her Key Drivers

energy drivers she had since grown to care about, she noticed trade-offs she had never considered before. Although the job ranked high on her desire to have an impact on others—she loved the positive influence she had on her campers—it did not afford her many learning opportunities. Understanding trade-offs we've made in the past reminds us that no job is perfect. It also forces us to acknowledge which sacrifices we're no longer willing to make at this point in our lives and to reckon with the changes in workplaces (such as the explosion of virtual and hybrid work after the COVID-19 pandemic) that have affected how we evaluate trade-offs. The reverse is also true, of course. You may notice that in your recent roles you have been missing certain energy drivers that you used to have and that still matter a great deal to you. Noticing these voids is important.

Conventional wisdom would suggest force ranking the energy drivers themselves. But that's another pitfall to avoid. There are too many interdependencies among them to allow for a simple ranking. We do, however, recommend bucketing them into three broad categories (see activity below) to develop a sense of what's critical, what's negotiable, and what's dispensable for you at this moment in time as you consider your next job move.

Activity: Bucket Your Energy Drivers

With your role rankings in hand, create three buckets for the energy drivers you've identified in your job history. The first should contain must-haves for your next job. The second bucket should contain nice-to-haves—benefits that would be great in an ideal world but that you're willing to sacrifice to get things that matter more. And the third bucket is for the energy drivers that are least important to you at this stage in your life and career.

This exercise will help you move forward with a reasonable

decision if you can't check off every box in a future job—which is a likely scenario. Almost no one gets everything they want—and if they somehow do, then they tend to just want even more. Assuming you don't land a job that addresses every energy driver, you can also consider how else you might fulfill the nice-to-haves through other endeavors, such as personal relationships, volunteer commitments, and side hustles. You may also discover in this process that your current role is better than other opportunities out there. Sometimes the grass on the other side isn't as lush as it seemed at first glance. After you have identified the energy drivers in your must-haves, look at how they are reflected (or not) in your current job. If there's significant overlap, then you're likely looking to build on how your job energizes you. Which means that your quest is probably to regain alignment or take the next step. But if there's a significant gap, then you're likely looking for a reset on how your job energizes you, which means that you're probably looking to get out or regain control.

If your bucketing insights are fairly consistent with your quest assessment results (from the tool at jobmoves.com), that should assure you that you've done this activity correctly. But even if there's a significant discrepancy between the two, that's not a bad thing. Perhaps your circumstances have changed since you completed the assessment, and this is a great time to retake it. Maybe the initial pushes or pulls you've identified for your quest aren't quite accurate, or some of your "not sure yet" responses have started coming into focus. Or maybe you are convincing yourself that certain energy drivers are more or less important than they in fact are right now. In other words, use this activity to check your earlier work so you can proceed confidently in line with your actual priorities around what you want to do and experience in your next job.

What Your Prioritized Drivers Say About Your Current Quest

When Clara did this bucketing, the energy drivers she deemed critical were doing intellectually challenging work, having learning opportunities on the job, making an impact on people, and gaining time for hobbies. Her negotiables consisted of having a wide variety of tasks, autonomy, the opportunity to collaborate, and time to think. At this point, her dispensable drivers were getting to exercise her curiosity, doing physical tasks, and generating new ideas.

When she considered these roughly grouped energy drivers—particularly those in the first, critical bucket—she realized that she didn't want a *total* reset in how her job energized her. In her present job, she had plenty of time to rock climb, and she was able to have a positive impact on people—more so than in any job she had held previously. Hanging on to those things in her next role was a top priority.

Nor was Clara simply hoping to build on her current job. It wasn't giving her nearly enough intellectually challenging work or ample learning opportunities. That meant she sat somewhere in the middle of the axis for how she wanted her next job to energize her relative to her current one (see Figure 3.1 in Chapter Three). And that suggested she probably wasn't looking to get out from her current job at all costs or, predominantly, to regain control.

Those realizations had an immediate impact on her search. Because she wasn't dying to get out, there was no reason to rush. Our admonitions for her to slow down made more sense now. She could set aside her nagging thoughts about whether she was staying in her current role too long. Recognizing that she wasn't looking to regain control led her to ask another question entirely: Did her still-unknown pulls toward her next job involve resetting—or building on—how her *capabilities* were used? Answering that question is the focus of the next chapter.

FIVE

STEP 3:
CATALOG YOUR CAPABILITIES

 Now that you have a sense of where you are along the vertical, motivation axis of the quest map (in Chapter Three), it's time to sort out where you are on the horizontal axis: How do you want your next job to make use of your capabilities?

Alex was already fairly sure where he stood on this question. After all, he loved the work he did currently, and he hoped that a new role could similarly leverage his skills and experiences. Working through his energy drivers and drains had confirmed that.

Clara had much bigger unknowns when it came to capabilities. She wasn't even sure which ones she had developed so far in her career, which meant she had no idea which ones she wanted to keep developing or leave behind. She also didn't know if she wanted to pick up any new skills—or how any of this would relate to what she was doing currently in her physical therapy job. She needed help structuring her thinking.

So did Avery, a professional in her late twenties who found herself at a capabilities crossroads. She was steeped in technical expertise with undergraduate degrees in computer science and engineering from a prestigious university and a master's degree that went even deeper into data science and information technology. She had worked for nearly a decade as a software engineer at a large tech company before being promoted to product manager. Now she was feeling stressed. The people she managed were struggling to solve problems independently and begging for her technical guidance. But Avery's managers were pushing her to focus *less* on using the technical problem-solving skills that she had honed as an individual contributor. Instead, they wanted her to become more skilled at managing her team and triaging the demands that came their way from other parts of the business.

If you have any of the confusion or questions that Avery or Clara had at this stage, this third step—cataloging your capabilities—is tailor-made for you. And even if you don't, like Alex, don't skip it. Employers speak in terms of capabilities and base decisions on them. While we're not yet ready to focus too much on what employers want—the "supply side" of the job seeker's market—this step does begin to prepare you for that as well.

Cataloging your capabilities is a matter of basic accounting.

Tallying Up Your Assets and Liabilities

This step, like the last, pulls from your résumé, but this time the focus is different. Instead of digging into each role's tasks and accomplishments to understand what motivated you and brought you energy, you'll shift your attention to the responsibilities within each job. From those, you can discern the skills you've developed and refined over time.

Some equate capabilities with aptitudes and strengths. But they're not the same thing. Aptitudes and strengths are one's natural talents and temperaments. They tend to be abstract qualities, such as "detail oriented," "analytical," or "idea developer." There are assessments that offer insights into these. For example, the now-classic Ball Aptitude Battery was developed in 1975 so that test takers could understand how their talents align with different environments. Many companies have used the battery and the research behind it as part of their career-recommendation engines. We've also found Strengths-Finder to be useful in helping people understand their strong points.

But such assessments fill in just part of the picture. Although capabilities are partially rooted in innate strengths, they also stem from acquired experience, knowledge, and achievement. As a result, we are capable of far more than what an assessment says our strengths are. Context is what turns abstract traits into applied, relevant capabilities. Figure 5.1 gives some concrete examples of how aptitudes/strengths and capabilities differ. Being detail oriented, for instance, may make you more capable of doing certain jobs, like quality assurance work, but less capable of others, like leading a big team. Although aptitude and strengths tests may help you identify careers that appeal to you, they aren't typically designed to assess capabilities in context. That's what examining your role responsibilities will help you do.

FIGURE 5.1

Aptitudes vs. Capabilities

Aptitudes/strengths are relatively abstract.	Capabilities are contextually grounded.
Analytical reasoning	Accurately predicted competitive dynamics in the music industry
Numerical computation	Constructed equity trading algorithms using applied math models
Spatial thinking	Designed collaborative professional workspaces using latest CAD software
Empathy	Managed large customer service teams during peak times
Communication	Successfully coordinated complex teams in crisis situations

Taking stock of your capabilities by looking at your past responsibilities will, of course, help you define what you're able to offer an employer today. But it also should raise questions about whether you want to continue developing the same skills in your next job. How does that relate to what you learned in the last chapter about the activities that bring you energy, given that your capabilities and what motivates you are interdependent? As professionals, we often like to lean in to our expertise and continue to learn in domains where we have had some success. So it stands to reason that what drives our energy will have some connection to the capabilities we both enjoy and want to continue developing. Another way to say this is that our capabilities, to some degree, both drive and constrain our pursuits. If we can understand what our capabilities are, then we can further define what's desirable *and* what's realistic in our career.

When Avery looked at the responsibilities listed in her résumé, her technical capabilities leaped off the page: data analytics, Python, and industry knowledge, to name a few. But she also saw evidence of emerging managerial skills. How should she start to systematize what she was capable of doing? And what would it take to maintain or further develop those capabilities? She couldn't do everything. To remain up to date on all her technical skills, for example, she would need to invest a lot of time. But might that mean she wouldn't have enough time to be a good manager? How would she make "good" trade-offs to keep succeeding—and how would she resolve these tensions she felt in her current role?

To see your current capabilities more concretely—and understand the investments they require—it's useful to think in terms of professional assets and liabilities and create your own career balance sheet.

For those who have no accounting background and are wondering what a *regular* balance sheet even does, it tallies up a company's assets, liabilities, and equity. For a company, assets—such as cash, inventory (products that will be sold), accounts receivable (money that customers plan to pay), property, and equipment—are things acquired in the past, at a cost, that are expected to produce future value. Liabilities—such as accounts payable (money that will go to suppliers) and debt—are obligations that companies have taken on to fund (i.e., pay for) their assets. If assets exceed liabilities—if a company could sell all its assets and generate more than enough value to pay its liabilities—then the remaining value is equity.

What does all this accounting jargon have to do with career planning? Simply put, individuals have assets, liabilities, and equity, too. And your balance sheet today, like a company's, will define the capabilities you have accessible to you over the next several years.

It is at this point that many people fall into that conceptual trap we mentioned earlier. Assets are not strengths. They are investments we have made in ourselves to stay relevant to our current and future employers, such as mastery of a particular skill or a certain set of connections in our networks. They also lose value over time. Some depreciate quickly, like cars and electronics, and others less so, like airplanes and buildings. Either way, without further investment, assets become less relevant, and therefore less valuable, over time until they reach the end of their "useful life" to us.

Liabilities are not weaknesses. They are the trade-offs we make— borrowing from the future to invest in the present—in order to be relevant to the job we want to do. You might have spent some money, time, and effort on a training that added to one or more of your assets—that's a liability. Or, to be frank, the time and money you have spent on this book, instead of other activities (like doing more work in your current job or spending time and money on family and friends), is a liability. If you don't have liabilities, then you probably haven't been doing enough to build your assets. But if you place bets on assets that don't fuel the kind of growth you want—in other words, you keep taking jobs that build on capabilities inconsistent with what you want to do and be known for—you'll end up with too many painful liabilities and not much future value in return. That's how companies—and careers—go bankrupt.

Across the job switchers we've coached, we've observed a consistent pattern: Without prompting, very few focus on their assets and liabilities. Most fixate on strengths and weaknesses instead—and often feel stuck in their jobs as a result. But because those traits are so closely tied to inborn talent, upbringing, and formative experiences, they are relatively static and restrictive. When people create a balance sheet and shift their thinking to capabilities that can be developed to stay relevant, they suddenly feel freer to move. They also feel more capable of proactively shaping and intentionally choosing which investments and trade-offs to make in their careers and quests, which is what we want. This knowledge will help you finish defining your current quest in the next chapter and begin crafting prototypes for your next job in the chapter after that.

The potential for growth—changing your capabilities based on what you do and learn—is critical. The reality is that the types of expertise that are valued change—both over time and from setting to setting. Given how rapidly and profoundly technology is transforming work, the shelf life of knowledge and skills will continue to shrink. That means individuals are continually having to upskill and retool as the world evolves. Up to 375 million working adults worldwide, for example, are in likely need of upskilling and reskilling—or switching occupations. Everyone will be at some point. Yes, there are evergreen skills, like communication and empathy, but even those are becoming more specialized. Your balance sheet allows you to flag areas in need of investment and development.

This tool can help you avoid being promoted to your "level of respective incompetence"—the so-called Peter Principle. To illustrate how, let's return to the detail orientation example. For some-one who is detail oriented, maybe it's been an obstacle to creating innovative strategies, but perhaps it's also why they've been so good at executing such strategies. So that individual has a choice: continue to grow that execution asset or invest in developing some-thing different. Being deliberate about that choice is what you need to do to complete this step and answer the question of whether you want your next job to build on or reset how your capabilities are used.

As Avery began working on her balance sheet (see Figure 5.2), she listed her assets. These included the tangible skills she had de-veloped. She also wrote down the intangibles, like her degrees from prestigious institutions, which signaled an ability to learn quickly, persevere, problem-solve, think critically, and so forth. She then recorded her liabilities—the trade-offs she had made to invest in her current assets.

FIGURE 5.2

Avery's Balance Sheet

Assets	Liabilities
Data analytics skills (7 years)	College loans
Mastery of Python (4 years)	Not enough time with husband
Industry knowledge (3 years)	Haven't seen enough of friends
Network of coding experts (2 years)	Lack of investment in health/ exercise
Master's and bachelor's degrees from prestigious universities (10 years)	
Global experience (10 years)	
Multilingual (5–10 years)	
Experiences leading coding teams (10 years)	

Once Avery had listed her assets and liabilities, we asked her to estimate the useful life of each asset to get a sense of how quickly her investments were depreciating. She thought her data analytics skills would remain competitive and sharp for seven years, but—because of the rapid evolution of how software was being created—her coding skills would stay relevant for only four and her industry knowledge would depreciate even faster without further investment. The asset she thought was depreciating the fastest, however, was her network of coding collaborators. Without spending time and effort to keep it up, she felt it would slip away in two years. She thought her degrees would last longer because of their prestige in the marketplace, along with her capabilities as a team leader and her global work experience. Her ability to speak other languages, however, would depreciate faster without practice and exposure.

Activity: Build Your Balance Sheet

Now that you've seen what one balance sheet looks like, you can create your own.

In the table you created to identify your energy drivers across your career (see Chapter Four), look at the row where you listed your responsibilities for each role. Those will help you identify the skills you've developed and exercised along the way that may be important assets. Then ask yourself: How did I "fund" those assets and others, such as my education and my networks, and what obligations or trade-offs have I incurred in the process? Those will be your liabilities.

From years of running this exercise with thousands of job switchers, we've found that it's useful to list eight to twelve assets and eight to twelve liabilities. You needn't generate precisely the same number of each—Avery didn't. Instead, focus on doing a true accounting of what matters. When creating balance sheets for organizations, accountants determine which items are "material" and omit things that don't clear that bar. The same principle applies here. Just get the big picture right so you can decide what types of roles and organizations would best suit you at this stage of your career.

Once you have drafted your lists, estimate the useful life of each asset. Avery's estimates were context specific. Yours should be, too. Be brutally honest with yourself about depreciation. The idea of this balance sheet is to start to make the trade-offs clear. You want a realistic picture of what's required to maintain, build, or develop an asset for your career trajectory.

After you've taken a first pass at your balance sheet, ask a mentor to do a congenial audit. What assets and liabilities would they include if they were you? Does your list line up with theirs? Individuals are often prone to overestimating or underestimating their capabilities. A reality check from someone who is willing to be honest is helpful. Also see if they agree with your useful life estimate for each asset. Perhaps you've been too generous with how long assets will remain relevant and how many of them are evergreen? This conversation should further clarify the trade-offs you've made to get where you are now and present a clear-eyed and accurate view of your current assets. That will be critical a couple chapters from now when you start to build out possibilities for what you could do next.

Investing for the Future

Look at your balance sheet and ask yourself: How closely do the assets and liabilities you've listed match what your current role is asking of you—the "responsibilities" row in your résumé table? As Avery considered this question, she acknowledged that in her project manager job, she had not yet struck an optimal balance. Her technical assets outweighed her managerial ones. That was not a big surprise. She had spent years as an individual contributor during which she honed her technical expertise and far less time managing teams and working cross-functionally. Now she faced a choice: Did she want to continue to invest in remaining relevant as an individual coder, or did she want to leverage her growing skills to take on more leadership roles—perhaps by moving to an organization, like a late-stage start-up she was eyeing, where she would be doing more team and content leadership than coding? Having recently married, she realized she couldn't continue to invest so heavily in the technical side *and* do more on the managerial side. The sacrifice in terms of time required in the future would be too great. She was already feeling burned-out as it was. She had to choose.

This was an important realization. All too often, when we think about the assets we want to develop, we make grandiose statements about all the things we'll learn in the coming years. A foreign language? No problem! Coding? Sure! Social media marketing? Why not! And yet, how many times do we follow through? That's why recording your liabilities alongside your assets is so critical. It makes the trade-offs real. Is a skill you think would be useful worth the investment in time, effort, and money? Those are scarce resources. When you choose to fund one investment, you are choosing not to fund another. Those decisions have implications for how relevant your capabilities will be to different kinds of jobs in the future.

As Avery studied the liabilities side of her balance sheet, she considered what it would *really* take to stay relevant doing her current job and what it would take to build the assets she thought she wanted for the future. And then she asked herself another critical question that you should ask as well: Do you want your next job to draw on your current capabilities or to take you in a different direction?

To answer that, it's useful to revisit your energy drivers. How do the activities that have landed in your bucket of must-haves for your next role correspond with the assets in which you could choose to invest?

For Avery, having hours of "head down" time working on code by herself had been a joy at the beginning of her career. She still derived satisfaction from it. But it had also become something of a drain as it interfered with things she needed to do as a leader—meetings with people in other functions across the company, one-on-one conversations with her team members, strategic planning, and so on. She increasingly found herself energized by the opportunities to collaborate, problem-solve across the company, and think strategically. That work wasn't necessarily a higher calling for her; she still believed her higher calling was solving technical problems with technical solutions. But it *was*, she thought, integral to her current quest.

Then she turned back to her balance sheet. To make her priorities concrete—and clarify that she couldn't do it all—we recommended bucketing her assets (both her current ones and those she wanted to acquire) into the same three categories we used for the energy drivers: the critical must-haves for her next job, the negotiable nice-to-haves, and the dispensable assets that were least important at this stage in her life and career. Her list looked like this:

Critical assets:
Experiences leading coding teams
Experiences working cross-functionally
Strategic decision-making

Negotiable assets:
Global experience
Data analytics skills
Master's and bachelor's degrees from prestigious universities

Dispensable assets:
Multilingual
Network of coding experts
Mastery of Python
Industry knowledge

When she looked at this list and what her current role was asking of her, what she wanted in her next job became much clearer. She wanted to build on the capabilities she had started to develop in her project manager role—not reset to do the sort of work she had done earlier in her career as a coder. That most likely meant she was looking to take the next step in her career or to regain control. That insight shaped what she considered doing next and the types of jobs she began brainstorming.

This step was likewise illuminating for Clara. But unlike Avery, she *was* looking for a reset in how her job made use of her capabilities. The assets Clara was using in her physical therapy role didn't line up with all the must-haves that brought her energy at this point in her career—in particular, work that challenged her intellectually and opportunities to learn. Meanwhile, some of her other assets, such as her master's in neuroscience and her research and lab skills, were essentially sitting on the sidelines. If used in the right way, they were the sorts of things that could allow her to challenge herself and learn more in her next job. This realization meant that she was ready to identify her current quest—the step we describe in the next chapter.

SIX

STEP 4:
NAME YOUR QUEST

 Like Alex and Clara, you have worked out roughly where you fall on the vertical (motivation/energy) and horizontal (capabilities) axes of our quest map. Now let's revisit that map in Figure 6.1 to plot your location.

Alex was almost sure at this point that he was looking to regain control. And Clara felt pretty confident that she was looking to regain alignment. Using the map to name their quests was clarifying for both.

It helped Clara realize she wasn't looking to take the next step in the physical therapy field through more education. As her positioning on the horizontal axis reflected, she had little appetite for building on the capabilities she had developed as a physical therapy assistant. Instead, she wanted a reset through a new job that would use her capabilities differently. She had some clear non-negotiables to that end—she couldn't fall back into a role where she wasn't learning new skills or being challenged intellectually. And as her location along the vertical axis indicated, she was unwilling to give up the work-life balance her current job afforded her. Time for outside interests was way too energizing to sacrifice.

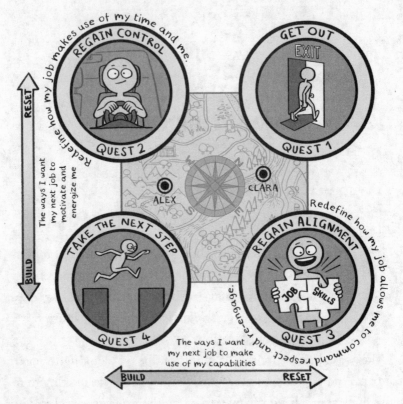

Figure 6.1
Plotting Where You Are on the Map of Quests

Identifying her quest to regain alignment highlighted some risks, however. Although Clara would be okay taking a lateral step in her career if it allowed her to reset how her capabilities were used, she wasn't willing to take a step backward or switch career paths entirely once again. Also, given her quest, there was a real danger that she could land in a job where her skill set wasn't being utilized properly, which meant she might find herself in yet another job search within a few months.

As for Alex, considering his nonnegotiables on the vertical axis—having more time for his family, for example—is what brought his quest to regain control into focus. That, too, came with risks. It would be quick and easy to jump into just any role that respected his time. But he knew he shouldn't do that simply because time was ticking. He wanted to build on his assets in a meaningful way.

Naming your quest will highlight some risks for you as well.

For example, if you're on a quest to get out, you should leave your job soon. But being in a rush could land you in another job that doesn't energize you and leverage your capabilities. Make sure to review the energy drivers and career assets that are most important to you right now (the "bucketing" work you did in the previous two chapters) so you won't relive the past in your next move.

If you're looking to take the next step in your career, the road ahead likely feels clearer. Here the biggest risk may surprise you: your aperture on what you could do next may be too narrow to optimize how productive or significant that step can be.

We address such risks in the next chapter, when we work with you to create role prototypes. But first, we need to make sure that you are reasonably clear on what your current quest is—and that you have a solid understanding of the pushes and pulls acting on you and what they mean for your job move.

Reassess Your Quest for Progress

In Chapter Two we introduced you to an assessment tool to help identify the forces behind your most recent job move—and to start feeling your way toward your current quest. Now, with a clearer sense of what's propelling you toward something new, it's time to revisit that tool at jobmoves.com. By analyzing your energy drivers and drains and the capabilities in which you want to invest, you have gained a lot of insight about the pushes and pulls acting on you. Look again at the most common pushes and pulls in Figures 2.2 and 2.3. Pick three to five pushes *and* pulls that you believe are "definitely a factor" in prompting your current quest. Then go through the rest of the list and determine which are "somewhat of a factor," "not really a factor," and "definitely not a factor." If you're still unsure, you can of course select "not sure yet," but note that the more forces you label "not sure yet," the less accurate your quest fit scores will be. Enter your selections for each push and pull in the assessment tool and see if you get a match with the quest that you've plotted on the map above.

If they line up, you've got a clear understanding of what's pushing and pulling you on the job switcher's timeline. You can proceed with confidence that your energy drivers and career assets are in tune with the progress you desire.

If they don't line up, that's not a bad thing. On the contrary, it means that a safety check in our process has prevented you from racing ahead with ideas that aren't true to the progress you're seeking right now. Step back to reconsider your priorities. Perhaps you haven't been as honest with yourself as you need to be in analyzing your energy drivers and assets for your next role—which ones feel critical, which are less important, and which ones you're willing to live without. When you fill out our online assessment, in addition to getting a set of results about your potential quest, you will also receive more information and context about that quest, which may help you identify other tensions you're feeling. You can use that feedback to revisit earlier steps in the process. For instance, you can ask yourself *why* you thought a certain push (say, "When I don't respect or trust the people I work with") was more important than another (like "When I don't feel challenged or am bored in my current work") if that seems to contradict your critical energy drivers and assets. Maybe you'll decide it's really not more important—and that simple adjustment is all you'll need. Or maybe you had it right at the outset so you should try re-bucketing your drivers and assets. If your reassessment seems totally out of line with the work you've done, you can also go back to a mentor and ask them to interview you again to better identify the forces acting on you at this point in your career.

To be clear, the results from our assessment tool shouldn't represent the final word. It's just one way to unearth the forces acting on you and to identify your priorities and guardrails. In any case, your circumstances may change as you move through this process. You could get a new boss. Your company might go through a restructuring. There might be material changes in your life outside your job. Your true quest won't be solidified until you actually make a job move.

So the final word is yours. You're the one hiring your next job. Our exercises and activities are just meant to deepen your awareness of your priorities and build your confidence that you know what you truly want as you march through the job-switching process. That's important to do before we begin the next step, in Chapter Seven, which is where we use the insights you've gleaned so far to create a wide range of job prototypes for what you might do next. Hence the safety check here. You don't want to base your prototypes on the wrong sets of drivers and assets. Spending a little time to reassess your quest now will save you a lot of grief later.

SEVEN

STEP 5:
PROTOTYPE AND
DESIGN YOUR FUTURE

 With your quest identified, you're ready to use all the information you've gathered so far in our process to imagine a wide range of possibilities for what you could do next. This step, creating prototypes for your next move, takes advantage of what designers call *divergent* thinking. The goal is to create contrasting visions of your future. By doing so, you'll deepen your understanding of what would be a good choice for you at this stage of your career and *learn before switching* what each of these options that sound appealing actually entails. Then in the next chapter, we'll use *convergent* thinking to narrow down your list of possibilities.

Building Divergent Prototypes

In the world of product development, after learning about what kinds of progress customers want to make in their lives, successful designers build prototypes to test their early ideas. They experiment with multiple rough mock-ups that they can change easily. Those who don't follow this step tend to miss the mark when their new product enters the market prematurely, as their hypotheses about what *could* work outpace their knowledge about what actually will. That's one reason why, each year, over 90 percent of consumer products fail after they launch.

Career choices benefit from experimentation, too. That's because if you focus on postings too soon, you're likely either to get overwhelmed by the variety of possibilities or to end up overly constrained by the first options you consider. Negotiation experts would say this premature closure to other options comes about because of "anchoring"—the idea that individuals attach too much importance to the first offer they see. Network scholars and economists would warn about social pressures to conform to obvious choices. Management researchers would likely remind us that exploiting—or leaning into—existing options could prevent us from exploring alternatives.

Could a divergent approach lead you to prototype a dream job that doesn't exist? Yes. But because the point of the prototypes isn't to *find* a job at this stage, that's a perfectly acceptable outcome. You're starting to put flesh on the bones of your quest to clarify the trade-offs you're willing—and unwilling—to make to get the progress you want. Learning is the goal here. You will, two chapters from now, turn your attention to the "supply side" of the job market. For now, however, there is still work to be done to define the ideal outcomes of your quest.

As you "mock up" an array of potential futures, these should range from roles you hope exist somewhere out there to those you're actively considering to novel paths you don't know much about but are interested in exploring. In our experience, people often want to stop with just one plausible prototype. But trust us—that's the hard way to do this. Creating "the one" is exceedingly difficult. What single role could be perfect in every way? And it sets you up for disappointment later when real-world options don't precisely line up with expectations and you don't know how to make trade-offs to unlock progress. Crafting multiple prototypes is more productive, both in the short term and in the long run. It helps you uncover the interdependencies and trade-offs inherent in your quest.

Although we're not always great at identifying exactly what we want to do in life, the human brain is quite good at ruling out certain options when it sees them alongside others. That's why we have menus in restaurants and A/B testing in marketing. Prototyping a range of career moves clarifies our thinking about which things are more or less important to us now and what makes sense as a next step.

We tell the people we advise that they can keep revisiting their prototypes as they learn more about new career possibilities—and more about themselves. Prototypes can be adjusted. They are moist clay, not dry cement.

For now, however, the task is to come up with three to five exciting, well-articulated possibilities (see activity below). Don't focus yet on what may or may not exist in the current job market. Remember: We're still working on the demand side, which is what *you* want (not the supply side, which is what employers are posting). If you can first clarify what you ideally want to do and recognize the trade-offs you're willing to make to do that, then when it comes time, you'll search the real job market with greater precision and make smarter decisions. When you know what you're looking for, it's a lot easier to find.

To give you a sense of how divergent your prototypes should be: Clara's ranged from becoming a science journalist to serving as a physician assistant to working as a rock-climbing instructor or even a rock-climbing professional. All were roles she thought would provide a reset in how her capabilities were leveraged. For the most part, they weren't what many people in her circle would expect her to do next, and some of them were inspired by conversations she had with people she normally wouldn't feel were close enough to her for career-related questions. The latter two prototypes would also mean a radical change in her career, which was something her likely quest suggested might not be prudent. She took that into account, but didn't worry about it yet. The next step in our process would help control for that.

Alex's prototypes started in predictable fashion for someone looking to regain control: managing product development for another company and starting his own business. He also built prototypes around working as a teacher and a musician—roles that sounded intriguing to him. He hoped to use our process to learn if they would allow him to build on his skill set as well as gain more control over how he did his work.

Clara and Alex both brainstormed freely and ventured well beyond their wheelhouses and perceived constraints. That's something we encourage at this stage. This is not the time to tell yourself, "I couldn't do that because I couldn't practically make that transition happen." This is the time to dream.

Activity: Create Your Career Prototypes

After reviewing the energy drivers and assets that you prioritized in Chapters Four and Five, brainstorm a list of jobs that might deliver your critical "must-haves." Those will be your early prototypes. To get started, imagine scenarios in which you would have:

- the same role, but at a different company
- a promotion within your company
- a role in a new function
- a role in companies of varying sizes and maturity (small versus large, start-up versus established)
- a role in a new industry
- a role you've always thought could be interesting but have never explored

This work will likely take some dedicated time over several days or a couple weeks. If you were already offered a new job—perhaps that's what pulled you into this job-switching process—then include that role as one of your prototypes. You can also use generative AI to help you brainstorm. For example, Ethan Mollick, an expert on AI and a professor at the Wharton School of the University of Pennsylvania, built a GPT that can create a list of a few dozen divergent ideas in minutes. Just tell it about your current job, your current quest, and your must-have energy drivers and assets and how they relate to what you do currently. Then ask it to brainstorm some possible jobs. People outside your immediate circle can play a similar role.

Once you have sketched out several options, you must flesh them out to create true prototypes that can be tested against the things that matter most to you.

To help build out each one, we've included a template in Appendix C. Or you can fill it out at jobmoves.com/jobprototype. As you work through the template for each role, ask yourself:

- Why do I think this option will align well with my energy drivers and assets? Which ones in particular does it support?
- What assumptions am I making for that to be true? What things am I really uncertain about?
- In what ways do I think this option *won't* align well with my energy drivers and assets?
- What assumptions am I making for that to be correct?
- To see more accurately where the role actually will/won't align with my energy drivers and assets, what questions should I ask people who do this kind of work?

You'll use the questions you generate from the last bullet to find out what each job is like in practice. Although your energy drivers and assets have helped you imagine an array of exciting jobs, you don't yet *know* if they involve activities that would drive your energy or that would leverage your assets. Through informational interviews, you'll learn what each job is really like to complete your prototypes.

Finish Fleshing Out Your Prototypes

You've done some good brainstorming. Now let's see how accurate your early prototypes are. To check, you'll line up informational interviews with people in jobs like the ones you've mocked up. Chances are you'll be having these conversations anyway as you "network" to learn about jobs and gain access to new opportunities. But we provide a structure for the "asks" and for the conversations themselves—which can make this part of the process feel less daunting.

Requesting targeted interviews

For starters, we recommend tapping your existing connections. Reach out to mentors and others in your professional and social networks to see if they know people who hold roles like those you've prototyped. You can also search social media sites like LinkedIn to find individuals who hold these roles. Once Alex and Clara started looking closely at their LinkedIn contacts and at friends of friends, they both found many people who would be good resources. Yes, it was challenging to get going—combing through contacts isn't the most thrilling task. But when they did, both were surprised by how useful their existing networks were.

Having identified people you want to talk to, you'll then ask a shared contact to introduce you. From personal experience, we know these asks can be difficult. To make them easier, we've included letter templates in Appendix D (and at jobmoves.com /prototypeinterviews) that you can modify to fit your circumstances.

When a shared contact introduces and vouches for you, it increases the likelihood that the person you want to talk to will agree to a conversation.

With that said, you can also write to people out of the blue (Appendix D has another letter template for this) and ask them to talk. You might be surprised at how often people will say yes to an informational conversation with no strings attached—one that allows them to share their own story with somebody who has similar interests.

However you reach out, make it clear that you're not going to ask them for a job. You just want to learn more about what they do. Otherwise, they may hesitate to connect, especially if they don't know you. Keep your request simple, but be clear about what you'd like—thirty to forty-five minutes of their time.

One woman we coached struggled with this task. As an entrepreneur who had run her own one-person consultancy for over a decade, she valued having the flexibility to choose which projects she worked on with clients. But she hadn't managed the business well. As she was nearing retirement, she realized there were some financial issues that she needed to remedy—and that she just didn't have the energy to do on her own. She decided she needed to give up some flexibility and work with a more established firm. As she built out her prototypes, we asked her to do some informational interviews. When one contact she emailed didn't respond, her reaction was to say, "Well, I tried that. Guess we should give up on this step and move on." If not for one of our colleagues prodding her, she wouldn't have sent a follow-up note a week later. When she did, she wrote simply, "Dear [interviewee's name], Just wanted to make sure you saw my first note. If you have time to chat, I'd welcome the opportunity." That note resulted in a reply—and the scheduling of a conversation.

The bottom line? We know this can be a difficult step, and we know it takes time. But it's time spent deliberately. Rather than aimlessly sending LinkedIn messages, you will make your requests for informational interviews far more targeted and focused than they typically are. And you'll need fewer conversations as a result. There's no secondary agenda of looking for an "in" at a company or in a function or industry. This is purely about understanding the experience of doing the job. We'll talk more about interviews in Chapter Nine. In the meantime, these early conversations should have real purpose behind them so that you're doing *better* networking, not *more* networking. With this deliberate, targeted approach, you'll have a clear, thoughtful answer as to why you want to talk specifically with each person—another benefit that will lead to more people saying yes.

Conducting focused interviews

Just as your interview with your mentor or friend (in Chapter Two) wasn't conventional, neither are these conversations. Many informational interviews meander around the topic of how someone came to their current role and only vaguely touch on what it's like in practice. They tend to focus on how the interviewer can get a similar job, perhaps at the same company, even if that's not the intent.

For the purposes of career prototyping, informational interviews should be hyper-focused on what people *do* on a daily and weekly basis and how those activities pertain to the energy drivers and assets that are important to you.

Systematically drill into the energy drivers you've prioritized. For example, as you may recall, one important driver for Clara was feeling that she was making an impact. For her, that involved building relationships. So she asked a series of questions about patient interaction during an informational interview with an emergency medicine physician assistant (EMPA):

> To what extent do you interact directly with patients and their family members?
> Do you follow up with patients after they are discharged?
> How much time do you spend with patients on average?

Clara learned that the EMPA generally did not have ongoing relationships with patients. She was responsible for triage and acute treatment but often never saw the patient again—or even learned what happened next in their treatment. The EMPA's own desire for impact was satisfied. She treated patients in dire circumstances, after all, and they needed immediate support. But that didn't align with what Clara wanted. Although she wasn't surprised by this in retrospect, the conversation clarified something for her. The physician assistant role—one that she knew well in the context of a rehab clinic—could align very differently with her drivers in other settings, such as emergency medicine.

Given how much work you've done to understand what each of your energy drivers means to you, don't settle for surface-level answers to your questions. Press for details and examples to get a clear picture of whether the work involves the things that give you energy. If someone says their job is creative—and creativity is important to you—ask them what that looks like in their day-to-day work. Then explain what it means to you. Perhaps it's about being free from the traditional constraints and processes in a workplace so that you can do your job in innovative ways. Or, as was true of one senior innovation leader we advised, maybe it means moving from "vertical" creativity (within your current silo) to "horizontal" creativity (across a wider span of the organization and its products). Then ask: Does the person you're interviewing have a job that allows them to be creative in *that* way?

Follow a similar script for assets: Which skills, experiences, and credentials do your prototyped roles actually leverage and value? You may be surprised at the answers you get in your interviews. Clara thought she would need a PhD, for example, to be hired as a science writer. She was pleasantly surprised to learn that her master's degree in neuroscience was more than credible.

You can also have your interviewee walk you through a typical day or week in their job and talk about how that work schedule intersects with other aspects of their life, such as family time and personal interests. This line of inquiry can clarify some of the assets that are actually used in a job, as well as how a job's daily activities line up with the things that drive your energy. It will also reveal some of the trade-offs people have made, both at work and elsewhere, and how they feel about those decisions. Because you've already been discussing their job in light of your priorities, it would be natural for them to explain their daily or weekly calendar in those terms, too. But if that doesn't happen organically, explicitly bring their attention back to what matters to you—as in, "In a typical week, how many opportunities do you have to engage with people beyond your immediate team?" or "When during the day are you able to put your head down and focus quietly on your own tasks, without interruptions?" Homing in on the calendar like this gets at what people actually *do* rather than what their title says they *are*. Also try asking how they make decisions about what they do and don't do to understand the extent to which they've shaped the job to suit their needs. You might be able to do the same.

Because you are building a wide variety of prototypes at this stage, success in these interviews doesn't mean finding *the* right fit. It means gaining insight into the energizers, capabilities, and trade-offs you would likely encounter in each job. After each conversation, write down any updated thinking on whether and how this role aligns with your desired energy drivers and assets.

Reflecting on what you learned in your interviews

A completed prototype has four core elements: what the job is, what you would do in it, how it aligns with the energy drivers that matter to you, and how it aligns with the assets that matter to you. For example, one of the prototypes Clara developed was about becoming a science writer. Through her interviews, she realized something important. There was a big difference between working as a freelance journalist and working in-house at a science publication. The former, she learned, would allow her maximum flexibility to pick and choose assignments, but it wouldn't offer any guarantees of a stable income. The latter would provide a more predictable income but less freedom to pursue her own story ideas. So she built out prototypes for each, the simplified versions of which are outlined in Figure 7.1.

What If the Prototypes You Design Feel Too Risky?

Some people feel anxious, even paralyzed, after they've done the informational interviews and developed several prototypes. This can happen when all the possibilities they've outlined feel like too big a leap—in one way or another—from what they're doing now. Whereas some see exciting opportunities to reinvent themselves, others see only risk.

A certain amount of hesitation is to be expected. As we discussed in Chapter Two, almost the moment you start to think about switching jobs, anxiety sets in and threatens to impede progress. You start to think about all the things that the new job might not do for you. But in some circumstances and for some folks, risk aversion runs much deeper. In these cases, despite their dissatisfaction with what they're doing presently, they just aren't ready to make a big switch because the pushes and pulls they're experiencing don't overcome their entrenched habits and their anxieties about the unknown future.

FIGURE 7.1

How Clara Split One Career Prototype into Two

Job Prototype A: In-House Science Writer	
What is it?	**What will I do?**
» Full-time staff writer at science-focused publication » Assigned to a specific beat	» Produce a set number of articles per week » Write both short- and long-form pieces » Research topics my editor assigns by interviewing sources and reading peer-reviewed journal articles » As I gain experience, pitch my own story ideas » Provide background research for other content in the publication

How well will it align with my energy drivers?
1. Offers intellectually challenging work
2. Provides learning opportunities within a narrow beat
3. Get to work with colleagues regularly and, over time, develop relationships with them
4. Should offer predictable schedule and stable source of income to pursue hobbies
5. Doesn't allow for much autonomy, at least initially, as I won't get to choose the topics I cover

How well will it align with my assets?
1. Leverages existing research skills, in particular my ability to read, understand, and distill peer-reviewed articles
2. Uses knowledge base of existing scientific research to understand what's truly novel. (Depending on beat, could also draw on my knowledge base in neuroscience specifically.) And uses my knowledge about research methods to translate the process into something more accessible.
3. Requires lots of writing; not necessarily among my developed or desired assets
4. Get to use my skill set of interacting well with people outside my team, specifically scientists
5. Doesn't leverage my capabilities in creating new systems

Job Prototype B: Freelance Science Writer	
What is it?	**What will I do?**
» Writer for various publications » Self-employment on a full- or part-time schedule	» Pitch, research, and write articles for science-focused publications » Dig deep into topics on which I'm knowledgeable and passionate (get to cover neuroscience field!) » Manage a business (self-employed)

How well will it align with my energy drivers?

1. Lots of opportunities for intellectual challenge and growth across broad range
2. Because I will be working solo, I won't have much impact on others personally
3. Although I will get to network to learn about story ideas, I won't necessarily collaborate regularly with those interesting people
4. More time for hobbies outside of work because I can arrange my schedule to suit me, but income will be variable, which could make hobbies more challenging at times
5. Offers lots of autonomy: I pick and choose what I research and write about

---

How well will it align with my assets?

1. Leverages existing research skills, in particular my ability to read, understand, and distill peer-reviewed articles
2. Uses knowledge base of existing scientific research to understand what's truly novel as I pitch ideas and try to make them accessible
3. Requires lots of writing and pitching of story ideas; neither is necessarily among my developed or desired assets
4. Get to use my skill set of interacting well with scientists and editors across publications
5. Doesn't leverage my capabilities in creating new systems

If you fall into this camp—as many of the people we study or coach do—we suggest building a few more prototypes. This time, consider much smaller steps you could take to make progress on your quest. In other words, lower the magnitude of the forces holding you back by eliminating a big, dramatic move.

Learning before you switch that your quest is real but your next step should be more incremental than radical is a valuable discovery. Use it to your advantage! If you completed the activity above, you may have already built a couple of these modest prototypes—a lateral move within your current organization and a familiar role in a new company. But you may need other small steps to consider. Here are three options:

You may recall in Chapter Two that we described Clara's decision to leave the neuroscience lab and work in the rehab clinic as a *jobcation*. A jobcation isn't quite a vacation—but it has some similarities. It's a step back or sideways in a career to give yourself time and room to figure out what you want next. You can think of it almost like a working sabbatical. For Clara, it was a way to take a break from the grind of the lab and reassess her priorities. That's exactly what it should be—a place to pause, breathe, and take stock. An interim or project-based role can serve a similar function.

A second option is a *side hustle*. This is exactly what it sounds like—a way to do something you're passionate about on the side. Because you don't have to give up your day job, you don't have to sacrifice stability or other priorities. Remember that assistant women's NCAA basketball coach from Chapter One who took a stable full-time job to pay the bills and save up for the family he wanted to have? He still loved basketball and wanted it to be a regular part of his life. So he refereed basketball games in his spare time. Because his main job wasn't that stressful and had predictable hours, he could pursue his passion through the side hustle. Lots of people these days have gigs on the side—a start-up they're tinkering with, some free-lance design work, a rock band they perform with on weekends, or volunteer roles for nonprofits. A side hustle is a great way to achieve some priorities you have in your life without "betting the farm." And sometimes our side hustles eventually turn into full-time jobs when they feel more secure and the anxiety around them declines.

A side hustle is also a great way to learn before switching about some of your prototypes while you are still in your current role. Doing this takes advantage of timeless insights from the research of Herminia Ibarra, a professor at London Business School. Among her nine unconventional strategies for reinventing one's career are two recommendations that are relevant here: "act your way into a new way of . . . being" and "identify projects that can help you get a feel for a new line of work or style of working." The basic idea is to create what we call "prototype bubbles"—periods of time when you can try out new ways of doing things, even in a context where they don't naturally fit—and see how that goes. In essence, you pretend to be a different version of yourself—and by trying on that hat and the behaviors associated with it, you get to sample a new role. This will yield far more actionable information than just introspection—thinking over and over about whether something might be a good fit. Doing these projects or activities while in your current job allows you to "experiment seriously without making a commitment." For instance, if you want to see what it might be like to jump into project management and you're currently a coder, you might find a side project for a nonprofit organization where you could play that role and see how it fits with your prioritized energy drivers and assets.

A third option is to take a *half step*, like seeking more education or training, to learn more about a particular field or about yourself before committing to a new job. Feeling your way is much more productive than remaining paralyzed with inaction. Indeed, for those lacking a clear sense of purpose, the best way to figure out what you're meant to do isn't to think about it. It's to act. When one individual with whom we worked quit her job in frustration, she didn't have something else lined up. But that enabled her to engage more fully in her part-time MBA program—an important stepping stone in exploring what she could do next.

No matter where you land on the risk-aversion scale, by this point in our process you have several prototypes that offer a variety of things you could do next in your quest. Both Alex and Clara felt excited by what they had brainstormed and learned. The blue sky that they had painted felt alive with possibilities. But it also felt a bit overwhelming. Weren't there too many possibilities? This is where our next step comes in—to help you prioritize, focus, and narrow the choices before you.

EIGHT

STEP 6:
CONVERGE ON YOUR PATH

 You've sketched out a range of divergent possibilities for what you could do next. Now it's time for our next step: to *converge* on one or two that make sense at this stage of your career. We'll base this work on how all your prototypes line up with the energy drivers and assets you prioritized. This step also serves as yet another useful check on the quest you've identified. If where you land in this step feels "right" to you and consistent with what your inner voice says you'd be excited about doing next, then you're probably headed in a good direction. If it doesn't feel right, you can simply (and much more swiftly this time) go back through our process so that you land a place that's more consistent with what progress means for you at this point in your life. This kind of iteration tends to be valuable. Either way, you'll know what to go looking for when you start to scour real job openings in the next section of the book.

Narrowing Down Prototypes to Prioritize Next Steps

To start, look again at your bucketed energy drivers and assets from Chapters Four and Five. Just as you force ranked past jobs on each energy driver—on a continuum between "not present at all" and "fully present"—you'll use that same scale to *rank your prototypes* on each energy driver *and* asset (see activity below). In the process, you might discover you don't yet have enough information to rank things accurately. That's okay. When this happens, it just means you need to flesh out your prototypes a bit more. You could do another informational interview or two to fill in what you don't know, for example, or huddle with thought partners to reanalyze the data you've gathered. At least you've identified that gap in knowledge before taking a new job. That's a critical part of learning before switching.

People ask us if they should rank all their prototypes, even those they've mentally eliminated from serious consideration in the course of their informational interviews. We recommend ranking everything. That's because it further clarifies your understanding of what your priorities are and why. The greater the contrasts between your prototypes, the deeper your insights will be around what's driving you right now. In other words, the process of converging from a handful of prototypes to just one or two isn't "wasteful." It's how you'll learn. More wasteful is skipping straight to "the answer" that isn't the actual answer at all. We encourage you to include your current job in the prototype rankings as well because it's something you could continue to do if you decided it would be better than pursuing other pathways.

Ranking all your prototypes also puts a finer point on how willing you are to make certain trade-offs to get different jobs. For Clara, rock climbing professionally would mean sacrificing the ability to grow intellectually on the job and limit her opportunities to have a personal impact on others. Although she loved having time for hobbies like rock climbing outside of work, having her hobby become *part of* her core work didn't line up with the capabilities for which she wanted to be known in her career and the assets she wanted to continue to develop. And in her gut, it just didn't feel right. None of this was surprising given that she was on the Regain Alignment quest, but it was useful data that helped confirm Clara's priorities.

Finally, this part of the process builds a bridge between what caused you to switch jobs in the past and what will motivate you to switch in the future, because you'll now be able to see how both your past roles and your prototypes stack up on the energy drivers and assets that matter to you. As we mentioned earlier, the things people care about shift over time. This can happen slowly or suddenly. Either way, our process allows for that movement. Maybe your life has changed quite a lot, and your reflection about your priorities is just now catching up. Perhaps you used to enjoy travel, but now with a family at home, that seems far less (or more!) appealing. Such shifts will come through in your rankings of past and potential roles.

Whatever your situation, once you've ranked your prototypes on each of your energy drivers and assets, one or two roles should rise above the rest. In most cases, those front-runners confirm one's quest. That's because the prototypes we design and gravitate toward reveal important information about the progress we're seeking.

Remember the two lawyers who had similar backgrounds but very different desires for their next move? The prototypes one attorney converged upon were a Department of Justice job and an in-house counsel role. Both reflected her growing frustration with the rigid, progression-driven life at her firm and were consistent with her quest to get out. The other attorney's convergent prototypes were switching to a new practice group within his firm and switching to a new law firm. They reflected the energy he felt with his current job and his desire to lean into the capabilities he was building. That dovetailed with his quest to take the next step. Both attorneys emerged from this activity with greater confidence that they knew what progress looked like for them at this moment in their careers.

Clara had a similar experience. As she worked through the rankings, she eliminated the rock-climbing roles and the physician assistant and freelance science writer roles. What was left was working as an in-house science writer. It was consistent with her quest to regain alignment in the way her job used her assets while building on the things that gave her energy. The role was one in which she would learn and be challenged intellectually; she would be trusted to do great work; and her experience and credentials would be valued.

Activity: Rank Your Prototypes

To force rank your prototypes on each of the energy drivers and assets you've prioritized, you can use our spreadsheet at jobmoves .com/converge, which will do the math for you. Or you can follow these steps and tally up the results yourself:

1. Write down your energy drivers and assets from Chapters Four and Five: your critical must-haves, your negotiable nice-to-haves, and those that are least important at this point in your career.

2. On a scale of 1 to 10, score your current job and your prototypes on each of your must-haves. For example, if you've flagged "taking on more leadership challenges," "having a seat at the 'strategy' table," and "learning new skills" as critical energy drivers, score each role according to each of them, and do the same for your critical assets. Then multiply each of those scores by 3.

3. Score your current job and your prototypes against your mid-tier energy drivers and assets (the negotiable nice-to-haves). Multiply each of those scores by 2.

4. Score your current job and your prototypes against your bottom-tier energy drivers and assets (those that no longer seem very important to you). Multiply those scores by 1.

5. For each role, add all the scores together. This will give you a relative weighting of options.

The higher the final score, the more closely aligned the role is with your stated priorities. Your current job, for example, may end up with 205 points, and one of your prototypes may end up with 260 points.

But don't take those numbers as the final word on what you should or should not do. If the role with the highest score gives you an allergic reaction, that's a signal to do a little more thinking. Maybe your circumstances have changed in the past few weeks. Or maybe a prototype that feels more "right" scored too low. You might need to re-bucket your energy drivers and assets. Alternatively, perhaps certain trade-offs you thought you'd gladly make suddenly don't seem plausible—as in, a skill you thought you wanted to learn feels like too great a stretch upon further reflection, given what the day-to-day would entail. The scoring is a way to check and refine your intuition.

If you feel a disconnect, we recommend revisiting the results from the assessment you did in Chapter Six to reexamine the pushes and pulls in your quest. Yes, those might be changing. Or they might be aligned with a narrative about *something you want to be*—or think others want you to be—rather than a job you *actually want to do*.

Preparing for Real-World Testing

The point of career prototyping isn't to give you *the* answer. It's to force you to think about the ins and outs of potential paths that hold some appeal. You carefully consider what you would do day-to-day and see whether that's truly in line with what you want next and the trade-offs you are willing to make.

This approach allows you to make an educated choice in accordance with what gives you energy at this moment in your life and the assets you want to use or develop. Many of the people we've coached took several weeks to work through all the steps outlined in this section of the book. Most reported in an anonymous survey that it was time well spent. Once you've landed on one or more prototypes that seem promising, you're ready to move on to our next few chapters and match them with real opportunities.

In our courses and workshops, we often ask the icebreaker question: "If your eight-year-old self had correctly predicted what you would do professionally, what would you be doing today?" We've done this dozens of times with all kinds of audiences, and yet the answers tend to be the same: astronaut, pilot, celebrity, sports star, doctor, inventor, teacher, and so on. Kids' career predictions rarely come true because they don't incorporate the trade-offs inherent in what it means to do those jobs. One of us, Michael, wanted to be an astronaut, for example, at a young age, only to learn later that he wasn't suited for the work one does in a weightless environment!

As kids—and, let's be honest, as adults—we all love to dream. But if you have followed our process so far, you have much more than a dream. You have one or two balanced, nuanced prototypes that speak to what's driving you to switch. Now let's test them in the real world.

PART III

GETTING TO WHERE
YOU WANT TO GO

Although we encourage you to keep tweaking your prototypes until you've identified at least a couple of promising paths to explore in the job market, we don't want you to fiddle with them indefinitely. Perpetual fussing is avoidance. It's often a symptom of anxiety about the future—and that, as we've discussed, is a major obstacle to change.

Obsessing isn't progressing. The only way to learn more about your purpose and passions is to shift toward a bias for action—which allows you to test and learn.

In this section, you keep testing the prototypes you've created and refined. But this time, in Chapter Nine, it's against real opportunities in the job market. Then in Chapter Ten, you learn how to tell your career story like a pro so you can go get the job you want. Finally, in Chapter Eleven, we provide tips for navigating the job hunt itself—and help you summarize all you've learned about yourself and your quest for your current and future employers.

NINE

STEP 7:
EMBRACE TRADE-OFFS
IN THE JOB MARKET

 Armed with a career prototype—in-house science writer—and an understanding of what trade-offs she would probably need to make to get this sort of job, Clara left one of our coaching sessions feeling good. But in the days leading up to our next conversation, her thoughts took a negative turn: Were such jobs available right now? Even if they were, why would anyone hire her to do this work? After all, just because she wanted a certain job didn't mean her capabilities lined up with what a given job required. And what if the trade-offs she *thought* she was willing to make weren't really viable? These nagging questions stemmed from an understandable fear that her prototype might look nice on paper but not pan out in practice.

If you're wondering the same things, rest assured. All the work you've done so far has prepared you for this moment—particularly the informational interviews you've conducted to figure out how your prototypes line up day-to-day and week-to-week with the energy drivers and assets that matter most to you. With your priorities clarified (although not solidified!), the next step in our process is to see if the career possibilities you're envisioning match real options. That means shifting our attention from all the things you'd like to do and experience to what you can realistically "be," in the language of the supply-side of the job market.

When you get to this stage, it's easy to say, "Okay, got it, I'll start applying to everything that looks like what I want to do!" That was certainly Clara's temptation. Movement feels good. Sometimes it masquerades as progress. But it's better to take things slow and have more conversations with more people about what's really out there. This isn't busywork. On the contrary, it will optimize your time—your most precious resource.

Think about how people get hired. Estimates vary, but according to LinkedIn, 70 percent of jobs come through personal connections. Many job openings aren't even posted on web-based job boards. That means you increase your chances of landing a job that closely matches what you want by making the most of your network, not by blindly playing the numbers game and applying to as many jobs as you can online.

But even before you get to the point of applying to jobs, your network can play two other key roles. First, it will help unearth real, often-unlisted roles that are close matches for your prototypes but that you might not know about otherwise. There could even be several opportunities at your current employer that, at least at a surface level, match your prototypes, but you didn't know existed. Second, your network can help you breathe life into static postings so you can get a true sense of them. Because most job descriptions focus on long lists of requirements like knowledge, skills, credentials, and work history that may or may not translate into doing the job well, you can't rely on them to gauge "fit"—that ever-elusive concept people use (and often, unfortunately, misuse) to decide who will and who won't succeed in a given role in a specific organization and culture. Even job descriptions that nod to fit—as in, "We're looking for a team player" or "We're all about balance here; no workaholics need apply"—are often filled with generic lists and empty clichés. They shouldn't be trusted at face value.

As a result, in this step, we're going to leverage your network to find potential matches and then once again do informational interviews. But now the purpose is to hone the prototypes you've converged upon into a realistic set of enticing choices with even clearer trade-offs. Will this prime your network for when you're ready to apply to jobs? You bet. But we'll dig more into that in the next two chapters. For now, talking with people is how you translate the opaque "supply-side" language of the job market into a concrete understanding of the progress you can make in a particular role. It's also how you weed out opportunities that are more attractive on paper than in real life.

Networking for Jobs That Fit Prototypes

With your top prototypes and priorities in hand, start scouring job boards and LinkedIn to see what might match what you want. Even more important, though, is to reach out to friends, family members, colleagues, and acquaintances to learn what opportunities *they* see that might align with your quest. As you have these conversations, don't just connect with those who know you best. Research has long shown that our "weak ties"—people with whom we interact less frequently—often provide unexpected professional value in our lives, as they possess "access to new information, supports, and opportunities" that we aren't exposed to in our regular interactions with those closest to us. It is precisely because these weak ties are more removed from our daily lives that they deliver information about job opportunities we wouldn't otherwise stumble across. This is important information, but it's also information we don't need every day.

Job seekers who have more established careers may think that they are less in need of such interactions, but that's a mistake. They need to see beyond the insular professional worlds they've constructed around themselves. Research suggests that building a career often creates a self-reinforcing cycle of success. You start with a role that initially represents a good fit. Then you build your skill sets and network of relationships. But that means that networks often end up being quite narrow—what academics call "path dependent"—because they are highly contingent on that first job and the roles that followed. When you want to get perspectives, advice, and—in this case—opportunities that extend beyond your current world, you need weak ties to broaden your access. They're more likely than strong ties to help you find and test real-world manifestations of the prototypes that stray from what's expected of you.

Weak-tie relationships also have lower stakes attached to them. They allow you to bounce ideas off people in a safe, casual setting and try out new work identities and approaches. It doesn't cost much to experiment within these relationships. Strong ties are a different story, however; they hem us in. For example, people are often afraid to confide in their confidants. In one study, participants were far more likely to share what was really on their minds with weak ties they barely knew. These conversations were often spontaneous, as individuals were looking for empathy. The risk of talking about a challenge they were having or something they wanted that wasn't on their traditional path felt much lower with people they knew far less well than with close friends or loved ones.

Why does this matter? Because you have to be open and truthful about your quest to find real roles that could be a good match.

Networking only with friends and colleagues in your inner circle for roles they would *expect* you to seek isn't necessarily going to help you make the progress you want at this point in your life. It's by talking to others more freely that you'll bring the most surprising opportunities out of hiding.

So if you find yourself worrying about approaching someone you haven't talked to in ages, get over it. We're not saying it's easy. Cultivating weak, or "instrumental," ties can "make us feel dirty," as one group of researchers phrased it. And networking *for a job*, those same researchers found, often makes us feel even dirtier—inauthentic or even immoral. That's because it is premeditated and professionally focused, as opposed to something we're doing more organically to develop friendships. Not everyone responds this way. The study showed that people in high-power jobs—like your boss—don't feel as dirty when they network for professional gain as those in so-called low-power jobs do. And yet it is precisely the people with less power who need networks to move up.

What can you do to get past your hesitation? For starters, remember that you're not actually looking for an "in" to get a job at this stage. You're looking to understand whether there are real jobs that line up with your prototype and what they are actually like. We share more about how to do the latter below. But to get over your hesitation, also remind yourself that you've already done a lot of the work. Your ability to efficiently and effectively communicate what you are looking for should have improved considerably since you started this book. Now you just have to reach out. You can once again use and modify the appropriate letter template in Appendix D to ask for a conversation.

When you do connect, focus on learning and personal growth, what you have in common, and what you can offer the other person. You've already adopted a growth mindset to analyze your last job move, to bucket your priorities for your next move, and to create and converge on your career prototypes. Having done all that work, you have something rich, not just transactional, to talk about. You're not merely showing up to ask for a favor. You're sharing what you've discovered about your quest and seeking information about how realistic your top prototypes are. The other person will learn something, too—not only about you but also about a new approach to career planning and how it relates to your common interests. Theoretically at least, you wouldn't have this weak tie if there weren't some common ground to bring you together.

What's more, by coming to the conversation as prepared as you are, you'll inspire confidence that you're likely to succeed in your quest—and everyone wants to be able to look back and say they helped a winner. Job switchers don't come across as a burden to weak ties when seeking their input. Quite the opposite. In our interviews and coaching sessions, we've found that weak ties look at conversations like these as opportunities to help someone thoughtful who deserves to make progress. They even occasionally see the person who reached out as a potential hire who could help them—or someone else in their professional network. Weak ties often know of someone who is trying—these days, desperately and often unsuccessfully—to fill an open job. Perhaps you're the answer to that search.

Everyone approaches networking slightly differently. Clara started with LinkedIn to see who might be connected to her roles of interest. She looked not only at the current titles and companies of her connections but also at their past experiences. It took time, but she found it energizing as she learned of the breadth of experiences just in her own network. Through this search she discovered that an old acquaintance from college had worked at National Geographic. Although they had been in touch only a few times since graduation, Clara decided to reach out—and her acquaintance reconnected readily.

Clara didn't just use technology tools to start conversations. She spoke openly about her search with her "strong ties"—such as her close friends and her sister. They in turn connected her to people they knew who worked in roles similar to the one Clara wanted to explore. The more Clara traveled down this road, the easier finding the right people to talk to became—and her networking search became far less intimidating.

Unpacking a Job Description

Your weak ties don't just help you find opportunities that appear to match your top prototypes. When you learn about new opportunities, they can also provide valuable perspective to help you understand if the jobs are as enticing as they may seem on paper. As we mentioned earlier, most job descriptions don't spell out what you'll do day-to-day. Even more to the point, none are written with you in mind. That means it's up to you—with help from your network—to figure out how each role will or won't line up with your priorities.

Unpacking a job description entails doing almost exactly what you learned to do in Chapter Seven: interviewing someone in the know to determine whether the role really delivers on your critical energy drivers and assets and to understand what trade-offs you would likely need to make if you took the job. As you'll see in the activity below, the main difference is that this time you're exploring roles that actually exist, not reality-checking ideal jobs you've crafted in your head. But because you've already had practice, you'll be better at it now that it "counts." To help land these interviews, you can use Appendix D again. Just modify the letter template to include the precise opportunity about which you're hoping to learn. At this stage, you're still not asking for an "in" or a referral, so you can keep that line in there.

Clara's interviews at this stage helped her see opportunities with much clearer eyes. At the start of one of our sessions, she joined our Zoom chat visibly excited. She had just come across what read like the perfect job to her: expedition coordinator for National Geographic. When we asked what she liked about it, she talked about how the work related to travel—something she loved from her time in Ireland and crisscrossing the United States. She talked about how she could once again work with the scientific community, which would allow her to use her degrees. And she positively gushed about the reputation of National Geographic as a research brand that people knew and trusted. Was it different from her science writer prototype? Sure, but she had found it because she was looking at places that employed science writers. And this job wouldn't have the writing component that she wasn't even all that excited about developing. Might this be the perfect job?

We echoed Clara's enthusiasm. Then we asked her to unpack what the job would actually entail and how that lined up with the energy drivers and assets most important to her—an exercise she had mastered with her prototypes. When she talked to her college acquaintance who had worked at National Geographic, she went through each energy driver and asset of importance to her. During that conversation, Clara learned that the day-to-day work of an expedition coordinator was more about purchasing tickets and handling logistics like airport pick-ups and drop-offs for other travelers. It was less about working with scientists and using her scientific research background. Although National Geographic is certainly an intellectually stimulating place, this specific role wouldn't offer opportunities for intellectual challenge and learning from scientists. And whereas many people might find purchasing tickets and handling logistics for travelers a way to have personal impact, doing those things didn't line up with the kind of impact Clara desired.

Although she initially felt disappointed, she was glad she had learned before switching that the job wouldn't measure up to her quest for progress. She had avoided making a mistake in her career journey. Part of her takeaway, she told us, was that she would love to go on one of National Geographic's expeditions, but she wasn't interested in coordinating them. That, in turn, helped her see that a bunch of other roles that she had discovered through conversations with her network would likely have similar drawbacks.

Another individual we coached—a recent MBA graduate who worked as a parts buyer at a large automotive company—did similar research to unpack job descriptions that seemed to align with what she wanted to do. Through her graduate studies, she had developed an interest in business strategy. When she converged on her prototypes, having a strategy role rose to the top. But that prototype was still quite generalized and disconnected from the job market. There are lots of strategy roles in companies and consultancies. What specific kind would help her make progress on her quest? And was she qualified for them right now? When she began looking at postings, she needed help processing the descriptions, which were riddled with abstract language about "transformation" and "critical thinking." Equipped with her desired energy drivers and assets— she wanted to be creative, to learn and be challenged appropriately, to work independently, to develop her strategy skill set, and to be able to make recommendations about a company's product line given its evolving position within an industry—she scheduled a conversation with a manager in a strategy role at her company.

This wasn't a close colleague. They worked in separate units and functions and knew each other only in passing. That bit of distance made it feel less risky to reach out, especially because she didn't want to signal to her own boss that she was unhappy in her current role. Instead of asking what *the manager* most liked about *their* job, she framed the conversation in terms of her own quest for progress and the postings she was finding. In what ways would these roles allow for creativity? How did the manager's own job allow for it, and did their definitions of creativity match? What about her assets—how did those line up with the expectations for different postings? And so on. This approach gave her information to test her abstract impressions about strategy work and find out how she herself might experience these roles. She followed the same informational interviewing process that you learned in Chapter Seven to flesh out prototypes. And she used similar questions to the ones she had used for that purpose, but with greater specificity as she tailored them to real roles and job descriptions.

Have conversations like this with a range of individuals as you explore the market and network your way into identifying real roles with potential. And remember, the goal is—to borrow a phrase from the product development world—to analyze the feasibility of your top prototypes. These interviews are meant to minimize surprises. There's a little more pressure now to get things "right" than when you were interviewing to create the prototypes. Still, you haven't made a move yet. That means you can keep testing feasibility with more interviews or revisit your priorities—unless of course your get out clock is *really* ticking.

Even after you've switched jobs and found a good fit for the time being, it's smart to keep doing this sort of interviewing. The more you practice it, the better you'll get at sizing up the real market and spotting roles that match your priorities. Building that pattern-recognition skill helps you know when to start searching in earnest next time as well. And it gives you confidence that there are various ways to make progress as you've defined it. Having this type of conversation on a regular basis—say, once every couple of months—also increases the number of weak ties you have. That means your network becomes more diverse—in terms of skills, backgrounds, geographies, organizations, functions, and so forth—and you expand your access to information, opportunities, perspectives, and ways of making progress in the future. Over time, this work can even help you identify and create a personal board of directors for your career, which is much more effective than searching for that one "perfect" mentor.

Activity: Prepare for Your "Supply-Side" Research

Before conducting an interview to unpack a real job posting, carefully consider what you *think* it means in light of your quest:

1. Write down why the role could be a good fit based on how it seems, on the surface, to match up with your energy drivers and assets. Spell out which ones you think align with the role. For example, one person we coached was intrigued by a property manager role. She thought it might line up with some of what was important to her, namely having flexible hours and not being chained to her desk. She made a note of those potential upsides as critical assumptions to test when she spoke with people who actually performed the role. You should do the same.

2. List the ways you think the role probably wouldn't be a good fit for your drivers and assets.

3. Jot down the aspects of the role you're really not sure about. For instance, the individual in the example above wondered if

the property manager role would involve having profit-and-loss responsibility for a property, because that was a skill set she wanted to develop.

4. Now write down the specific questions you want to ask to check your assumptions and learn more about your uncertainties.

By organizing your thoughts like this in advance, you'll ask sharper questions and keep your conversations focused on the things that matter most to you at this point in your life.

Why Trade-offs Are Good

After you've conducted the interviews about jobs that do exist, do what you did with your divergent prototypes: plot these real jobs against the energy drivers and assets of importance to you and see where they fall compared with your current and imagined roles. As you do this, you will learn some truths about trade-offs.

First, it will become increasingly clear that there is no perfect job. We said that earlier, but as you talk with more people who do the types of jobs you're exploring, you won't have to take our word for it. Utopia doesn't exist. For anyone. Better to learn about the downsides of roles ahead of time than to wait until you've already switched.

Second, you'll start seeing trade-offs as positives. Many people view them as "settling" for something suboptimal and laden with disappointment. They then make one of the biggest possible mistakes in a career: They decide that, because there is no perfect option now, they should just take the one that offers them the most prestige, money, benefits, and power in the hopes of a better slate of possibilities in the future.

But intentionally making a trade-off isn't settling. It's an empowering choice because it's based on information you've acquired and weighed—and it unlocks the progress you want. You get to decide what you are or are not willing to change in your life. You get to say what you are willing to give up so that you can get something greater than what you have right now. This psychological framing puts you in the driver's seat: *you* get to choose what job you hire next. Because of that, just like the way you can fall in love with the shortcomings or "imperfections" of your spouse or partner, perhaps you'll come to even appreciate some of the idiosyncratic shortcomings of the job you ultimately and deliberately take.

The trade-offs you pick are informed by what energy drivers and capabilities matter most to you right now. You may be letting certain skills or areas of expertise languish, either for good or just for now. That's perfectly appropriate. Making choices about what *not* to do frees you to pursue your quest. By consciously understanding these trade-offs, you're also making yourself a better fit for the employer and role you ultimately choose. Because you've vetted the job beforehand to make sure it aligns with your priorities and you have no illusions about what the job doesn't have, you're more likely to make a choice that's better for both of you. That's something else you get by learning before switching—a fit on both sides.

The MBA grad at the automotive company discovered this after conducting a series of interviews over a couple of months to scope out several strategy roles in her current organization. Going into the conversations, she had two prototypes of interest to her. One was a strategy role at a large company, and the other was a strategy role at a community-based nonprofit. One of the unknowns still looming over these two prototypes was whether she was in the "regain control" quest or the "get out" quest. Either way, she was sure she wanted to reset how her job made use of her capabilities. She was eager to jump into a role where she could learn from a trusting manager. What she had vacillated on was whether she wanted to build on or reset what energized her. Job security, directly supporting those in her community, and being trusted to do her best work were some of the energy drivers that kept changing buckets as she iterated on her priorities.

Conducting the interviews, however, about jobs that actually existed, figuring out for which ones she was qualified based on her current assets, and comparing them across her energy drivers persuaded her that her quest was most likely to regain control. That led to several insights. To start, she realized that her top priority was security. For her, that meant earning a solid salary in a stable job that wasn't subject to the whims of a fickle manager, a vulnerable company, or a volatile market. For that reason, she decided that continuing to work at a large, established company was desirable, which heightened her interest in internal roles and helped her make a trade-off: although she had an interest in helping those in her community by working at a nonprofit, she wasn't willing to give up the security and stability that a job in a large company could provide. She could instead pursue her community work on the side, as a volunteer. She also realized it was critical to find a role in which she would be trusted to do her best work. To her, this meant that she could work remotely, take time to volunteer but still get things done, and not have her manager question her every move even as she was developing her strategy skill set. She was dealing with micromanagement in her current role, and she was sick of it. That was partly why she had wondered if her quest was to Get Out. As she continued to dig, she found two internal strategy opportunities and then zeroed in on the one where she would have more freedom and flexibility to do her work her way but still receive regular feedback. That meant she would be doing the right work on the right team, such that she would feel secure and be energized daily. That struck the right balance for her and the company.

Of course, finding a good fit where you know you can make progress is one thing. Actually getting the job is another. Once you've decided what employer and role you want to hire, you need to persuade *them* to hire you, too. To do that, you'll put everything you've learned about what progress looks like for you into a narrative that matches the progress your potential employer wants to make. Crafting that story is the subject of the next chapter.

TEN

STEP 8:
CRAFT YOUR CAREER STORY

 In an ideal world, you would simply go to the job market and find a no-hassle match with the prototype you've tested. Opportunities would just flow to you, given the clarity you have around what you want to do.

But like other matchmaking endeavors, finding your next job is never that easy. Part of the reason you have done so much work to get to this point is what organizations *think* you (and others) want isn't typically the same as what you actually want. As a result, they have trouble attracting the right people and managing and developing them effectively. We suggest some changes employers could make in Chapter Twelve. But for the foreseeable future you should accept that you are living in an imperfect world where you will have to *translate* your prototype into a career narrative that managers and organizations can understand, appreciate, and accommodate. That's the next step in our process—and the topic of this chapter. After you develop that story, it will permeate your résumé, your cover letters, and your interviews—all of which we discuss in the next chapter.

Even if you haven't yet found a real-world posting that fits your prototype, there's still great value in crafting a compelling narrative. Doing so can bring unexpected opportunities your way. That's what Alex discovered. Having converged on an ideal job prototype—a role within a consumer products business that would build on his current skills but allow him more flexibility in how he did his work—he began to share his story. He told hiring managers in other areas of his company about his desire to keep learning at work and developing novel digital products in an agile way, but with the freedom to work remotely and to structure his day in ways that would optimize his performance. As they heard his story, some wondered how they might be able to leverage Alex's capabilities and sources of motivation. One manager in a different division even created a job that would allow Alex to work from home while coaching the company's executives on how to move to an agile product development process.

When his current manager heard about that job offer, he called a time-out. He asked Alex what he wanted at work. So Alex shared his career story. He explained that every day he showed up excited to work—that he loved his colleagues and the products they developed together. He admitted how disappointed he was when he learned that he would have to move to keep his role. He and his wife had evaluated the options and trade-offs and realized they just couldn't uproot themselves, so he had taken advantage of the transition time to think about what drove his energy and what drained it. He had thought about which of his skills he wanted to continue to develop and which were less important at this moment in his career. And he had identified some must-haves: the ability to keep growing, the flexibility to do his best work, the opportunity to help a company develop digital products in an agile way, and the chance to do that work without moving. Alex also laid out the trade-offs he was willing to make in order to get that type of job—and even briefly described some of the exercises in this book so that his manager could better understand what Alex had learned and how.

After hearing Alex's story, his manager said, "You know, if that's what you want, we have this other thing we've been cooking up. We hadn't told you about it yet because we weren't quite sure what it would look like. We want to create a cross-departmental role to help build our capabilities in agile and tech-powered innovation throughout the whole research and engineering group. Even though your current department is relocating, this more centralized role wouldn't require you to move. I bet we could adapt it to fit most of what you're describing."

Alex was stunned. It didn't check off every single box, of course. The role would require some travel and hybrid work to collaborate with those who had to relocate. But everything else he wanted was right there—and he wouldn't even have to switch units, let alone companies. He could continue to do work he loved without moving. An offer was soon put together, and he took the job. The trade-offs in periodic travel were well worth all the things he would get to do.

Learning how to tell your story to the world—so that managers inside your organization (like Alex's) and those on the outside can understand what you want to do, why, and how you'd contribute—is your next task. Don't worry, though. You don't have to be a born storyteller to craft a good narrative. You can take your cues from one of the best storytellers in the world: Pixar, the renowned animation studio.

Taking a Page—or Seven Lines—from Pixar

In 2011, Emma Coats—a storyboard artist at Pixar—tweeted twenty-two guidelines to make anyone a better storyteller. Although the whole list went viral and was a hot topic in the professional writing community for months, the part that has received the most sustained attention is her fourth point, about creating a "story spine" to provide narrative structure.

Given that the human brain is wired to learn and retain information through stories, turning your quest for progress into a story is an effective way to get noticed and be understood. The story spine will help you create and tell this story well.

Just as you will continue to hone your career narrative, Pixar spends years writing, rewriting, and then writing again each story it tells in its films. And each time, its writers use the following Mad Libs–like template, which captures the seven core "frames" of a story spine:

Once upon a time _____.
Every day _____.
One day _____.
Because of that _____.
Because of that _____.
Until finally _____.
And ever since that day _____.

When we use this technique with students or mentees, we ask them to fill in these seven blanks *twice*. First, we have them craft a story spine about their *past trajectory*, typically focusing on a key transition that brought them to where they are today. For some, filling in each blank takes only a sentence; for others, a paragraph. Given the work you've already done, this exercise should be straightforward and also, our experience suggests, clarifying.

Here's an edited example of a past trajectory story spine from one of our students, a firefighter who came to us at a critical point in his career, when he was struggling to figure out whether he wanted to become a fire chief. This story spine focuses on how he came into his current role as a first responder:

Once upon a time I was undecided on where I wanted my future career to go. I was just going through the motions at work. I would get up, have the same routine, go to work, deal with the same people and the same problems, and have little satisfaction.

Every day I would not look forward to going to work. While there, I would wish I was home. I would constantly look at the clock and count down the hours. I would leave work feeling unfulfilled. All of this continued for a while until . . .

One day I decided that I needed to make a change. What I was doing was not a career; it was just a job. I decided I wanted to go back to school and give back to my community. I started to volunteer as a firefighter. This was a way to both give back and also receive further training and education to pave the way for my future.

Because of that I started to feel more fulfilled. I felt like I was actually making a difference in my community and that this could be the career I was looking for.

Because of that I completed my bachelor's degree as well as further firefighter training and applied to be a firefighter. I went through the application process a couple of times.

Until finally I was hired as a firefighter by the department I had served as a volunteer in the community where I grew up. I continued getting more education and training and pursued more of a leadership role. I became a senior firefighter. Then I became a lieutenant. I was recently promoted to the management team as a division chief of safety and professional development.

And ever since that day I've been more fulfilled in my career and felt a real sense of accomplishment. I've also tried to apply what

I have learned throughout my career to help develop employees and grow the department. But I find myself wondering whether it is time for me to take the next step in my progression toward being a more influential and more senior leader.

We've found that writing a story spine about a pivotal moment in the past prepares people to talk about their larger journey in thoughtful, concise terms. Because your mentor interviewed you in Chapter Two about your most recent career switch, you already have the basics of that particular story, grounded in "The Timeline of a Job Switcher" (Figure 2.1). The notes from that conversation should spell out how you moved from your first thought about switching to whatever change you made. You can use those same events and phases to fill in the seven blanks in the story spine template.

Then it's time to construct a second spine that describes what you want next in your career—as Alex did before telling others in his organization about his quest. Yours might begin, "Once upon a time, I had a first thought that it was time to move on from my current job . . ." and proceed from there. If this spine comes out more abstract than your past spine, you're not alone. After all, you're sharing a story about your intended future, which hasn't occurred yet. But if it's so abstract that people can't follow the thread, you probably haven't quite landed on a solid prototype for your next role. Your spine about your quest for progress needs to be clear, concise, and actionable enough that hiring managers can easily see how well it matches what they are looking for and you can readily envision yourself living into the narrative. In other words, this story spine is both a communication tool and yet another check in our process to make sure you really understand your current quest.

Here's the firefighter's edited second story spine, which builds directly on his first one—like an outline for the next book in a series or for a film's sequel that reestablishes the protagonist's current position.

Once upon a time my desire to become a better leader caused me to keep pursuing further education and professional development.

Every day I try to apply what I have learned throughout my career to help develop employees and grow the department.

One day during my one-on-one meeting with the chief of the department, he shared that he was impressed with my work ethic, my desire to keep developing my skills, and my passion for making the department stronger. He then informed me that he would be retiring in the near future and that I should consider applying to become the new chief.

Because of that I realized that I could do more and be more than I had appreciated. It was clear my hard work was paying off. But I was also initially scared of the responsibility of being in charge of the department. The buck would stop with me, and I would ultimately be responsible for the actions, decisions, and changes that I wanted to put in place.

Because of that anxiety I took steps to address my concerns. I began to move out of my comfort zone and make more decisions internally to see what it would feel like to lead the department. I spent more time studying what it takes to be a great fire chief.

Until finally I realized that this isn't just a job I could do someday, but one that I feel I'm already prepared to do. I've done the work. I know the team here. They respect me. And I'm ready to make the tough decisions.

And ever since that day I realized I am not only ready for this role but also the right person for it. I know I'll be a good leader. I've learned a lot throughout my career, and the time is right to move to the next chapter. As a result, I'm applying to become the fire chief and director of emergency management.

Your story spines about your past move and current quest will together form the basis of your "elevator pitch"—a short statement, two minutes or less, about what you want to do next and why you're the person for a particular job. The concept of the elevator pitch, of course, isn't new. Although there's dispute behind the phrase's origins, many people credit Philip Crosby, a pioneer in the quality improvement industry, for coining the concept. In his classic 1972 book, *The Art of Getting Your Own Sweet Way*, Crosby wrote that "when teaching Quality Management, I always teach my students to learn an 'elevator speech.' This is an all-encompassing, action-producing set of ideas that you pronounce while on the elevator with the big boss for just 1 minute."

"Elevators" have of course changed a lot since the 1970s. You may have more or less time in them; more distractions to combat, thanks to smartphones; or even a different venue in which to make your pitch, such as a shared Uber ride or the first minute of a virtual meeting while waiting for someone else to join. But the ability to tell a quick, compelling story is as important as ever. Using story spines to sum up past career moves and future aspirations makes it much easier to create a concrete and memorable elevator speech that will accurately reflect where you are in your journey and resonate with potential employers.

Workshopping Your Story

Story spines and elevator pitches can take several iterations to get right, just like Pixar movies. Now is another great time to circle back to your mentors to see what they think of what you've constructed. Would they frame your past moments differently? How so? Is there room for confusion about why you made the move you did? And does your story about your current quest seem viable given what your mentors know about your trajectory so far? Does the story gel? Are your key energy drivers and career assets coming through clearly?

Creating a compelling narrative is challenging, even when you've had practice. In addition to sharing yours with people you know and trust, you can turn to technology for some automated "workshopping" support. As in Chapter Seven, artificial intelligence can help here. You can feed your text to a generative AI chatbot and ask for help making your story more concise, punchy, or moving. You can also try asking it to find the essence of your narrative or to translate it into a story for recruiters, mentors, or even kindergartners. Sometimes the simplest version of a story makes the best elevator pitch.

Worst case, the generative AI version ends up being garbage or inauthentic, and you don't use it. But if that happens, ask yourself this question: If the chatbot is struggling to make sense of your story, is there a chance that prospective employers would misinterpret it, too? Perhaps you have more work to do to clarify the narrative. Remember, the story isn't for you. It's for others. What others perceive in your story is what matters most—and audience perception is something that AI is often good at simulating. To help you further, you can even use an AI tool to read your story to you in a voice that sounds like yours, so you can have the experience of being the audience for your own story.

Even if you like what the chatbot does, keep testing your story on real people. As we've said elsewhere in this book, social interaction fuels career progress. Others can ask questions that will reveal confusing aspects of your narrative. They can suggest ways of sharpening your thinking and your message. You—and they—will know when your story is market-ready because your résumé and every other part of your application package will snap into focus. At that point you can apply for specific jobs and fine-tune your story for each posting that seems promising.

Harkening back to the question we asked in Chapter Eight— "If your eight-year-old self had correctly predicted what you would do professionally, what would you be doing today?"—we've noticed that once a narrative clicks into place, there is often an artifact from childhood that is consistent with what people want to do now. Even back then, when you didn't give trade-offs much thought, you knew things about yourself that might now make your career narrative "just make sense." One individual, for example, wrote about how he had worked his whole adult life to create a résumé that would impress others and had bounced around a variety of jobs. When he became editor of a prestigious fashion publication, a friend from elementary school showed him a homemade fashion magazine he had created back in the day. The friend's mom had found it while cleaning out the house. The editor took it as a sign that deep down, he had always known what he wanted to do.

Such signs needn't be quite so precise to add useful texture to a career narrative. An architect who was obsessed with Legos as a kid, an interior designer who constantly rearranged his bedroom as a teen, a veterinarian who used to spend hours and hours hunting for interesting critters outside—you get the idea. Connections like these can help explain why a role feels right in your gut. These moments in our childhood are rarely predictive. Instead, they're told in hindsight. You didn't mess up by not knowing sooner that you ought to follow a particular clue. But once you know what path you should be on, these connections to your childhood can add a feeling of authenticity to your story spine. And that feeling will enable you to share your story with confidence—and to stride forward into the job market, the next part of your journey.

ELEVEN

STEP 9:
APPLY FOR JOBS
YOU'D LIKE TO HIRE

You've made it to the final step in our job-switching process: applying for roles that align with the progress you want to make. "At last!" you might say. "I'm ready to move forward on my quest."

You are indeed. This chapter doesn't replicate all the great tactical advice on the nuts and bolts of job searching that you can get from the many blog posts, podcasts, message boards, articles, coaches, and books that are out there. It instead highlights just a few tips to make sure that what you've learned through our unconventional job-moves discovery process translates to the crowded marketplace for jobs. With a precise sense of what progress looks like for you, it would be a shame to not make that progress.

Busting Through Application Filters

Given that you have more clarity than most about why you are the right fit for a particular job, how do you make your application stand out from the hundreds or thousands of others? Even if you apply through a personal connection, which we recommend, you will still need to convincingly convey what you have to offer.

In many companies, human beings don't do the initial screening of job applications, cover letters, and résumés. It's instead done by software called an applicant tracking system, or ATS. This software looks for certain keywords as evidence that a given applicant is a good match for a job. If the ATS sees enough of a match between the job description and the documents you submit, then you make it through the filter.

The practice of using applicant tracking systems is well established. So what do you do to make the first cut? View the job description as a cheat sheet, says Tom Dowd, the director of career coaching at Guild, which helps companies leverage education to upskill their workforce and improve career mobility. Dissect the posting. What are the key skills, experiences, and credentials listed as requirements for the job? As you customize your résumé and cover letter, incorporate those items that are mentioned early and often. Those are likely the most important things for which the ATS will screen.

The takeaway here? Don't get too creative when you write your résumé and cover letter and fill out your application. At the screening stage, there are no points for originality. Tailor your language to reflect the critical requirements for each posting.

What if you don't meet 100 percent of the requirements? That's okay, Dowd told us. You don't need to possess every single skill. Almost no one does. That's especially true given that job descriptions these days often include long laundry lists of skills cribbed from past job descriptions, competitors' postings, and anything else that seems even peripherally relevant. In essence, employers are hunting for unicorns—which don't exist. So if the fit seems good overall, don't torture yourself over skills you don't have or try to "spin" them into being. Instead, emphasize two or three capabilities that the job description suggests are top priorities and that match your assets. Look at the story spines you've created and the work you've done to understand your energizers and assets. Translate all that into language that echoes those essentials in the description. You've already done informational interviews to gain market-based insight into why the role you're applying for is right for you—and to pinpoint how you can make a valuable contribution. You're ready to make the case.

With that said, it's worth addressing one of the trickiest challenges these days: breaking into a new industry by applying for an entry-level job. All too often, entry-level postings ask for several years of prior experience—which makes little sense. In those situations, highlight the relevant "transferable" skills and experiences you *do* have (and, to the point above, do so using the language of the job description). Show how the work you've done in other contexts sets you up to do the work that the job description suggests is important. As you connect those dots in your résumé and cover letter, quantify your experience. For example, if a description asks for one to three years of experience, sum up at least that many years' worth of relevant work in other settings, volunteer or school projects, or side hustles—anything that fits the skill profile the employer wants.

People often struggle to figure out which capabilities from one industry might apply to entry-level jobs in another. But this shouldn't be as difficult for you. Having cataloged your assets (your experiences, skills, and credentials) and prioritized them to determine which of your prototypes would make the most sense as a next job, you have already identified both gaps and connections between capabilities developed in the past and work you want to do now. Incorporate those insights into your positioning as a candidate. For example, let's say you have never fielded pitches for start-up businesses. If your prototyping has led you to seek work in the world of venture capital, you could shine a light on your experience assessing "intrapreneurial" product ideas within your organization and your track record picking winners. To fill a gap, you could even engage in a relevant side hustle now—say, a gig that involves market research or financial-data analysis—and include that in your résumé to show that you are continuing to build your assets. Write explicitly about all this in your cover letter. The idea is to make sure that an applicant tracking system and, if you get through the initial screening, a human being can easily see how you meet the critical requirements.

If your application is filtered out and you don't get invited to interview for a job, don't be discouraged. As much as it shouldn't be, at this stage it is partly a numbers game. Keep applying for roles that fit or come close to your prototype, keep tailoring your career narrative, and keep looking for personal connections that increase your odds of success. As you do so, you will ultimately get past the screening stage.

In the meantime, you'll also want to prepare to tell your story "live."

Interviewing Like a Storyteller

To begin preparing for interviews, study and rehearse your story spines. Chances are high that you will have an opportunity to share your elevator pitch about your career journey (see Chapter Ten). You want to be ready to present a pithy version when that moment arrives. Career coaches—like media coaches—often advise going into an interview with a handful of messages you want to deliver. The seven frames of a story spine serve as a useful template for figuring those messages out and articulating them succinctly.

Next, anticipate which questions you'll most likely get and prepare answers for them. If you're applying for a job at a consulting firm or for a strategy role at pretty much any type of company, the hiring manager might conduct a "case" interview, in which you're presented with a hypothetical problem you could face on the job and asked how you would solve it. If that's the type of interview you'll have, you'll probably know beforehand. But if your interview is more general in nature and you haven't been asked to prepare anything in advance, the most straightforward way to get ready is to scrutinize your cover letter and résumé against the job posting as if you were the employer. What would *you* want to know more about if you had to assess fit for the role and the organization? Where do you see gaps in your experience or skills? If you were looking for a reason to take your application out of the running, what would it be? Look for those potential holes or weaknesses in your narrative so you can practice addressing them clearly and confidently. Your interviewer is probably less prepared for this conversation than you are, and yet they care just as much about looking like they know how to do their job and evaluate you. The easier you can make it for them, the better you will do.

For example, if you're trying to break into a new industry, you're likely to get a question about how you'll get up to speed. Practice a few versions of an answer. Think about how each response maps back to the story spines you've created. Draw on that narrative to illustrate how and why you will be able to contribute when you get the job. Perhaps you've successfully switched functions or areas of focus in the past and you've derived energy and motivation from what you learned in the process. You could describe how that same desire to keep learning is compelling you to explore a new industry now—and point out specific ways in which your experience in a different setting equips you with fresh insights about how to do or manage the work effectively. You could mention, as well, which tools you used in the past to quickly learn about a new function and talk about which tools could similarly help you gain your footing in this role. And take this opportunity to talk about the informational interviews you have done with people in this role and what you learned when you pressure tested if the job was a good fit.

There are several common interview questions for which you should also prepare (see Appendix E for a list). You might, for instance, be asked to explain how you overcame a particular challenge or to describe actions you took to achieve a certain set of outcomes or results. In your answers, you can again leverage the story-spine structure from Chapter Ten. Ground each response in the details of the roles you've held—the "once upon a time" and "every day" parts of your narrative. Then, in the "one day" part of your story, describe how something changed, a problem erupted, or an opportunity to do something different emerged. Next, briefly describe the steps you took to tackle that situation. Then point to the results you achieved—the "until finally" plot point—and cap that off with the skills, dispositions, or character you built or showed that's relevant to the open position.

Toward the end of a job interview, most interviewers will ask if you have any questions for them. Here's where you can shine. Don't forget—you're trying to figure out if *you* want to hire *them*, too. That means you should interview them. Use the same types of questions you asked in your informational interviews (see Chapter Seven and Chapter Nine) to learn how the job lines up with the work you want to do. Your questions will reflect how much you've done to figure out what really matters to you. You're not just asking questions to feign interest. Use this conversation as an opportunity to learn more about what trade-offs you'd need to make in order to do the job—and then, after the interview, assess whether those are trade-offs you'd happily make. If they aren't, then this isn't the job for you. One person with whom we spoke shared how he took a new job for significantly less pay. When we asked him why, he was able to articulate all the other things he would get that were of importance to him. When he reported to work on his first day, he wasn't worrying about the money he gave up, because he consciously made that trade-off to secure his nonnegotiables.

Although you probably shouldn't talk about the trade-offs you're willing to make in your first or second interview, knowing what they are will put you in a much better place as you move toward negotiations. You'll most likely discover that the job description isn't rigid. Employers, too, need to make trade-offs when they hire people. Huddle with them to see if you can shape the job to include your must-haves. And before you accept an offer, make sure you and the employer agree on how those needs will be met. By clarifying expectations up front, you'll improve your experience (and your employer's) once you're working.

And always write a personal thank-you note after every interview you have, whether it's a formal job interview or an informational one. Send it right away while the conversation is still fresh in both your minds. Gratitude alone won't get you a job, but it can help. And not showing your gratitude for the time someone spent with you can certainly hurt.

Sharing What Makes You Tick

We wrote this book to help you make progress in your career, and making progress isn't just landing the job—it's also doing that job well. To that end, there's another tool that can benefit both you and your employer. It's a **personal cheat sheet**, a quick guide that details the best way to work with you. In the same way that the latest gadget on the market comes with a one-page reference sheet to help people get started quickly and productively, a personal cheat sheet sums up how others can get the most out of you—so that you're all successful.

The concept of creating such a guide for business leaders and managers—popularized by a 2013 *New York Times* article about creating a personal user manual—has gained traction in recent years. People are creating these sheets to share with their teams, their recruits, and others. Many leaders have told us that this enables them to form stronger relationships, build sturdier collaborations, and achieve higher levels of individual and group performance. At the same time, some have wondered if creating and sharing a personal cheat sheet will look too self-involved or entitled. That's a common reaction to this exercise. And it's a real risk. That's why it's important to understand the why behind this work—and to remember that deciding whether and how you share it is important, too.

First, view it as a useful way to organize and summarize deep insights you've learned about yourself—for yourself. As you're applying for positions, a personal cheat sheet clarifies in your own mind how you can best contribute: In what circumstances do you thrive? Which activities bring out the best in you? What do you bring to a job and how? Even if you don't share this sheet with anyone, it will distill your career narrative into points you'd like to make during interviews about why a job is a good fit for you—and why you're a good fit for the employer. A personal cheat sheet also gives you a starting point when you're ready to make another job move down the line, because you'll have captured much of what you've learned about yourself in the course of this book in one place. Rather than reinvent the wheel, you'll be ready to build on that foundation with your latest insights as you cruise through our process again.

Second, if you decide to share this work with your manager, colleagues, or a potential boss, do so with the intention of either asking for feedback on the sheet itself or making yourself more valuable to them at work. And consider following up by asking for similar insights about working with them. If you share your sheet with a prospective employer, explain that it's to help you both gauge fit more accurately.

To determine whether seeing such a sheet is wanted or appropriate in any circumstance, take a cue from Alex. Remember when he shared what he had learned through our career process with his manager and other managers inside his company? Rather than simply send over a sheet about himself, he told his career story in person. His personal cheat sheet was merely a supporting visual. In essence he said, "I found this process that allowed me to lay out my career, reflect, and think about the things that really drive me, and I'd love your feedback." For Alex, emphasizing that this was coming from a place of self-reflection was key. He had captured his insights in a virtual whiteboard, but had he just shared that file without any context, eyes would have glazed over. Instead, he referred to his laptop screen while he spoke with people to illustrate some of the points. He listened to their responses and looked for body language that suggested where to lean in or back off. As he told us, "I didn't take them through too much of the process in depth."

He also talked with people about where he gets the most energy and how he sorted out those priorities. When one manager in the company started nodding his head in agreement, Alex asked what was resonating, which gave the manager a chance to offer feedback and synthesize his take on what Alex had learned. This person then said, "You know, Alex, you're a transformation champion. That's how I would describe you." Since then, Alex has used that phrase to describe himself because it encapsulates many of the things he likes to do.

By approaching these conversations as someone who wanted to learn, Alex was able to head off the risk that people would think he was too self-involved or entitled. Hiring managers who say yes to having this type of conversation are likely to be impressed by your initiative, self-awareness, and clarity about what you really want in your career. And if the information in your sheet ends up taking you out of the running for a role, you've avoided a career move that you probably would have ended up regretting.

As the management scholar and consultant Peter Drucker pointed out, understanding and communicating how you work best is imperative for your productivity—and a good manager knows this. As Alex observed, it can also be central to your happiness, because it often involves defining and pursuing what holds meaning and purpose for you. Most employers want that for you, too (at least in theory—we'll get to what they can do better in practice in the next chapter). When you thrive, they tend to thrive, too. When you're unhappy and not performing well, you're probably going to be less productive and useful to your employer. When there's a good fit, you're both generally happy. When there's a bad fit, both sides feel it. It's hard to hide something that isn't right—and why would you want to? No one benefits. That's why savvy employers are willing to make trade-offs themselves and change the specifications of a job to get the right person for their team or organization.

On that note, your cheat sheet can play one more critical role once you land a job. In the "preboarding" and "onboarding" stages, it can give your new colleagues insight into how you like to work and how you perform your best. Again, though, before sharing it, ask if it would be useful so it's not perceived as unsolicited homework— even if it's "just one page"—that places you at the center of everyone else's universe. Revealing so much about yourself can be challenging. But if you treat and describe your guide as an unvarnished look at your foibles and quirks as well as your capabilities—and if you give it only to those who want it—it can unlock progress not just for you but also for them, by painting a realistic picture of how to get the most out of you.

The good news? You've already done the heavy lifting required to create your sheet (a process that's easier than it might sound, as you can see in the following activity). The steps you've accomplished so far—to identify what brings you energy and what drains it, to tally up your professional assets and liabilities, and to unpack which energy drivers and assets you want to lean in to going forward—have generated lots of rich, granular data about which contexts allow you to be your best self and which ones are likely to put a damper on your performance and enthusiasm. That information has practical value for everyone you'll work with in your new role.

Activity: Create Your Personal Cheat Sheet

There's no set format for the personal cheat sheet. Alex did his on a virtual whiteboard because he preferred something more visual, but you can create a simple document if you'd prefer. Just do what feels authentic to you, and make it concise—no longer than one page or screen.

The simplest approach is to take the work you've already done in previous steps and flow it into one sheet. For example, you might:

- List the activities and circumstances that drive your energy;
- List the activities and circumstances that drain your energy;
- List your current assets;
- List the assets you're developing;
- Specify what colleagues can do to earn your trust and make you more productive. Are there values that you hold dear that others should know about when they work with you?

Appendix F offers an adapted template that we like to use with our mentees—although you don't have to follow it. Feel free to get creative as you do this exercise. We offer examples of personal cheat sheets from people we've coached at jobmoves.com/cheatsheet.

Supplementing Your Earlier Work

As you create your personal cheat sheet, you may find it useful to supplement the work you've done earlier to identify energy drivers and drains and to take stock of your professional assets. You might consider, for instance:

> the conditions in which you like to work and how those might shift depending on what you're doing (e.g., quiet/loud environments, own/shared space, cool/hot spaces, virtual/in-person/hybrid)
> the times you do your best work (e.g., mornings or evenings)
> the ways you like to communicate (e.g., phone, text, email, collaboration apps)
> the ways you like to receive feedback (e.g., be blunt and straight with me, do it face-to-face, include specific examples, be timely, do it at the end of a project)
> the things you need to be productive (e.g., space to generate new ideas and be creative, time to reflect, authenticity to be open, consistency to support logical thinking, a spreadsheet for everything)
> the things with which you struggle (e.g., too little/much interaction for extroverts/introverts, too little/much critiquing and debate, trying to execute something without understanding the wider purpose, unnecessary process and red tape, standards that are unrealistically high, concerns about quality, being/not being on time)
> the things you love (e.g., rolling up your sleeves and diving in, generative and risk-taking team cultures that drive action against a stated purpose, organizing team-bonding events and offsites, trying something new, hearing what others are working on, being a mentor, discovering new talent)

> the unique "miscellaneous" things that people who know you well would say about you (e.g., your true north is based on intuition/logic, your favorite saying is "practice what you preach," you don't like/drink coffee, you bring your whole self to work, you are usually just thinking deeply when you look grumpy, it takes a while to get used to your sense of humor, fairness is really important to you, you will often call out the elephant in the room).

These prompts are meant only as inspiration, not as blanks that must be filled in. The goal is to sum up how you work and collaborate best. You are the best judge of what matters most. Make sure you unpack the examples and words that you do use so that a reader who isn't you will really understand what you mean. You learned in Chapter Four to unpack your energy drivers—to clarify what concepts like "impact" and "flexibility" mean to you. Do the same thing here.

Ultimately your personal cheat sheet is about the essentials. Limit yourself to one or two pages so people can reasonably digest and apply the insights. Write down 80 percent of what matters in 20 percent of the space you think you need. We've found that less really is more here. It forces prioritization. We've also found that it's important to think both about your "installation instructions" (how someone new should get to know you) and about your "operating instructions" (what people who already know you should remember about working with you). There's no need to separate these in your personal cheat sheet. There will be overlap. But giving some thought to both will help you create content that's more useful to more people.

As with other activities in the book, you can refine your cheat sheet by reviewing it with someone who knows you well and also revise it over time as you and others learn more. This can be a fun and collaborative exercise—perhaps over a glass of wine on a Friday evening with your life partner. It's even a great team builder to do with current colleagues in a job where you're happy.

You can also offer to help your colleagues create their own cheat sheets if they show interest. In fact, as people come to you for career advice more generally, you might find yourself sharing various ideas and exercises from this book, and we'd like to make it easier for you to do so. That's why our next (and final) two chapters are about how you—as a manager, a human resources officer, a career coach, or a sounding board for a friend or mentee—can use what you've learned here to help others make progress in *their* lives.

PART IV

HELPING OTHERS GET WHERE THEY WANT TO GO

By now, congratulations on a new job may be in order. At the very least, you've learned how to navigate your career journey and make your next move. After working through what energizes you and which assets you want to invest in, you've identified your current quest, prototyped a range of roles that excite you, explored the inherent trade-offs, and reconciled all that personal insight with the real job market. And you've learned the art of telling your story to hiring managers and others who can help you make progress in your life.

You're sitting on a lot of know-how—know-how that can benefit others.

In this section, we show you how to help those around you: first by working with your organization to align its talent development efforts with the kinds of progress employees want to make and then by supporting your family, friends, colleagues, direct reports, and mentees in their own quests for progress.

Alternatively, if you are a mentor, manager, or friend who just wants to know what to do to support those around you, these next two chapters cut to the chase. As we wrote in the introduction, feel free to start here and consult the earlier chapters as needed.

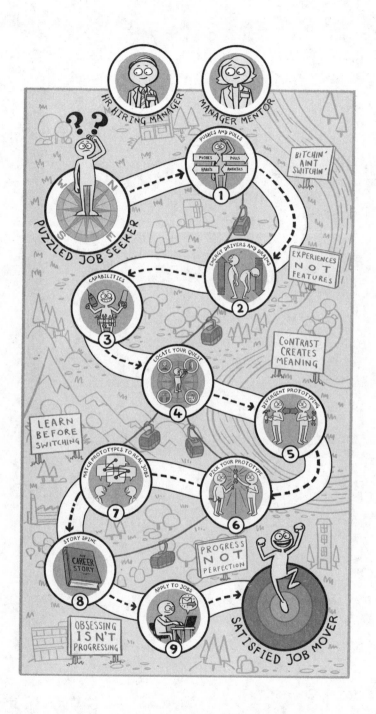

TWELVE

BUILD A TEAM YOUR EMPLOYEES
WANT TO REHIRE EACH DAY

This one's for the managers out there.

If you've found the process in this book personally useful, you can—like many job switchers we've coached—put it to work for the people on your team. "But wait," you might be thinking. "Aren't we trying to prevent the good employees from leaving? We're already having enough difficulty getting the good ones to stay!"

This paradoxical idea—retaining your top talent by setting them up to move on someday—makes many managers anxious, even when we assure them that everyone benefits. If you consider managers' and employees' priorities separately, it's true they can be hard to reconcile. But think about where they intersect. Just like individuals navigating their careers, teams and organizations are on their own quests for progress. They have missions to fulfill, customers and other constituencies to serve, books to balance, and results to deliver. To accomplish all this, they hire people. And the people who use our process tend to "hire" employers with quests that align with their own. By sharing that process with your team members and supporting them in their quests for progress, you're making it more likely that they'll rehire your team each and every day, as long as their quests and yours continue to be mutually reinforcing. That means you'll be supporting your organization, too—even though you're bound to experience some short-term pain when strong contributors venture off in a new direction.

Retention is a long game, and it matters a great deal. Although human capital doesn't show up on a company's official, audited balance sheet, talented workers are worth more than ever in the knowledge and service economy. As we noted in the introduction, even with the rise of automation and artificial intelligence, companies are still desperately looking for talent. A Harris Poll released in March 2023 found that 91 percent of hiring managers expected to face staffing challenges in the year ahead. Nearly half, 45 percent, said they had positions they couldn't fill—the highest percentage Harris had ever seen—and one-third worried about keeping good people.

Americans spend around 90,000 hours, the equivalent of 3,750 twenty-four-hour days (that's more than ten solid years, not accounting for sleep), at work over their lifetimes. In a competitive labor market, our analysis shows, most people won't consciously take a job where those hours won't serve their interests, purpose, and goals. So while managers search for the right people to tackle specific jobs in their organizations, they must also think hard about what jobs those workers need to have done in their lives—and how to establish mutual benefit so that what the employer needs to get done also helps employees in their own quests for progress.

Although we don't have all the answers, a few takeaways emerged from our research. After sharing our initial findings with dozens of chief human resources officers and other managers, we asked what they would do differently as a result of what they had learned, watched some of them make those changes in their organizations, and then observed the outcomes. As managers continue to report back to us, we look forward to gaining further insight into how employers become places that employees want to hire. So far, our findings fall into three buckets:

1. Use the pushes and pulls to create a workplace your employees rehire each day.
2. Collaborate with HR to support the progress people want to make.
3. Develop a "shadow" job description that speaks to the quests.

Let's look at each one.

Use the Pushes and Pulls to Create a Workplace Your Employees Rehire Each Day

At a conference session on putting purpose into work and learning, Marie Groark of the Schultz Family Foundation made a critical point about retention: Good employers and managers are constantly in the business of re-recruitment because they realize that employees always have the choice to stay or leave as they grow and evolve in their careers.

The job switcher's timeline reflects that insight (see Figure 12.1 for a refresher). As we explained in Chapter Two, although there are tipping points that provoke individuals to actively search for their next role and then to switch jobs, each quest for progress is an accumulation of forces—of *pushes* away from the present and *pulls* toward something new—that eventually move someone from thinking about change to making it happen. As the head of talent at a large financial services firm told us, the pushes and pulls we've shared with you in this book "explain why so many are passively looking right now . . . and thus on their way to silent quitting." She added, "The forces also describe what the leaders and managers need to do in order to reengage [them]." The code for understanding why people grow passive and disgruntled and then switch jobs is right here.

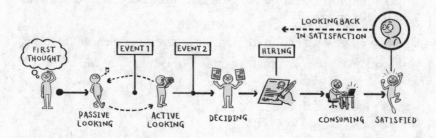

Figure 12.1
Revisiting the Job Switcher's Timeline

Go back to the lists of common forces in Chapter Two. Note again how few of the pushes—the factors that compel people to leave a job—are explicitly about money or benefits or climbing the corporate ladder. Those things often *correlate* with switches. And sometimes they coincide with two major obstacles to change—anxiety about an unknown future and entrenched habits of the present—just enough to delay a switch. But they aren't root causes for leaving or staying. As one chief human resources officer (CHRO) who heard us present our findings aptly termed it, they're "window dressing." That may be shocking to anyone who views career progress as a linear ascent within an organization. But that's a limitation of traditional supply-side thinking in the job market. Employers on that supply side may be good at dressing up the status quo to make the habit of the present temporarily more appealing, but the pushes and pulls on the demand side often win out over time. People seek progress in their lives—and their work is a key part of that. If you understand this as their manager and dig into the underlying forces that have led them to switch jobs in the past, you can manage them more effectively and make your organization a far more attractive workplace day-to-day.

What does that look like in practice? For starters, you can have candid conversations with your team members about the common forces that cause people to switch jobs. One software company in the United Kingdom, IDR Solutions, now incorporates the pushes and pulls into the organization's employee development and review processes. Employees are encouraged to talk openly about what motivates them and what might cause them to leave so that their personal goals can be better reflected in their job goals. As the CEO, Mark Stephens, told us, this approach sets workers up to have less emotional and more productive conversations about what's blocking their progress and enables managers to "pre-empt people leaving for the wrong reasons because we failed to diagnose an issue early."

Joe Carver, who heads up leadership development at the Puget Sound Naval Shipyard, has taken a similar tack. He uses our online assessment at jobmoves.com to help people identify what quest they were on when they left a previous job. Did they want to get out, regain control, regain alignment, or take the next step? (See descriptions in Chapter One if you haven't already worked through our process yourself.) He likes this tool because it labels the experience, not the person. When personality tests sort people into categories, he told us, they lead people "to act a certain way because I'm a 'certain type.'" They can also be gamed more easily than a dynamic assessment that's based on past experiences. He added that an assessment that produces different results for different job switches shows individuals that their career journeys are dynamic as well. After his direct reports have taken the assessment, Carver then follows up with one-on-one conversations to understand why they left a past job. If they left for negative reasons, he works with them so that the same thing won't happen on his watch. He engages in deep listening to envision what those past pushes looked like in that employee's context. Carver told us that, in his experience, it's most helpful to talk about people's hardest or least favorite job switch. The reason for this may stem from a useful design-thinking principle: it's easier to see deeper insights at the extremes.

Carver doesn't stop there. To show he understands the past pushes, he acts on the information. For instance, he might sit down with an employee to brainstorm ways of giving them more agency in how they do their work—and then incorporate those ideas when creating future assignments, development goals, and performance targets. He also examines the pulls that enticed individuals to join his team so he can deliver—and keep delivering—on what brought them there. In his regular check-ins, he continually asks questions like, "What should I be doing or be aware of to help you be more successful or give you more challenges here? Or help you stay engaged?" As with the pushes, Carver gives team members opportunities to shine in ways that align with the pulls to their current role and allows them space to learn and grow into their definition of progress. And when he sees that team members have fulfilled their pulls and that he can't offer them ways to continue growing within their current role, he finds that it's far better to have an upfront conversation about what's next for them than to delay their inevitable departure. That way employees don't stall in their quests for progress, and his team doesn't stagnate from their loss of energy and productivity.

Carver does one other interesting thing. He sees value in going through the findings in our book as a whole team. He says it's a morale booster—perhaps because it shows that their leader thinks the insights will benefit everyone and because it gives them a shared vocabulary and set of tools, so they aren't waiting for him to provide guidance. It's not just about him helping them with their pushes and pulls—it's about them helping themselves, too. By using a many-to-many rather than a one-to-many approach, he gets more leverage. This method also makes it clear that he's not using the process to quietly put a few "problem people" on a kiss-of-death performance plan. Rather, he's holding up the pushes and pulls as principles that will help the whole team—and its individual members—make progress.

Collaborate with HR to Support the Progress People Want to Make

When we present our findings to CHROs, they often say, in so many words, "We already KNOW much of this! We just wish that the managers in our company understood these things as well." They also note that our process involves a lot of reflection and wonder how they could get managers and employees to devote sufficient time and effort to it.

Although we agree that most managers could be doing more, it shouldn't all rest on *your* shoulders. You need support, too. Ideally, you'll partner with HR in the following five areas to systematize much of the process we've laid out. With this kind of collaboration in place, as employees make progress in their own quests, they can also become stronger assets to the organization.

1. Identifying employees' quests

In most organizations, people expect talent to follow strategy. The company creates a strategic plan, and investments in human capital follow suit. Some organizations call this "cascading" their talent strategy from their enterprise strategy. The problem, however, is that careers move too fast for that maxim to apply across the board. Traditional strategic plans typically span five years, whereas the average person changes jobs more frequently. So talent acquisition and development processes must be relatively fluid. The employee life cycle is relentless. Both HR and managers must continually support the onboarding of new hires while also facilitating the ongoing development of current employees and the transitions of still other employees out of old roles. To streamline these efforts, you and HR can work together to help people identify what quests they were pursuing when they signed on the dotted line—whether they've changed jobs within the company or just joined. That makes it easier for HR to put together a talent plan that can accommodate individuals' evolving pushes and pulls while still satisfying the organization's strategic need for a more stable flow of talent. The progress sought by the individual and the organization needs to remain intentionally interdependent, in other words.

Unfortunately, when employers fill jobs, they tend to focus almost exclusively on the functional elements of the candidate's career journey—for instance, the skills that person has acquired along the way, how they can deliver on the organization's key performance indicators (KPIs) to contribute to the bottom line or mission, what their job title will be, and how much money they will be paid. These things are important. But to create a workplace where employees will come in each day ready to do their best, you also need to recognize the social and emotional reasons they hired the role and the employer.

Because the four quests we've gleaned from our research take into account the functional, emotional, and social dimensions of a career move, helping people identify their current quest *is* an act of compassion and empathy. It also gives you, the manager, a clearer sense of what's driving them and what "fit" means to them. By making the quest explicit to all parties and aligning around it, you can better customize and curate individuals' internal sponsors and champions, career guidance, skill development, and other supports. And HR can expand its tool kit for gauging where each employee belongs in the organization—not just at entry but on an ongoing basis.

In organizations that are doing this well, quest identification starts during the "preboarding" period before the new hire's start date. HR can have people take the assessment at jobmoves.com, add the results to their individual files, and incorporate discussion of their pushes and pulls into the protocols for reviews. These are great activities to assign to an HR business partner—the HR professionals working directly with managers—as it will help them establish productive relationships with employees early on. Employees who are switching jobs within the organization can be asked to take the assessment again as part of their transition. This will make it easier for managers to have candid conversations about what their employees want to do in their next role, which is one of the most important, but also difficult, conversations to have. Indeed, doing this can also allow HR to reshape part of an employee's role rather than moving them to an entirely new one, which would give an organization and its individuals added agility. For too long, leadership development has been defined not by employee pushes and pulls but by the availability of predefined roles. Using our assessment can help create the data to correct that. Finally, if HR pairs people across the organization in mentor-mentee relationships, this information can be used to better inform the mentors. That way their connections and conversations will be more useful and grounded in each employee's context.

2. Helping employees craft their stories

Several HR executives told us that one of the biggest challenges employees face is telling their career story well. This makes it challenging for employees to make a compelling ask of their current or prospective employer as they hunt for jobs or look to develop themselves. As a result, both HR professionals and managers spend significant time coaching individuals on how to craft a narrative and boil it down into an elevator pitch. In the end, it's unclear whether the pitches are authentic to the employees—or just employees playing a hiring or promotion game by saying what they think HR and the manager want to hear.

You can simplify matters by teaching the story-spine technique outlined in Chapter Ten. As a manager, you can do this in one-on-one or group meetings with your team members. But you can also ask HR about including this material in training for new hires. Having a "development elevator pitch" at the ready won't just help people communicate what they want when they're asking for new opportunities. It will also give you a deeper sense of how they can contribute and what trade-offs they would be willing to make to gain or keep what matters most to them.

To amplify the effect of this work, some organizations pair it with a strengths-based assessment (as mentioned in Chapter Five, we like StrengthsFinder, but ask your HR folks what they recommend). Organizations often fixate on finding individuals who lack significant weaknesses, rather than looking for people with outstanding strengths and then building teams around them to accentuate the strengths and offset the weaknesses. With input from a strengths diagnostic, managers and employees can have more focused conversations about what everyone on the team brings to the table. Then you can have people update their elevator pitches to reflect their strengths. They'll be better equipped to make progress in their own quests. And you'll have a clearer line of sight into meaningful contributions they could make to the organization, which will allow you to ensure that others on the team can complement their unique combination of strengths, weaknesses, and desired progress.

3. Making personal cheat sheets an organizational tool

When we introduced the personal cheat sheet in Chapter Eleven, we cautioned job seekers against sharing it with others in ways that might look self-involved or entitled. With support from HR, managers can remove that potential stigma by having *everybody* on their team create one and share it. That way everyone will know what makes each member tick. The places we've seen these tools work best are in organizations where leaders use them consistently within and even across teams—and revisit them to keep them updated.

Several years ago, Ethan worked with an organization that had its one hundred most senior leaders—starting with the CEO—all craft, share, and workshop their personal cheat sheets to accelerate individual and organizational transformation. One of the HR leads told us a month later that this activity was "a great start" for these leaders' journeys, as it generated "deep conversation about how to develop their people to achieve their transformation."

4. Designing roles for real people

This next recommendation for working with HR flows from the previous three. Remember how (in Chapter Ten) Alex's manager carved out a new role for him so that he wouldn't have to leave the company? That manager created a job in Alex's image to meet a need inside the organization in a way that matched his assets, energizers, and life priorities.

All too often, organizations cobble together roles based on established assumptions about what they "should entail." Or a manager and HR put together whatever roles they need to combine to convince a compensation expert in the finance department that the role can be "graded" at the title and pay level they want. But when you understand employees' quests, you can make roles more malleable to better utilize people you value rather than try to force square pegs into round holes. There are a couple of straightforward ways to do this: You can examine the tasks inside a set of jobs, identify where they can be broken cleanly, and mix and match tasks with employees to build new roles that play to people's strengths and desires. Or you can start with the quests, narratives, and cheat sheets of your superstars and reverse engineer those into roles you want to fill.

Zappos, the online shoe and clothing retailer, provides a more extreme example of flexible role design. When then-CEO Tony Hsieh announced Zappos's move to Holacracy in 2013, the media were captivated by the idea of no managers. But when people looked past the hype, the real innovation—and opportunity—lay in how roles were designed and allocated. The average Zappos employee went from having one role before the transformation to having 7.4 roles afterward. In truth, more thinly sliced roles initially complicated things. It became harder to keep track of who did what, to reallocate roles when needs changed, and to pay people fairly. Employees had to create new systems—an online role tracker, an internal labor marketplace, skills badges pegged to compensation guidelines—to solve these problems. But as our research shows, a key benefit was that Zapponians could craft their own jobs within the scope of the organization's overall strategic needs. And in interviews with them, we found that they did so based on what we now call—in this book—their particular quests for progress.

Chances are your employer won't fully embrace a role-selection system like Holacracy. Few companies do. But the more finely you can slice roles and tasks, the more opportunity you'll have to design jobs that find the sweet spot between organizational needs and individual progress. What your organization considers a side gig in terms of an employee's overall role can be a main gig for that employee—and that's okay. Of the 7.4 average roles that a Zapponian held, the one that the employee thought was most fulfilling and the one that Zappos thought was most essential did not need to align, as long as they all got done.

When we shared this observation with highly experienced HR professionals, a few came back and asked politely, if critically: "Isn't this just repackaged 'work on good job design'?" Is it indeed a new bottle for old scholarly wine dating back to the 1960s and 1970s? In fairness, there is some truth to that. But technology has made it far easier today than it was back then to support individual job enrichment. We have social enterprise tools now. We have virtual learning tools. We have more robust ways of measuring employee engagement, productivity, learning, and even happiness. We also have AI undermining traditional career paths and therefore requiring everyone to get more creative about progression. As future-of-work scholars predict the continued disaggregation of career paths into gigs, agile operating systems, and other channels for talent to flow smoothly from one kind of work to another, managers and their organizations will gain more tools to engage and develop people, whether you call it job enrichment, job crafting, or, simply, helping employees make progress.

5. Prioritizing long-term over short-term development

The moment an employee lands in a new role, their current quest continues as they do the actual job and experience satisfaction (or not). But they also begin building toward their next quest (see Figure 12.2).

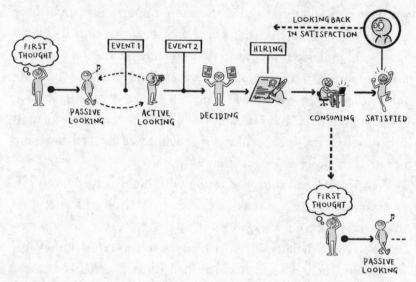

Figure 12.2
As the Job Switcher's First Timeline Ends, the Next Soon Begins

A career journey isn't simply a series of short-term quests. It's a longer arc in which quests overlap and interact in ways we can't know in advance. To effectively support your employees in their development, talk openly with them about their long-term trajectory rather than just their next step—even if it means they'll ultimately make progress by leaving your organization or your team.

As employee tenure has become shorter over the past several decades, companies have moved away from investing in long-term talent development out of fear that people will take their new skills and insights elsewhere. We certainly understand that fear, particularly in a tight labor market. Yet adopting a short-term view is even riskier. It makes it harder to identify opportunities to keep people engaged, motivated, and productive beyond the very next step in their careers. Also, as one chief learning officer put it when he spoke with us, "What happens if you *don't* train your employees and they stay?"

Taking a longer view of development boosts employee satisfaction—and that's good for business. Glassdoor research found that a one-point improvement (out of five points) in employee satisfaction garnered a 1.3-point uptick on the customer side. Restaurateur Danny Meyer, who owns establishments ranging from New York City's Gramercy Tavern to the Shake Shack chain, has found the same thing: Treating employees well leads to happier customers. HCL Technologies' former CEO Vineet Nayar is another prominent leader who embraced an employees-first, customers-second strategy. So what we are saying here, at least in its basic form, isn't news. And it can be a cliché—especially if you're only head nodding at it by giving people the occasional free lunch and extra time off over the holidays. But if you treat employees well by investing in their current and future progress, then you're doing something special. Many managers and HR leaders are telling us that's easier to do now that they have a shared language around the four quests and the pushes and pulls that move people toward making progress. And because it is easier, they are not just doing it once. They are periodically and systematically keeping it up to date. Like a great editor, employees, managers, and HR should wield a red pen as they revisit the nine steps in this book to keep the learnings and outputs up to date.

That brings us back to a critical point we made at the beginning of this book. Career progress isn't the same as progression within an organization. The two *sometimes* line up. Witness the work of the America Opportunity Index (AOI) to measure how well US public companies do when it comes to worker economic mobility. AOI cites examples like Demetrus Hayes, a vice president at AT&T who started his career there in 1994 as a sales associate: "AT&T offered a pathway for Hayes to advance without a college education, and when he expressed interest in pursuing a degree in business administration . . . the company paid for his studies."

But lifers are rare these days. In most cases, career progress spans multiple employers. And employers should support that journey—no matter where it leads. Even if a valued employee's current quest is Get Out, who is to say at this point that they won't eventually want to "get back in" (what HR calls a boomerang)? Or that their departure won't create new opportunities for the organization? Consider how professional service firms benefit as their alumni join other companies and then later find reason to hire the old firm to support their new employer. Wherever people are going when they head for the exit, take the time to meaningfully understand why they are leaving—not just with a standard exit interview or exit survey but with the quest assessment mentioned above. What quest are they on now? And where might that lead them down the road?

How can HR help you promote your team's long-term development *before* people leave? It's well known that employees often don't avail themselves of the various professional development and other continuing education opportunities that employers offer. For example, although many US companies offer tuition benefits for enrolling in higher education, less than 3 percent of employees enroll nationwide. Our data suggest that if HR worked with managers like you to align learning opportunities to individuals' quests, there would be more uptake. What's more, anticipating the inevitable day when your top performers will leave, HR could help you prepare a boomerang strategy so that the organization could be ready to hire them for their *next* next job.

Consider this story from a CHRO we know. One of his direct reports liked working in talent, but she wanted to try new things within that space. She thought the best way to broaden her scope would be to move into a role like his, but the CHRO wasn't retiring anytime soon. Her family also wanted to live somewhere new. (By now, you can probably sense the pushes and pulls and maybe even predict where this is going.) Another company took advantage of the situation and offered her a job as head of HR in a location that suited her family. Her boss offered advice as she weighed the offer, supported her when she accepted it, and even mentored her when she left. Just fifteen months later, after she had satisfied her need to try new things and had also discovered how much she missed her old organization and the people who worked there, she boomeranged back with HR's support, and her former—and now current—boss agreed to let her stay in the new location and work from there.

In this way, job move "failures" can become success stories for employers and employees alike. It's much more common than you might think.

Develop a "Shadow" Job Description That Speaks to the Quests

The application process has become so standardized that most employers don't question it. There's the top of the funnel. Sometimes several thousand résumés pour in after a job description is posted, and software helps sort people out. From there, candidates enter the middle of the funnel, where HR and hiring managers review résumés to determine which people get assessments and interviews. Then *those* candidates enter the bottom of the funnel, where they are assessed and interviewed before someone receives a job offer. It's a fairly universal set of steps, but it needs a serious rethink—especially if you're trying to create a workplace that prospective employees want to "hire" in their quests for progress.

Perhaps the most fundamental problem to solve is the job description, which kicks off the whole process. It's usually a hodgepodge of skills, qualifications, and platitudes about work style and culture cribbed from past job descriptions, competitors' postings, and requirements for pay and title grading at the desired level of the role. The whole thing is so vague as to be meaningless—and the role is impossible to fill as described. Think of the myriad entry-level postings that call for "two years of experience," for example. Or all the job descriptions that require college degrees when current employees in the same roles lack them. If you peruse enough job postings, you sometimes get the feeling that employers are seeking unicorns. It's no wonder that prospective employees feel they need to puff up their résumés to make themselves look like superheroes. And yet people on both sides of the process—employers and candidates—know that these posts don't reflect reality. They're playing a game of unicorns and superheroes, and it does nothing to ensure a good match.

The origin of the job description dates back more than a century, with its roots in scientific management theory—a body of work attributed to Frederick Taylor. Observing the factories that dominated the industrial economy, Taylor set out to measure the precise time it took to do different jobs and tasks. From there, it was relatively simple to spell out the work that would be done and its requirements. Employers then published these descriptions in newspapers to find workers. Early job descriptions were short, because newspapers were paid by the line.

When job boards went online and charged one flat fee regardless of length, brevity became less important. Descriptions swelled. As Maury Hanigan, the CEO of SparcStart, a job marketing platform, notes, "The unlimited-length job posting could have been an opportunity to provide detailed and useful information about jobs; but generating original content is difficult and time consuming." Companies' legal departments got involved in writing and approving the descriptions, to the detriment of recruitment. As Hanigan points out: "[Job descriptions] are the basis against which an employee is evaluated, and potentially fired. They were never intended to be marketing documents and work poorly in that capacity. It is comparable to real estate agents selling a house by posting the mortgage documents." The purpose of the modern job description, then, is to give legal and HR departments more flexibility and protection, not to bring in employees who will thrive.

Given the litigious nature of decisions around employment in our society, this is unlikely to change anytime soon. That means hiring managers must work around these vague, bloated descriptions to make good matches between people and roles. One way of doing that is to focus on *experiences not features*, as we advise job seekers (and house hunters) to do in Chapter Three. When sharing descriptions with people in and beyond your network, instead of just posting links on social media, provide the practical context that's missing. You can do the same in your phone conversations and interviews with candidates.

Ideally, the job descriptions themselves would spell out what the employee would do day-to-day. But even postings that make some gesture in that direction usually don't offer a realistic picture. Consider this one (disguised from the original that appeared on LinkedIn):

Serve as a key member of leadership team. Play critical role in developing, accelerating, and communicating agenda for executing vision. Be responsible for coordinating and advancing company-wide priorities and projects. Duties include leading staff units in C-level office, developing and implementing key initiatives; managing special projects and crisis situations; collaborating with senior officers to advance priorities; involvement in comprehensive communications planning and stakeholder engagement; leading and partnering with key staff, faculty, and leaders on special projects, operational decisions, policy development, and communications planning.

The description goes on for another few (vague) sentences and then moves on to requirements:

Bachelor's degree; at least ten years of experience in publications or communications; excellent writing, editing, and project management skills; an appreciation for the distinctive culture and values of the organization; ability to strategize creatively and collaboratively; ability to make complex information comprehensible and compelling for a wide range of readers and to write effectively in many styles depending on audience, content, and platform. Proficiency with Microsoft Office, Drupal, social media platforms, and Adobe Creative Suite; initiative; and judgment and discretion when dealing with complex, confidential, and sensitive information.

This is roughly half of the listed requirements. You get the idea—and if you've ever posted a job, you probably already knew. Although there are plenty of skills and credentials, there's no sense of what the daily and weekly specifics of the job will really be like. And without more context, the requirements lack meaning. For example, the definition of "excellent writing" can vary quite a bit depending on the type of writing—marketing? technical? academic?—and the intended audience.

By focusing on what someone will do—much as you would in contract agreements for gig workers—rather than what they'll be or what they'll need to have, you can help job seekers gauge whether the role is compatible with their current quest: the activities that bring them energy, the assets they want to invest in, and the trade-offs they're willing to make in their lives. With that level of specificity, you'll also encourage prospective employees to represent themselves more accurately in their résumés and interviews—to better describe their energizers, their assets, their relevant past experiences, and the outcomes of that work. Both sides will get a clearer sense of fit.

Working around the listicles in job descriptions can have another surprising benefit: diversifying your candidate pool. As we noted, postings sometimes attract thousands of applicants. Organizations like having those big numbers at the top of the funnel. Many believe it will increase transparency and bolster diversity. Yet despite those intentions, most jobs are still filled by personal connections. So the influx of online applications creates false hope—and an unnecessarily cumbersome process. It also places a heavy burden on the software to identify the most promising hires. That rough cut of candidates doesn't reflect *true* fit, so managers lean into their network connections for applicants, which can undermine diversity, especially if the network ties are strong. You can mitigate those effects by describing what people will actually do in the role. Allowing applicants to self-select with greater accuracy shrinks the pool of generically plausible candidates midfunnel and should give you much more to go on than who knows whom.

Making Progress Is a Team Endeavor

As managers gave us feedback on our findings and advice, they confirmed something we suspected from the beginning: Our process works best when it involves both self-reflection and collective insight. As we said earlier, it ought to be a social endeavor. By embedding the exercises into your organization's recruitment and development efforts—that is, by making them more social—you and your HR team can create room for both types of reflection. If this thinking is all left to the individual, it's still valuable. But the insights won't be as rich. And the employer won't benefit nearly as much from them. In your calls for job applicants, in one-on-one conversations with prospective and current employees, in periodic team meetings, and in ongoing development discussions with individuals, you can meet people where they are in their career journey—without sacrificing your own goals as a manager. If that results in a culture where people are more articulate and more vocal about their paths to progress, then they will talk more, collaborate more, and do more together. These behaviors don't happen organically. Most find talking to others at work about their individual development a daunting, overly vulnerable, and unpleasant task. Yes, this involves work, but it pays off in better matches between people and roles, happier employees working in concert with their quest and purpose, and stronger performance long-term.

At this point, you may be saying to yourself, "Wait, they want me to spend even more time on this at work? I am already overloaded, and this new generation of workers seems to have an insatiable and impatient need for constant feedback, advancement, and growth. It's unrealistic." In one session with the top five hundred leaders of a leading global financial services institution, one senior executive expressed her exasperation by exclaiming that she was tired of a generation who expected to be "massaged like Wagyu beef" in order to be retained.

Here's the counter. Although this may seem like a lot of work, the old adage of working smarter, not harder, applies here. Too many retention and development efforts by managers end up being forgotten because the structure required to create collective, lasting traction is absent. Touchpoints may be individually valuable, but they do not add up to a meaningful career trajectory without a structure that managers and employees use consistently. Our recommendations in this chapter are less about increased investment than about increased structure, so that the investment bears meaningful and lasting fruit.

Progress—for organizations as well as individuals—is what we're after. Progress that takes into account people's lives, not just within a single company or role but across their entire careers. Progress that influences both how an organization motivates a person and how it makes use of what they have to offer—and includes health and wellness, personal and professional relationships, individual interests, and other needs and desires. Progress that is appropriately paced, so it satisfies both the lockstep of an organization's strategic needs and the impatience of the employee's desires. That kind of progress—best understood by assessing individuals' struggles, circumstances, and goals so people can enthusiastically rehire their current job day after day and better hire their next job down the line, as well as the one after that—makes for quests worth pursuing together.

THIRTEEN

PAY IT FORWARD

One of the biggest mistakes people make in their quests for progress is not engaging others in the "messy middle" of their self-development efforts and job transitions. Many of us hide our shortcomings, our anxieties, and even our aspirations from colleagues and friends.

Yet when we make job switching social—by apprising others of our goals, soliciting their ideas about how to achieve them, and asking for their feedback as we try to put those ideas into action—progress comes within reach far more quickly and reliably. Without tapping their networks and relying on the advice of colleagues, friends, mentors, and managers, people risk working in a vacuum with limited information and insight.

Most of this book has equipped you to engage socially as the person being mentored and advised. But eventually, someone is going to ask you to be *their* interviewer, *their* coach. That's your chance to pay it forward. If you find this thought daunting, we understand. We know firsthand what it's like to be asked for career guidance—and to worry that you might lead someone astray in a series of major life decisions. It's a lot of responsibility. This chapter is about making you feel just as prepared to help someone else hire their next job as you now are to hire your own.

Finding Your Way as a Career Mentor

A CEO we know doesn't even like to use the word "mentoring" because the implied level of obligation scares people off. He talks instead about "sparking relationships."

No matter what you call it, investing in someone else's professional growth is a commitment. In our work, we've found that the energy required to effectively mentor a job switcher hinges on several variables. These include the mentee's drive and motivation, the distance between where they are in life and where they want to be, the gap in experience between the mentee and mentor, and the relevance of the mentor's expertise and connection to the mentee. Even though serving as a mentor can be incredibly rewarding, it's a complicated equation. It's not something to undertake casually.

Still, there are simpler ways to support people in your work life and personal life. Whether you explicitly tell others about the steps in this book or just key in on certain places where you can offer them useful insights, you can help them make the progress they seek. This can happen through one-off conversations, occasional chats over a beverage or a meal, scheduled check-ins with direct reports, or more intimate discussions with friends or family.

You may have noticed in your own life that when you've consulted people for career advice, what they said wasn't all that helpful. Or perhaps those you lead, mentor, or befriend often ask you for such advice, and you struggle with what to say. Either way, you're not alone. As journalist Derek Thompson wrote: "With 160 million American workers across thousands of occupations in hundreds of industries, saying anything that is of use to all of them is practically impossible." He added, "My toes curl with embarrassment when successful people say anything along the lines of 'Just do these three things I did.' Autobiography is not advice. Given how poorly most people understand themselves, it's barely even autobiography."

So when you do get asked for career advice, how do you make it count? In our experience, it involves walking people through the right part of our process at the right time. If they are at the beginning of a job search and brainstorming possibilities for what they might do next, for example, you might suggest they identify the activities that drive and drain their energy and create a career balance sheet that reflects their current assets and liabilities (see Chapters Four and Five). Or if they are trying to understand why they keep getting stuck, you could conduct an interview that yields a deeper understanding of their overall career trajectory (as we described in Chapter Two). Making the process social increases the likelihood of progress.

In our years of advising people, we've never produced "the answer" to any career dilemma. We've just been in the room when the person seeking our help uncovered their right next move. If you're acting as a full-on mentor, you can offer support in all six of the following ways. If you're serving as a more casual adviser, you can skip to whichever ones make sense given the nature of your relationship and the needs of the moment. These recommendations loosely map to the steps in our job-switching process where it's easiest for an outsider to offer support.

1. Ask the first and most important question

Helping someone make progress doesn't just happen when that person is struggling in a role and looking to leave. It ideally starts much earlier. Good managers are already thinking about the next job for those on their team when they hire them. Great managers directly *ask* new hires what they envision doing next. It shows that they have each employee's best interests at heart and starts a conversation that can and should be ongoing.

We take this approach as coaches and mentors as well. In any conversation about past or present moves, we talk about the future, even if it's someone's first day in a role.

Why so soon? Because asking the question merely makes what's true explicit. All jobs are temporary, even the last one before retirement. Your mentee, friend, or employee won't be in any role forever. By acknowledging that, you open a bigger conversation about the pushes and pulls (see Chapter Two) that brought them where they are now, as well as their goals and priorities for moving forward. With that understanding in place, you can then ask: "How can I support you in those goals?" And if you're that person's manager, as we explained in the last chapter, you'll go further: "How can I make sure you have the experiences and knowledge you'll need to take your next step? How can we avoid the pushes that caused you to leave your last job?"

Taking that approach signals that your relationship will be a two-way street. You didn't hire this person solely to make progress as you or your organization define it. You also plan to invest in *their* quest for progress by addressing their social and emotional desires in addition to their raw functional needs, like money. Managers often avoid asking what employees want next out of fear of losing them sooner. As we shared in Chapter Twelve, we've found that doing so counterintuitively improves retention.

Most people won't have a precise answer to your question about what they want to do next. Even those with carefully drawn-up master life plans will find that most of those plans won't, to paraphrase former heavyweight boxer Mike Tyson, survive the first punch to the mouth. Your goal isn't to extract a definitive answer, though. It's to get people thinking more deeply and broadly about how to make progress in their career journeys. It's to create fertile soil for a fruitful first thought about switching jobs. As our own mentor, Clayton Christensen, often said, "Asking the right questions creates space in the brain for solutions to fall into." Without that question about the future, the space may not exist.

2. Conduct an interview

If you've asked a mentor or friend to interview you to understand what quest you were on when you last switched jobs (in Chapter Two), you know there's great value in having someone play that investigative role. Although people can interview themselves, we all have our blind spots and can easily miss telling details about our own journeys. Now it's your turn to supply a fresh set of eyes—and to guide the conversation toward deeper insight.

That doesn't mean you already possess that insight as an outside observer. On the contrary. When you conduct this interview, it's not your job to correct the person's career narrative, to offer your own ideas about why they've made certain moves, or to connect any other dots that they haven't explicitly connected. Instead, your job is to poke and prod to reveal whatever they aren't yet seeing on their own. Approach the conversation with humility and curiosity. Don't assume anything; ask questions about anything that's unclear. As you embark on the interview, remember that this is less about asking the perfect questions. It's more about listening with intent, searching for the forces that caused them to change jobs, and unpacking their answers so you have clarity.

At this stage, don't focus on what drove and drained energy in each job. That comes later. As a person who has finished the whole process already, your natural tendency will be the rush to the finish line, but like a good whodunit novel, you want to take your time to let the story unfold. For now, just look at the circumstances that caused them to think about leaving. After debriefing to identify which forces pushed them away from the old role and which ones pulled them toward a new role, you can encourage them to use our assessment tool at jobmoves.com to put a name to their quest for progress. And in a future conversation, you can revisit that same tool as they start to think about what current pushes or pulls might be causing them to think about switching jobs now.

We described this interview at a high level in Chapter Two, but the activity below provides a much deeper dive on the basic format we like to use. As you do this, we encourage you to resist the very natural temptation to make your progress theirs. You may now be the teacher, but that means you need to be even more patient.

Activity: Follow a Loose Script

Clear a two-hour block to conduct your interview and debrief afterward.

Set expectations for a casual, comfortable conversation. For instance, you might say:

There are no right or wrong answers.

If you can't remember something, don't feel comfortable talking about something, or want to change an answer, that's all okay.

Your interviewee should not prepare for the conversation. It's about their experiences. You're just there to help them understand those experiences.

In that spirit, you might say something like:

Let's pretend we're creating a documentary film about when you last switched jobs. We want all the details around when you first started thinking about switching, when you made the decision, and when you actually came on board. I'll begin by asking some pretty broad questions. Then there will be some places where I'll slow you down and ask for all kinds of little details. For example, when you talk about a certain realization you had or something that happened to you, I might say, "Who were you with? What time of day was it? Where were you?" Things like that. Think of it as capturing a close-up shot in our film so we can get the specifics and the mood just right. Does that sound good? It might feel overdrawn at points, but we'll have fun.

The goal here is to put the other person at ease. You don't need to use our exact language. Say what feels natural.

If you happen to be this person's manager or hold some other position of authority, provide assurance that nothing will be judged or evaluated and everything will be kept confidential. You might add:

This conversation is for your use only. If there is something you are nervous about sharing, it's completely up to you, of course. But I encourage you to share it because you can't yet know which details may lead to new insights.

In your first set of questions, ask for context about the other person's latest job move. Start by having them describe what job they had before, what their life was like then, and just a bit about what their job and life are like now. If they don't know where to begin, prompt them to set the scene:

What background information should I know to understand the basics? Just tell me whatever feels relevant, like how long you had been in your prior job, and when you switched, and where you were living at the time.

Although we want detail, we're not trying to get an exhaustive biography or playing the role of armchair psychologist to diagnose their job switch. The objective is to understand the events and reactions that surrounded the change. You need just enough information to put those things in context.

Let your interviewee talk uninterrupted for a bit. They'll probably want you to know certain things about their most recent switch—which may or may not be relevant to discovering what quest they were on. Let them get all those thoughts out of their head at the beginning of the conversation. Then you'll be freer to direct the interview to where you want it to go. Once you start to feel their energy slowing down, you can jump in to ask:

So tell me, how did all this come about? Do you remember the first time you thought that you might be ready to leave your prior job?

To be fair, the person you're interviewing might not remember or know at this stage. And if they do offer an immediate answer, it might not be accurate. To dig deeper, ask follow-up questions like:

What events led up to that moment when you and your boss had that shouting match?

You can also take your interviewee back to when they started the old job and have them play things forward:

What was your day-to-day like the first year or two?

As they work through the sequence of events, they may suddenly land on a key moment when they realized they wanted something new.

To jog their memory throughout the conversation, refer to other people in their story by name. If the person you're interviewing mentions a difficult conversation with their spouse, for example, use the spouse's name in your follow-up questions. Names trigger emotions, which can transport the person back to the moment they're trying to describe.

You want to understand their perspective. To that end, it's fine to show that you can relate (as in, *Yeah, that's happened to me, too*), but don't do this so much that they shut down because they feel as though you already know their story.

Scrutinize the circumstances that caused them to think about leaving. They might say something like, "I was just so sick of missing my daughter's softball game yet again because of a fire drill at work and then having to explain to her and my husband why I missed it. That's when I realized something had to change." That's some real energy you can dig into. Don't assume you understand it. You really want to empathize by listening deeply here. Play back what they said—and then push them a bit more.

Help yourself (and the other person) more deeply understand root causes by offering points of contrast. For example, to follow up on those missed softball games, you might ask:

Was your reaction about feeling guilty and annoyed at yourself? Or was there other pressure coming at you from other family members?

This isn't leading the witness. By offering two contrasting options, you can gain deeper insight into what was going on. If your interviewee pushes back and says, "It's neither! It was this!," then that will also be instructive. After exploring a set of contrasts, you can ask for more details:

How often were you missing family time for work?
Were there other important things you were missing because of work as well?

When did it start, and how often did it occur?
When did it become a problem?

Some interviewers find it helpful to tell themselves they are trying to figure out a murder mystery to stimulate their curiosity and their desire to deeply inquire and listen.

Flag the places where you don't fully understand what happened. As you work through the job switcher's timeline of events (see Chapter Two, Figure 2.1) and record your notes (Appendix B shows what these can look like), ask questions to fill any holes in the story. What really moved your interviewee from passive looking to active looking? What did they consider at that stage? What conversations were they having? What moved them to deciding? What led them to rule out options?

We've found that when people use general language to describe things, the natural tendency is to assume that we all understand what is meant. Don't assume. Contrast can once again be a useful tool. For example, if someone tells you that they ruled out a certain job offer because the manager didn't seem nice, ask what "nice" means to them:

Are managers nice when they are generous with praise? Or when they give you honest feedback without belittling you?

Although both might be nice, by providing concrete examples, you can home in on what's meant so you don't misinterpret anything.

If the person you're interviewing just starts to agree with you and answer in shorter and shorter sentences, change your line of inquiry. When you're being yessed, you're not getting the full story. Revisit something that you don't fully understand and probe for clarification. Or connect the wrong dots purposely and let them correct you to get things back on course.

At the end of their story, replay what you heard. Spell out the whole timeline and give your interviewee space to correct what you missed. And then take a short break before you debrief (see Chapter Two) to sort out which pushes and pulls led them to switch.

---

3. Assess energy drivers and drains

When people don't have a next step in mind—or their sense of what they could do next is all over the map—we've found that having them document their energy drivers and drains in their past jobs sharpens their focus. In Chapter Four, we asked you to imagine rotating your résumé 90 degrees to create a timetable that summarizes your career path to this point. Instead of just listing all the things you did in each job and the skills gained, you also identified the activities that brought you energy and those that depleted it. Walking someone through this activity takes only a few minutes and can add a lot of value. It reveals underlying sources of joy and pain at work.

To add even more value, offer to help flag five to ten recurring energy drivers and drains over the person's career. An outsider can make connections that may be hard for someone to see in the details of their own narrative. Again, this won't take much time—and it will set up your mentee, friend, or colleague for the rest of our process if they choose to follow it.

4. Probe and audit the balance sheet

Another useful exercise that can stand alone—if you want to pick and choose—is tallying up professional assets and liabilities in a balance sheet (described in Chapter Five) to capture what the individual is capable of offering an employer. There are two roles you can play here.

First, after having someone list their assets (that is, their skills, experience, education, and so on), ask them to elaborate: How long will it take each asset to lose its value without further investment? Which assets are they content to let depreciate? Which do they want to continue to develop? What future investments would be required to maintain or develop those assets? And do they really want to bank on those?

If you're this person's manager, the answers to these questions will help you as well. They'll give you insight into which assignments and tasks are most and least likely to engage your direct report. This doesn't mean that everything you ask them to do should further the development of their desired assets. You and your organization need to make progress, too. But you can include certain activities that meet your employee's needs. You can also work the desired assets into a development plan, which will create a valuable feedback loop. If your direct report seems disinterested in an opportunity or experience that you thought would help them develop a particular asset, you can start a conversation with them. Ask why the assignment isn't accomplishing what they want—or whether a particular asset they thought they wanted to develop isn't, after all, something they'd like to invest in building.

The second role you can play is in auditing the balance sheet: Do the assets and liabilities match what you've observed from the outside? Have they over- or underestimated their capabilities? Which assets would you suggest including? Do you agree with the estimates of the useful life of each asset, given where the world is headed? You might even try to do this as a small-group exercise, with other mentors, colleagues, or friends offering their views, for example, on depreciation schedules for various assets. Getting a variety of perspectives can help people shape their own thoughts about which capabilities matter most right now in their careers.

5. Help people make real-world connections

One of the most generous—and impactful—ways to support potential job switchers is by extending your network to them. For example, if someone is prototyping roles that intrigue them to get a realistic sense of what to expect (see Chapter Seven), you can introduce them to others who have held those or similar jobs. That might seem like a tiny contribution, but it takes a lot of pressure off those you're supporting. Asking for an informational interview is always easier with a quick intro from a mutual friend.

In our experience, people struggle to reach out on their own. They don't know how to write succinctly about why they want to connect. To make it easier on them—as well as yourself—you can point them to Appendix D (and jobmoves.com/prototypeinterviews) for template letters that can be revised to fit their circumstances.

In Chapter Nine, we suggested that job switchers should continue to network, even after making a good move, by conducting an informational interview every couple of months. On the flip side, so that others can learn from you, be willing to *be* interviewed a few times a year as well. And if you're managing others, make yourself available to your direct reports for these sorts of conversations so that they can more fully see how what you do lines up with the progress they do or don't want to make in their lives.

Given that people we don't know well often hold keys to new opportunities, you're doing others a great service by inviting them to forge more "weak" ties through your network—and by being accessible to those who are weakly tied to you. Such connections allow individuals to gain access to information, resources, and other supports they wouldn't otherwise have within reach. As we mentioned in Chapter Nine, people are often more willing to share what is really on their minds with connections they barely know.

That distance lowers the stakes and, we've found, can deepen the conversation.

6. Reality check the narrative and cheat sheet

The people you support can also benefit from your perspective when testing and refining their career narratives—work we describe in Chapter Ten. Give them feedback about what's confusing, what gels and what doesn't, and what's missing, given what you know about them. Allow them to practice telling their story to you, as if you're a hiring manager or recruiter. Although many career guides extol the benefits of doing mock interviews, people gain much more from the exercise when they learn how to seamlessly weave their narrative into answers to a variety of questions. That takes some experimenting and extra rehearsal time.

As you work with people to polish their story for the job market, also push them to be clear in their own minds about the trade-offs they're willing to make to get what they want. Now that they've done more research and thinking, would they *really* be happy with those trade-offs they've identified? Or would they be settling for something suboptimal—or even giving up a core requirement? Revisiting that question as they're preparing to apply for jobs can save them grief after they switch.

Finally, invite them to create and then share a personal cheat sheet—the "how to work with me" document we describe in Chapter Eleven. Doing so will prod them to think about what makes them more or less effective on the job and what values or settings are most important to them. If you're their manager, this will also help you bring out the best in them.

Use the personal cheat sheet to spark a conversation. If you know the person well, you're likely to have strong reactions that range from "Yup, that's definitely you" to "Do you really think *that's* what you bring to the table?" Asking questions where you see discrepancies between the person and the sheet invites them to engage in further reflection and refinement—whether you have this conversation with them before or after they switch jobs.

Going this deep also signals that you're serious about their personal and career development and success. It shows that you care about the answer to the central question we urged you to ask at the beginning of this chapter: "What do you want to do next after this job?" *That's* paying it forward.

Conclusion
WHERE ARE THEY—AND YOU—NOW?

Six months after we'd begun working with her, Clara looked up at her computer screen and smiled at us. She had completed much of the work we have presented in this book (see Figure 14.1). It hadn't been easy. But it had helped her move much more confidently through the job-switching process.

That process was anything but linear for her. Few job changes are. Clara had identified and explored a wide range of potential futures—from working as a physician's assistant in an emergency room to writing articles for science magazines to teaching people how to climb rocks. As she learned what these and other jobs actually entailed and how they lined up with her desire to regain alignment in her career, she realized she would have to make certain trade-offs. Working internationally, for example, wasn't going to happen. That had meant having a few serious conversations with her Europe-born boyfriend. That slowed down her job search until they decided that as long as there was flexibility for travel to Europe, they could make it work.

Shortly after reaching this conclusion, Clara heard from a former colleague about a job opportunity in the Pacific Northwest. It was a research associate position at a neuroscience research institute. Although the lab setting would be familiar to her—she had worked at a neuroscience lab in Ireland, after all—the work itself would be quite different. Rather than managing people and dealing with the politics among the scientists—both activities that drained her

Figure 14.1
Nine Steps to Making Progress in Your Career

energy—she would get to work on the research itself and learn new things she hadn't been exposed to at the previous lab. The role would also give her lots of flexibility to "work from anywhere," which meant time to pursue travel and outside hobbies like rock climbing. True, being a research associate didn't match the science-writer prototype on which she had converged. But with clear eyes about what she wanted in her next role, she was able to hold the position up against that prototype and say with conviction—before switching jobs—that this was an opportunity that could help her make progress.

As she talked through her career story with the people at the research institute, she sold them on how she could contribute and how the role fit in with the progress she sought. They extended an offer soon thereafter, which she accepted. She then jumped on that video call with us to share the happy news.

We were of course thrilled that Clara was making the switch—and that she went on to thrive in her role. But it's been even more gratifying to give her a process that she can repeat again and again to continue making progress and learn before switching. You now have that same set of ideas and tools at your disposal.

When we checked back in with Alex a couple of years after his job move, he was still happy building his company's capabilities in agile- and tech-powered innovation. But he said something that caught us off guard. He had returned recently from a competitive cross-country ski race in Norway. Cross-country skiing hadn't been on his list of things that gave him energy, nor had it ever come up in our many other conversations—so we were surprised. Had we led him astray in some way?

On the contrary, he told us. In his past jobs, he had come home completely drained and exhausted, having expended all his energy at work. He had none left to do anything else. But in his new role, he came home with more in the tank. It wasn't that his job was easy or that there weren't trade-offs. But because he had moved to a role that brought him energy, it created room in his life for new interests. The skiing was a happy incidental by-product of his job switch. He also shared that he had joined the board of directors for a local symphony orchestra, another surprise move that had further enriched his life and made the decision to remain in Wisconsin that much more satisfying.

Alex's main takeaway wasn't about work-life balance, though. He just wanted to make sure that he continued to do work that synced with the things that gave him fulfillment, happiness, and purpose.

If you've ever felt stuck in your career like Clara or forced into a move like Alex, you're in good company. A cottage industry has bloomed around surmounting such challenges. Much of the advice boils down to building resilience. To do that, many suggest developing and following a clear vision for what you want to do in your life—that is, having a sense of purpose with concrete goals and living in congruence with those. But that's not easy to do without a road map.

In this century, responsibility for leadership development has primarily shifted to the individual—and away from the employer. There are lots of reasons for that, including rising employee turnover rates. Now that people switch jobs more frequently, organizations have less time and incentive to invest in them. Although a certain amount of autonomy comes from owning one's development path, people have largely been left without the tools they need to do it well. It's a bit like being thrown into the middle of the ocean with no navigational aids and being told that it is a privilege to have the freedom to swim in any direction you choose.

Think of our job-switching process as a set of way-finding tools for forging your path forward. You can use it to avoid common traps, break out of ruts, continue to grow, and live your life in step with what progress looks like for you at any given moment. It's a process built upon the experiences of thousands of job switchers worldwide—people who have worked every imaginable job, people at all career stages and income levels, people with all kinds of educational backgrounds, family situations, and other life circumstances. And it's a process that has given many folks real traction in their careers and lives.

Now it's your turn to find *your* way. You're not any of the thousand-plus people we talked to and worked with in order to reach our conclusions. Each and every human being is unique. So is each job and each search for something new. But we've found that this process for making better job moves consistently empowers people. By working out what quest you're on, what drives your energy, which assets you want to develop, what trade-offs you are willing to make, and what story you want to tell about your career—and by checking your insights with others whose perspectives you value—you can understand what progress means for you, right now, in your life. And then you can achieve that progress in the next job you hire—and in every job move after that.

ACKNOWLEDGMENTS

This book and the three of us are all connected and indebted to Clayton Christensen.

As we described in the introduction, Bob first connected with Clayton in the mid-1990s. Together they developed the Jobs to Be Done theory, which helps explain why people buy the products and services they do. As a doctoral candidate at Harvard Business School, Ethan studied under Clayton and collaborated with him on various academic projects. Around the same time, Michael coauthored a book with Clayton on education, *Disrupting Class*; cofounded the Clayton Christensen Institute, a nonprofit think tank; and, over time, began working more on the question of how to help adults learn and upskill at work. Eventually, the three of us began to work together—on other books and articles, business courses, consulting engagements, and new ideas and models—to help organizations and customers jointly make the progress they sought.

As we wrote, Ethan made the first jump to connect the underlying Jobs to Be Done theory with helping individuals make progress in their careers. As a professor who gets asked for career advice all the time—frankly, all three of us do—Ethan wondered, Was he making the same classic error that often confounds product developers? Was his career advice noisy correlation—platitudes based on observable categories—rather than customized, targeted guidance? What would happen if he interviewed advisees the way Bob interviewed consumers—to explore why people "hire" new roles and employers and better understand *those* Jobs to Be Done? The result was his popular Developing Yourself as a Leader course. What's notable is that the course isn't just popular on the front end. More than 85 percent of those who have completed the course say they have found excellent value in learning to hire their next job, with roughly half doing so by seeking jobs outside their organization and the other half shaping their career trajectories on the inside. When Michael started using the book that he coauthored with Bob, *Choosing College*, to help guide his own career choices—not just those of others—we all realized we were onto something.

As we honed the course and dove into the analytics, we suffered a personal loss: Clayton Christensen, our mentor and collaborator, passed away just before COVID wreaked havoc on the world. Honoring who he was—his decency, his kindness and caring, his example of helping others make progress in their lives—was our impetus for turning our work in the classroom and in conversations into a book that could help many more people who are agonizing over their next career move. This book is truly because of and dedicated to him.

On the heels of our loss, Bob dove into more rounds of research to understand what *causes* people to switch jobs. We could not have done this work without Katherine Thompson by his side. Katherine not only conducted the dozens of interviews and coded the thousands of data points that helped us flesh out the dataset behind this book but she also helped design, iterate, and codify the process behind helping individuals switch jobs. She patiently coached cohorts of individuals looking to switch jobs through minicourses—and even more patiently helped translate Bob's insights and the stories of the individuals to the written word for Michael and Ethan.

Unlike academic journals, there is no peer-review process to approve the methods when you write a book like this. But like Clayton, Ethan is a stickler for research methods. As a result, this book is not based on anecdotes and personal experiences. From data collection to data analysis, we have used the same rigorous academic methods, quantitative and qualitative, that Ethan uses when he publishes his articles in academic journals. We couldn't have done that without Cara Mazzucco, Ethan's research assistant, by our side. Cara has been fastidious in helping us track down half-baked leads; synthesize research and insights from all the job switchers we've studied, taught, coached, and observed over the years; figure out how to turn high-level ideas into usable digital tools; and more. As part of our core writing team, we've been fortunate to have her. With the book finished, she is now looking for her next job, and we hope this book will prove useful to her in this search and those in the future.

We understand from other authors that when a book is published, it usually is yet to be read by more than a handful of people. Ours is different. This material has already been seen, in one form or another, by the thousands of people we have advised. It's with their generous input—and with their needs top of mind—that we've written our book. The ideas have been helpful to them. We—and they—hope these ideas will be helpful to you, too.

There are a great many people to thank as a result. Our publishers, Hollis Heimbouch and Kirby Sandmeyer, for believing in the idea behind this book and coaching us throughout the process. Our literary agent, Margo Fleming, who proved one of our best editors and toughest critics, never afraid to support us to the hilt or tell us directly when we were off base. Lisa Burrell, who provided skillful editing at several points in the development of the manuscript and helped us to understand what we were trying to say when we were struggling ourselves at times. Those who read drafts and provided feedback and insight at critical junctures (from reading every word to provoking us to think differently without even knowing it): Allie Feldberg, Amy Edmondson, Amy Jones Vaterlaus, Anjali Bhatt, Ariel Droesch, Boris

Groysberg, Bruce Dudley, Cary Friedman, Christina Wing, Clarke Murphy, Covell Brown, David Brunner, David Vieira, Edwina Melville-Gray, Emily Truelove, Erika Byun, Evan Terwilliger, Frank Barrett, Gale King, Helen Ramisch, Henning Piezunka, Immanuel Hermreck, Jack Gabarro, James Riley, Jeff Polzer, Jim Dowd, Jon Jachimowicz, Joseph Carver, Josh Budway, Joshua Margolis, Juan Batiz-Benet, Julie Battilana, Julie Boor, Karen Dillon, Katherine Roling, Kelly Smith, Kim Scott, L. T. Zhang, Lakshmi Ramarajan, Laura Huang, Laura Ruprecht, Leslie Perlow, Linda Hill, Lumumba Seegars, Lydia Marks, Marina Lee, Mary Fielder, Maya Hadziomerovic, Melissa Valentine, Michael Jordan Halbert, Mike Beer, Morgane Herculano, Nadia and David Rawlinson, Nigel Le Quesne, Nitin Nohria, Paul McKinnon, Peter Cappelli, Randall Stutman, Robin Ely, Rosabeth Moss Kanter, Rusty Zaspel, Ryan Raffaelli, Sam Unguren, Steven Moran, Summer Jackson, Teresa Amabile, Ting Zhang, Toby Bernstein, Tom DeLong, Tony Mayo, and Tsedal Neeley. We benefited tremendously from a global community of scholars who shared their thoughts with us, including faculty at the New Directions in Leadership Research Conference. We also thank Luke Newell for his ability to take our high-level concepts and turn them into the beautiful illustrations gracing these pages, and Renato Pavlekovic for building the complex Quest survey tool that accompanies this book.

In 2015, Bharat Anand tapped Ethan on the shoulder after a faculty meeting to ask if he would consider creating the first multisession virtual course in HBS's (then HBX's) virtual Live Online Classroom. If not for that moment, the Developing Yourself as a Leader (originally titled Managing Your Career and Managing Your Career Development) course, which has been essential to creating and refining the material in this book, would never have been created. We are grateful to Bharat for trusting a faculty member as junior as

Ethan with that responsibility and thereby giving us this opportunity, as well as many others on the HBS faculty—including Nitin Nohria, Jan Hammond, VG Narayanan, and Youngme Moon—without whom the Live Online Classroom would never have existed. Courses don't run or teach themselves, and as the creator and faculty chair of Developing Yourself as a Leader, Ethan knows just how many great moments would never have occurred (and how many near misses would have) had it not been for the incredible team of HBS faculty (Alison Wood Brooks, Anita Elberse, Ariel Stern, Francesca Gino, Jon Jacimowicz, Ryan Buell, and Ryan Raffaelli), coaching faculty (Allyn Gardner, Becca Carnahan, Bryn Pane'e Burkhart, Cici Barrett, Connie Walsh, Dana Keep, Diane Lapine, Eileen Stephan, Ildi Nielsen, Jackie Gosciak, Karen Baker, Katherine Rowley, Lee Hendrickson, Lew Weinstein, Nicola Pugliese, Patty Scanlon Levy, and Stephenie Girard), and leaders (Abby Rebello, Aileen Tschiderer, Alejandra Ruiz-Gordillo, Alex Most, Alexa Simon, Amelia Wright, Andrew Samel, Anthony Corsino, Ben Beckwith, Ben Didsbury, Blake Rivera, Bobby Sullivan, Brenna O'Connell, Brian Winnicki, Chad Jackson, Chris Judge, Cristina de la Cierva, Derek Keefe, Dustin Hilt, Eli Levy, Elizabeth Waterman, Emily Cronin, Grant Lacouture, Hannah Nestler, Jamie Thomas, Jan Abel, Jason Rosario, Jenna Brayton, Jennifer Reardon, Jerome Harris, Jonah Sobol, Jonathan Barrett-Parker, Joncarlos Villegas, Josh Lifton, Julia Henry, Jun Lee, Kate Milne, Kathy McSweeney, Katie Alex Stevens, Kevin Wilson, Laura Gendreau, Liz Flaig, Michaela Hummer, Mike Downing, Mike Soulios, Ned Barnes, Nick Mesenbourg, Nicole Alvarez, Patrick Mullane, Peter Shaffery, Ross Pearo, Scott Snape, Simeen Mohsen, Stephen Batts, Therese Cronin, Wendy Riseborough, Wyatt Cmar, and Yuri Dafonseca).

We'd also like to thank some of the folks who have "read" this book by living its process and seeing improvements in their careers and lives as a result. That includes everyone from the senior executives and leaders at offsites who have engaged with us to all the students in Ethan's Managing Human Capital and Developing Yourself as a Leader courses. We have also gotten meaningful feedback from many HBS alumni—at reunions, at an HBS Club of Toronto event, at an event for the HBS Human Capital Alumni Group, and across many interactions. We are lucky to have been along for the ride and indebted to all of them. And we now look forward to learning from you all as well, as you use the book to continue your own quest for progress.

A thank-you of course to our loved ones—the individuals who enable us to do the work we do.

From Ethan: I am immensely grateful for the loving support of my family, immediate and extended. My children, Covell and Clayton, and their mother, Maly, are my inspiration—I wrote this book in hopes that it would help them. My parents are not just my best readers and editors but also the people who taught me how important it is to make good job moves. The fact that they did so allowed me to grow up as I have. My faculty colleagues at HBS, especially in the OB unit, are my intellectual family—without exception, every idea in this book was sparked in some way by them. And finally, I am grateful that, at 6:30 a.m. on Thursday, February 15, 2007, I received one of the best unexpected wake-up calls of my life: Clayton Christensen called to offer me a spot in the doctoral program at Harvard Business School and, as a result, years later, I met the two greatest coauthors a first-time book writer could ask for.

From Michael: Thank you to my family—my wife, Tracy, and my children, Madison and Kayla, who continue to make all that I do possible. And who hopefully will benefit from the insights in this book as they navigate their own journeys. Also, a thank-you to my mom, who keeps me grounded, and my dad, who has inspired and taught me through his own job moves that you can do and be multiple things as your career winds through different areas of interest, passion, and value.

From Bob: Thank you to the fantastic team at the Rewired Group, including my partner, Greg Engle. And to my wife, Julie, and my kids, Marty, Mary, Henry, and Susie, for their love and teaching me through their own career journeys as we wrote this book. As grandchildren enter the picture and will one day navigate their own lives and careers, I hope the insights in this book prove to be a productive legacy for them that helps them continually make progress.

APPENDIX A
GLOSSARY OF PUSHES AND PULLS

This glossary offers detail on what each of the pushes and pulls encompasses through (1) the range of sentiments underlying each force and (2) real quotes that people said during interviews that capture elements of the force's meaning. The real quotes that we use could in some cases apply to multiple forces. We have categorized them here merely to illustrate the full breadth and depth of each force.

PUSHES

When I don't respect or trust the people I work with:

Sentiments underlying this force:	When my current work environment is "cutthroat" and/or encouraging borderline unethical behavior;
	When I feel like I'm running on a hamster wheel with bigger and bigger quotas each year;
	When I have to put on an inauthentic face in order to do my job;
	When I don't trust the people I work with;
	When people are yelling at me and it's not a civil work environment
Real quotes:	"I underestimated the importance of cultural fit. . . . I did due diligence on the people and culture within my function, but not in other functions and found them to be extremely political and self-interested."
	"My new boss was being unfaithful to his marriage with the CFO. So not only was the boss not supporting me, but I didn't want to work for someone who didn't share my strong family values."
	"I realized my new boss was sexist when he explained the male-dominated company by saying, 'I haven't found any females that are good enough yet.'"
	"I was spending way too much time with people I didn't like . . . I felt like I had to 'fake it' and tone down my extraverted personality."
	"When colleagues would leave for other firms, the senior members of the firm 'took them out to the square and shot them.'"
	"I worked in [college admissions], where we were paid to judge people. But this carried over into the culture. I realized I didn't need to put up with the constant judging and office politics."
	"There was gender-pay disparity, sexist comments, and a lack of willingness to share information."
	"I didn't enjoy or even understand the political dynamics, and so I felt I couldn't trust my colleagues."

When I feel that the work I'm doing has little or no impact on the company, world, or my life:

Sentiments underlying this force:	When I can't make important decisions myself;
	When it takes a long time to see the results of my work, or the fruits of my labor seem invisible;
	When I feel disconnected from the results/benefits of the work;
	When I am working long hours and they don't matter to me;
	When my work doesn't seem to get traction in my organization;
	When I'm good at the work but don't like it;
	When the work is primarily about numbers rather than people (or only about people without considering the data);
	When what I'm doing has little or no positive impact on the world, as I or my friends define the word "positive";
	When there's no tangible sense of long-term impact (adding jobs, growing the business)
Real quotes:	"I realized that having passion does not necessarily equate to having impact."
	"I felt stifled by the large company bureaucracy . . . and felt it diluted the impact I could have."
	"I felt removed from the day-to-day aspects of the company when in my global job. I didn't get to see visible daily impact."
	"It was hard trying to spread analytical management practices within a company founded and led by a celebrity."
	"One time I spent weeks deciding on a shade of blue for a soup packaging that was never going to move the needle. I wanted to create new food products aligned with industry trends, but the many layers of management above me were only interested in incremental change."
	"I couldn't see a straight line between my effort and the tangible impact on the company or world."
	"Once I reached steady-state and couldn't do the work I wanted to do and drive impact, I knew it was time for me to depart."
	"I had no levers to do that job well—no autonomy to move the needle."

When the way I'm managed day-to-day is wearing me down:

Sentiments underlying this force:	When I'm being micromanaged;
	When the rules at my job seem Big Brother–ish;
	When communication has to flow through many levels;
	When my compensation is restructured and I end up making less;
	When my quota is set by people who don't understand the market;
	When I'm managed by a stick, not a carrot;
	When I have an obnoxious boss;
	When my boss does or says something publicly that undermines the social contract we had about how I like to work
Real quotes:	"I had a congenial relationship with my manager, and we accomplished many things together. But I didn't have the sponsorship and support I needed to continue developing."
	"My boss had anger issues."
	"When I accepted my job, I negotiated fewer hours and limited travel, but then after my colleagues became envious, my manager made a negative comment about my flexible working hours in my performance review."
	"I reported to two different managers on two different teams at the same time. I felt like a floating island, since neither manager took full responsibility for my work and development."
	"My manager told me I was 'over-functioning' by providing too much strategic support to the president while working as an HR business partner. He said that the president was relying on me too much for business decisions."
	"My hiring manager was a micromanager. It came down to trust; I didn't feel like she trusted me. She even told me, 'Either we'll need to get you a new manager or you'll probably leave.'"

When my current company is struggling and the end feels near:

Sentiments underlying this force:	When morale is low in my workplace; When there is a lot of turnover in my workplace, or I feel like I might be left behind as others rush for the exit; When I'm afraid of where this is headed; When my current job feels unstable—I could lose my job if my project is defunded; When people are being laid off; When I don't know if I'll have a job tomorrow or not; When the business isn't doing well and other companies like ours are failing/being acquired/downsizing/etc.
Real quotes:	"[The company] was beginning to prepare for an IPO. I knew that the company would need stability for a longer duration than I was prepared to stay, and I didn't want to get trapped." "After I joined [the company], I quickly realized that the company was in legal and financial trouble, and that it wasn't a good company. I learned that it had been sued by the Federal Trade Commission, but recruiters hadn't informed me of this." "There were a series of restructurings that resulted in many colleagues either being laid off or leaving the company for better opportunities. I was in a field sales role at the time and had been considering going back to a corporate function, but these restructurings made me feel uncertain." "The company's stagnant growth made me question its long-term viability." "My company fired ninety percent of my division and did not provide coaching and support resources for those who remained. I could tell the company was struggling, and the restructuring process wore me down."

When I end up with a new manager and feel like I'm starting over:

Sentiments underlying this force:	When my boss/mentor leaves the company; When my work environment has been reset and the new leadership is starting over; When I was in the inner circle and now I'm not; When my mentor is fired and I feel like I don't have an ally inside; When I have a new manager who has a different working style than my previous manager
Real quotes:	"I felt like I was starting over again, and it didn't help that I didn't really like my new manager." "My former peer and friend got promoted above me, and I knew I couldn't expand my responsibilities with her micromanaging style." "I got layered by someone with less skill than me." "My manager left. She had been my lifeline in the company and the person who had my back, which was critical to navigating the political environment. I knew I was done." "I founded a company, but at the behest of an investor, a new CEO (my new manager) was put in place. He didn't listen to me, which drove the company down a path that did not align with the future I wanted or what I thought the company needed."

When I feel disrespected or not trusted:

Sentiments underlying this force:	When my manager takes credit for work that is mine;
	When I am not respected for paying my dues or earning a new credential;
	When I'm not respected;
	When the organization drops balls that are important to me;
	When my manager excludes me from more important meetings;
	When I've been passed over for a promotion without any justifiable reason besides tenure;
	When I'm not included in decision-making;
	When my manager and the people around me don't respect/recognize my contribution;
	When I'm doing a job way below my skills;
	When I am always negotiating to get my fair share, like having to fight for a large commission that is rightfully mine;
	When my manager treats me unfairly because of how I dress and my lifestyle;
	When I am passed over for a promotion at work twice
Real quotes:	"I wasn't given a promotion because it 'wasn't my time' and other candidates were 'older in the company.'"
	"The social contract I had with the company was getting out of balance. I wasn't getting the investment in my development in return for all my hard work."
	"I led a company that I founded, but since my identity didn't match that of the community I was serving, this mismatch did seed distrust among my team and contributed to me stepping down."
	"My managers were dismissive of my investment ideas. I felt unheard."

When I've reached a personal milestone in my life:

Sentiments underlying this force:	When I have only enough left at the end of the month for a few Starbucks coffees and now need to support more than that;
	When I want to make time for my education;
	When I realize I can't be a college student anymore and work three months at a time;
	When my aunt dies and I see the impact of our product;
	When I need a paid internship to pay my bills;
	When I need an internship to fulfill my college credits so I can graduate;
	When I am not willing to take an unpaid internship;
	When someone very close to me dies;
	When I'm done having kids;
	When my mom dies suddenly and I didn't get to say goodbye;
	When I feel like time is running out;
	When I finish my master's degree;
	When my mom no longer needs my help because her cancer is in remission;
	When I have to start paying my student loans;
	When I have a newborn who needs specialized medical attention;
	When I have been living here much longer than anticipated;
	When I've overextended my stay;
	When I'm thirty years old, and I've paid my dues

Real quotes:	"After both my parents died following my . . . graduation, I realized it was time to start doing something meaningful for myself and my family."
	"After I got married, I chose to relocate to San Francisco, where my husband's company was, despite being on the path to becoming the CEO of [the company]."
	"During COVID, my husband was overworked, and we couldn't travel, which is our shared passion. We weren't having fun. Two small kids, school being online . . . it was just not good. At some point you need to ask yourself . . . what is happening to my life?"
	"My spouse got a job offer in Hong Kong, so I left my promising career in marketing in the US and moved to a new country. I knew my career decisions weren't just about me anymore—they were about the portfolio of my family."
	"My wife got a job in San Francisco. So I moved to [a tech company] mostly because I wanted to stay married . . ."
	"My dad got sick so I wanted to move back to the United States."

When I've reached a milestone in my job or career:

Sentiments underlying this force:	When I keep hitting my goalposts for my project faster or more easily than I need to;
	When I feel like I have enough experience that I can apply for something else;
	When my service obligation is ending;
	When I feel like I've been there long enough;
	When I look at job postings and feel like I finally have the experience I need;
	When I've been able to coach in the big tournament;
	When I feel like if I don't make a switch now, it will be a long time before I can do it;
	When I see peers getting ahead of me
Real quotes:	"I timed my departure from [the company] to correspond with the middle of its five-year funding cycle, so my successor would have a runway to learn the ropes before needing to raise money."
	"After making partner at a young age, I left to get my MBA because knowing the amount of money I would be making if I stayed, I'd likely never go back to school."
	"When I attended meetings, I kept having familiar conversations and seeing familiar problems. My learning curve had flattened, and . . . what was next for my role was that I would've been a CMO for additional countries. . . . The role itself wasn't going to change that much."
	"I didn't want to be pigeonholed into the CFO path. I wanted to be a COO someday, so I left my finance role."
	"My boss proposed I transition to the CEO of Home and Community Care. It was a stretch role, but there were also components of the position that I knew I could add value to."
	"I realized that prolonging my career as a consultant would only delay my ambitions of P&L ownership at a budding tech company."

When my work is dominating my life and I sacrifice myself or my family to get things done:

Sentiments underlying this force:	When I can't control my own schedule;
	When my daily routines are inconsistent;
	When I haven't had any time for myself for the last seven years;
	When my current job requires me to travel/deploy frequently;
	When I am burned out on travel;
	When my life is not my own, and it is run by my job;
	When I can't earn vacation time;
	When I don't have a work-life balance and don't see my family enough;
	When my commute is several hours long;
	When my spouse struggles with my inability to help in a consistent or predictable way;
	When I'm having trouble fitting my priorities in;
	When I have no free time;
	When my current job requires me to move frequently;
	When I don't have time to do anything else but work;
	When my commute is long and complicated;
	When I don't have enough time/space to think about what's next because I'm so sucked in;
	When it's hard to manage a relationship because I'm working so much;
	When my job requires me to be "on" 24/7;
	When I have no say about where I am going to go next;
	When I realize I'm getting older and there's more outside of work I want to do (marriage, children, etc.);
	When I am getting older and realize the lifestyle of my work is not appealing (when I don't want to get drunk every night);
	When I feel like I've met my future wife and she's moved away

Real quotes:	"One month, I lost my car twice; that was the moment I realized that something was wrong and I was burned out." "As the CHRO, it was unsustainable for me to be the mother, doctor, and health professional of the firm." "As a consultant in the private equity group . . . I felt overworked and burned out." "I would wake up at 3 a.m. every day to film a show that aired at 3 p.m. My work schedule was grueling, and moving up in the organization only meant even more hours and even more stress. I felt overworked, isolated, and unsupported." "When I brought up work-life balance to my cofounders of six years, since I had a three-month-old baby at home, all they said was, 'You either work the same hours as us or you take less equity.'"

When a trusted adviser, mentor, or previous boss guides me toward my next step:

Sentiments underlying this force:	When a friend gives me a referral and a list of companies to explore; When someone I know recommends an opportunity to me; When I am supported by my spouse/partner; When a friend got a job doing it; When I have many resources like exit programs to help me figure it out; When someone close to me recommends a path that is blocked; When family members have also done the job

Real quotes:	"After talking to a trusted coworker, this sparked me to finally take initiative on something I'd been thinking about for a long time myself." "While at [grad school], a mentor encouraged me to pursue a job at [the firm]." "Two mentors helped me realize that an education NGO would enable me to learn fast and make decisions early in my career since they are usually very lean organizations." "My goal had always been to be a leader. Meeting with a coach led to an aha moment where I realized that I'd already been developing that skill set for over a decade and I was ready to become the leader I envisioned." "I had a lightbulb moment during a coaching session." "A co-VP said to me, like, 'You should really think about doing HR as a career. This really feels like your passion. You should be a CHRO.' I'm like, 'It's too late in my career to do that.' But I think that was a turning point for me. I think I mentally made this shift to say, 'What lights my fire? Like, what am I really passionate about at work? What feels fun to me?'" "I got a phone call from a friend who thought that I would work well with her boss. There wasn't even a job description for the role yet." "I was offered a job that I thought was beyond my ability, but my boss encouraged me to take it on."

When I am challenged beyond my ability, logic, or ethics:

Sentiments underlying this force:	When I am scared that I'm not doing the work correctly;
	When I am not good at my job;
	When I feel like I have no backup;
	When I don't think I can keep this pace up;
	When my sales quotas are getting higher and higher every year;
	When I am asked to do more than I can do . . . multiple times;
	When my responsibilities keep increasing but my compensation doesn't;
	When my manager is pressuring me more and more (and doesn't recognize other obligations);
	When I am held accountable to unreasonable standards;
	When my resources are constantly readjusted because of financial situation
Real quotes:	"One year into my tenure as CEO at [the company], I found myself feeling overwhelmed and overmatched, desperate to find a way out."
	"I was working on a private equity deal at [the company], and I recall a 2 a.m. conversation with my manager who was pushing me to solve for the answer the client wanted rather than what the data truly showed."
	"The HR department at my company was too focused on doubting employees and questioning why they might not be the right fit, rather than building them up and seeking growth potential."
	"I was responsible for orchestrating layoffs for 27,000 people. The work was challenging and new, so I wasn't bored, but I didn't find the restructuring process energizing."
	"I was mentored by the COO, and he told me that I need to become a tougher leader who introduces more productive tension within my teams. More of a jerk, effectively. This was despite the overall company culture, which celebrated collaboration, and was in direct opposition with my personal leadership style and beliefs."

When I don't feel challenged or am bored in my current work:

Sentiments underlying this force:	When I've repeatedly asked my manager for more work and haven't gotten it;
	When I feel like I am standing still compared to my peers outside the company;
	When I make a lot of money and I don't have to do a lot of work;
	When I'm not challenged because most of my work is outsourced;
	When I feel like I'm stuck in a rut doing the same thing over and over again;
	When I'm overqualified for my job;
	When I am bored and the challenges are few and far between;
	When I don't want to do the same thing I've done before;
	When my job is feeling monotonous and I'm stuck;
	When I'm performing better than everyone else in the office based on all the metrics;
	When I'm always looking to better myself and see if there is something else out there
Real quotes:	"I felt that the company was just throwing money at people-related problems, rather than actually trying to solve them."
	"My role was limited by my team's capacity, but I felt that I could do more."
	"The tasks I was doing weren't boring, but they required focus on very narrow problems that didn't sufficiently draw on all my experiences. I felt like I was wasting my uniquely acquired perspective."
	"I remember looking around at my arts management job, wondering, 'Is this it?'"
	"It felt like the movie *Office Space*. Everyone was just going through the motions."
	"I remember thinking in meetings, 'Oh my God, I've seen this problem five times; I know exactly where this is going to go.'"

When I can't see where to go or how to grow in my current organization (or it will take too long or be too hard):

Sentiments underlying this force:	When piecemealing my solution is not going to work;
	When I can see where my career path is headed, and I don't want to go there;
	When I feel trapped;
	When there's no opportunity for me to move up or grow;
	When I've maxed out my current position;
	When there are too many hurdles to make a career change internally;
	When the processes are very well established and very hard to change;
	When my promotion is more of a token as opposed to an opportunity for more responsibility;
	When I feel like it's going to take a long time to get promoted;
	When I know I'm going to leave after grad school;
	When I don't see a future at my current job;
	When I am not progressing like I had hoped and won't be able to make this a career;
	When my path to promotion is almost impossible for me to achieve

Real quotes:

"I never intended to be a career officer."

"The CEO wanted to exit sooner than I did."

"I couldn't imagine looking for a new job. I liked what I was doing and couldn't imagine anything better. However, I still started feeling like I could see the end of my path if I stayed."

"I wasn't ready to sell the company I founded, but I felt pressure from my investors to do so."

"Working in a male-dominated industry, I didn't feel like I fit in, I lost interest in my job, and I couldn't see myself growing with the organization."

"I realized that I would never be the decision maker I wanted to be at [the firm]. I didn't want to be on the sidelines, but I couldn't find a path forward that checked all my boxes."

"I'd contributed what I could to the company and didn't want to invest more energy there . . . something inside me clicked where I realized that I was a lot more capable than I gave myself credit for, and I needed to chart a path for professional growth."

"I had been coming to a realization that even though I still enjoyed a lot of what I did, I was having this, like, very clichéd moment of where you look up and you suddenly realize that you're not that excited about what's next. And that's a really important conversation to have with yourself: how excited are you about your boss's job or your boss's boss's job?"

When I feel that I have been on my own, ignored, and unsupported at work for a long time:

Sentiments underlying this force:	When I work in an environment with no standard operating procedures;
	When my bosses and I don't have much control over how the system works;
	When I don't have the tools or resources to do my job;
	When I was never taught how to work in a client-facing position;
	When I am not getting meaningful feedback on my performance;
	When my employer provides little onboarding or training to do my job;
	When I'm struggling to get the skills I need to help me grow;
	When the boss is focused on another part of the business and not me;
	When the employer seems to be helping everyone else advance, but not me;
	When other prospective colleagues are not like me (racially or otherwise);
	When the area I live in is very tight knit and it is hard to make friends;
	When I feel helpless;
	When I'm not listened to;
	When I feel that I'm a cog in the machine;
	When the culture is resistant to any changes and I'm supposed to be making changes;
	When my employer doesn't acknowledge my success;
	When I have no manager or a new manager who provides no support but pressures to deliver results

Real quotes: | "My other partners decided our company should focus on bigger deals such as leveraged buyouts, instead of growth and venture stage companies, which is what I specialized in. My deals were not prioritized and my concerns about where the company was heading were mostly ignored."

"While a product manager at [the company], I shared several product ideas but was ignored."

"I felt useless. I cried weekly. I felt like I was on a hamster wheel with no support or sense of belonging or purpose."

"[They] acquired my company but clearly didn't actively choose to hire me. I then felt excluded from decisions related to the company that I founded and was inaccurately blamed for things I had no influence over."

"When [my company] acquired [another one], my team was doing similar work and was sidelined. All the work we were doing became sort of second-tier. I was working long hours putting strategy documents together that nobody read or acted on."

PULLS

So I can have more time to spend with others outside work:

Sentiments underlying this force:	So I can be there for/spend more time with my family;
	So I can have the free time/flexibility to spend with my future kids;
	So I can get back to a community where I can make friends;
	So I can have a better work-life balance;
	So my spouse can count on me;
	So I don't have to commute as much;
	So I don't have to travel overseas;
	So I can have more control over my own time;
	So I don't have to travel as much;
	So I can build a relationship with my significant other for the future;
	So we can have children eventually;
	So I can spend more time with loved ones
Real quotes:	"I wanted to have more time to dedicate to social causes and to spend with my family."
	"I realized that it's never worth trading off your friends for your career."
	"I felt glued to my phone at all hours at my consulting company. I wanted to be able to set my own schedule so I could go to the gym and see my fiancée more."

So my values and beliefs will align with the company and the people I work with:

Sentiments underlying this force:	So I can be myself;
	So I can do work I care about;
	So I can work at a job that aligns with my interests and/or values;
	So I can follow my passion to try to be a coach;
	So I can love my work again;
	So I can work at a company whose mission I can buy into;
	So I can be part of a team with similar values
Real quotes:	"Working as VP of Social Impact at [the media company] was my dream job. I viewed media as an important cultural influencer and wanted to help make a positive impact in the world."
	"I grew up loving baseball. I interned within sports during my undergraduate summers. I love that sports can galvanize people and change lives. So, I was drawn to [the company] being a sports organization."
	"I am a risk-loving person, and I've always sought out high-risk, high-reward situations."
	"When I first heard [the company's] mission to 'make life interplanetary,' I thought, 'Sign me up. I'll almost pay you to let me be a part of that.'"
	"I did some deep self-reflection and I realized . . . my calling is education. Education has always been my personal passion . . . That's my thing. I have to go find something closer to my thing."

So my job will fit into my existing personal life:

Sentiments underlying this force:	So I don't have to go back to my hometown because I don't think there's anything there for me; So we don't have to move
Real quotes:	"I was drawn to New York because my multidecade friend group was there, and they kept me grounded." "I pivoted to be [his] speechwriter when I moved home to Delaware after the death of my father." "I thought about moving to NYC to work in finance, but the desire to be on the West Coast near my family was stronger." "I was working at [the company] in Oregon, but my husband was based in Minnesota, so I left after one year to work at [another company]." "I didn't see a path forward [there] because I didn't want to relocate my family. But [this other company] allowed me to stay in Chicago." "I felt that New York was more welcoming for gay men compared to cities in certain countries in Europe."

So I can reset my life and start over:

Sentiments underlying this force:	So I can get the strain and stress off me; So I can reduce the stress and be in a better mental wellness space
Real quotes:	"After fourteen years at my job, I was burned out and needed change. I felt pulled to restoration and reflection. I wanted to focus on myself and not my career." "I wanted something new, even if that meant getting a job I was overqualified for." "After my parents unexpectedly passed and I later got quite ill, I felt very aware of the energy I wanted to give. It would have been disappointing to leave [the school] and go back to what I was doing." "I thought it would be a fun stop for two years until I figure out what I want to do."

So I can acquire the skills I need for a future job or career (stepping stone):

Sentiments underlying this force:	So I can get the experience now for the job I want in the future (two to three moves out);
	So I can get my foot in the door of the industry;
	So I can get the time and flexibility to invest in myself;
	So I can go to school;
	So I can be in the know about the workings of the business;
	So I can be better;
	So I can learn some new skills (content development, marketing, etc.);
	So I can get an education that is meaningful to me (not check the box);
	So I can learn a new business;
	So I can grow my knowledge base and experience;
	So I can learn from my classmates
Real quotes:	"I pursued the [company's] leadership program because I wanted to gain general management skills for my entrepreneurial pursuit."
	"I wanted to become a CFO because I hope to leverage my servant leadership, finance expertise, and earnings to grow the foundation I started when my child died at three months old."
	"Something inside me clicked where I realized I was a lot more capable than I gave myself credit for, and here was the path for professional growth."
	"Entrepreneurship had always been in the back of my mind. It's something that I was very excited to do at some point in my life. . . . So having that motivation in the back of my mind was . . . like how do I get myself set up for that?"
	"I wanted to cement the finance skills I learned at [grad school] so I became a financial analyst at [the company]."
	"I wanted to move into product management, but with the bad economy and without previous experience in product management, I thought a strategy role at the company would be a perfect stepping stone."

So I can be acknowledged, respected, and trusted to do great work:

Sentiments underlying this force:	So I have the respect of my employer;
	So I don't feel like someone is looking over my shoulder and second-guessing me;
	So I have a management team that supports me with carrots, not sticks;
	So I can be respected and recognized for the work I do;
	So I am not disrespected
Real quotes:	"It seemed like marketing was going to be valued."
	"Life is too short not to be appreciated."
	"I rejoined the company I worked at before my MBA because I had an established reputation there and thought this would enable me to get ahead fast."

So I can find an employer who values my experience and credentials:

Sentiments underlying this force:	So I can use my degree and know-how;
	So I can use the skills I've been training for over the last six years;
	So people will appreciate me for my skills and my abilities;
	So I can make as much money, if not more;
	So I can make at least the same or more money;
	So I can see the opportunity for advancement;
	So I can be paid what I'm worth
Real quotes:	"I saw the [new] job as an opportunity to apply twenty years of experience to the role."
	"I had become too senior and too used to the lifestyle not to be picky in my next role."
	"The role at the [philanthropic] foundation seemed to bring together all the things I've done: strategy, DEI, and education."
	"I had never gotten a bad performance review and likely would have succeeded long term, but I didn't feel like a star. I wanted to be in a role that uniquely utilized my skill sets and enabled me to shine."
	"I was being hired for my skills. Leadership was willing to say, 'I don't know [what this role will look like], but I trust you to go and figure it out.'"
	"I admitted to the hiring manager at a big ski resort that I wasn't a 'ski bro,' but she said she wanted greater diversity of thinking to fuel the next stage of growth and valued my consumer goods expertise, which was a new addition to the team."

So I will feel that my job is a step forward for me and in the view of others:

Sentiments underlying this force:	So I feel like this is a step up; So I can take a step forward, not a step back; So I can catch up to my peers
Real quotes:	"I moved from [my old company] to [the new] because this was a clear step up in terms of P&L accountabilities, exposure to senior management, and global responsibilities." "I'd been involved at an arm's length in my family's company since I was a teenager, but I never had the confidence to join. I took on a variety of finance roles at other companies, and then finally took the leap to work at my family's company to prove to myself and my family that I could do it." "I got a call that I was short-listed for two of the top [military] positions. It was flattering when you're asked by [name] to do something. It was an indicator that they thought I could be [a high-ranking officer] one day." "Deep down, I wanted to operate and build, not purely invest. I couldn't stop thinking about my start-up idea, and I wanted to fulfill what I believe is my true purpose." "I was drawn by the opportunity to sit at the CEO table and be a strategic thought partner." "Looking at what was happening in the market on the West Coast, the tech scene was heating up . . . [All these tech companies were] taking off . . . so for me and my classmates at a consulting company, we definitely had this FOMO and thought, 'If we're going to be working in Silicon Valley, we need to be in the start-up world.'" "I felt ready to become a CEO after spending my whole career trying to grow as a leader."

So I will have the freedom and flexibility to do my best work:

Sentiments underlying this force:	So I can be creative in my work; So I can have variety in my work (teaching two subjects, coaching different sports); So I can do my job the best way I know how to do it (work from home, be able to watch TV, etc.); So I can create my own class; So I can work from home (at least sometimes); So I have time to do my work and not spend so much time in meaningless meetings; So I have flexibility around how and where I work; So I can have control over how I am compensated
Real quotes:	"I continually sought additional autonomy and flexibility to make my own decisions and be my own boss. I wanted to own my own time and live and die by the outcomes." "I was allowed to name my own noneconomic terms of joining [the firm]. Getting complete operational control of my own fund within [the firm] while getting access to the benefits of its platform was highly compelling." "Joining [the company] in its formative stages meant a lack of bureaucracy. I was given autonomy and did not have to take direction and do everything in a box. I was able to run my team the same way and hold them accountable but give them autonomy." "I never felt like I had ownership in the eventual decisions being made or the execution . . . for me, it was really important to have that ownership and control over the outcome." "I had a lot of roles where I felt like I could do a good job by doing activities, demonstrating progress, and being execution oriented, but the strategy was not defined by me."

So I can be recognized for my work's impact on people and the business:

Sentiments underlying this force:	So I can connect what I do to the meaningful impact it has on people;
	So I feel like I have an impact;
	So I can "live a great story" vs. "live a comfortable story";
	So I can feel like my work has an impact;
	So I feel like I am doing meaningful work;
	So I can help people and see the results of my work;
	So I can become a manager and coach others;
	So I can have more impact by being a project manager and designing processes
Real quotes:	"Tom Brady is CEO. Bill Belichick is the management consultant. The owner in the box is the investor. I realized that I just wanted to be Tom Brady."
	"Becoming the COO of [the company] was an exciting opportunity to build plumbing in the company. I wanted to institute processes and principles, organizational structure, strategy, etc., to turn the company into a true business, in the way I thought best."
	"I love designing, and with the [company] I could select the furniture, help with the design and feel of the hotel, and I liked that. Maybe it was me fulfilling my [cultural] identity."
	"I've always been driven to contribute to something larger than myself. The opportunity to effect real-world change at [the biotech company] was irresistible."
	"I moved from corporate strategy to product management because I wanted to have a more direct impact on the experiences that people have. It is these experiences that have an impact on people's lives."

So I will have a supportive boss who guides me and provides me constructive feedback:

Sentiments underlying this force:	So I have a manager who pays attention and cares;
	So I can work with someone I know will trust me;
	So I can have a boss who is invested in my development;
	So I can work for somebody who has been through what I've been through;
	So I can be trusted to do my job and not micromanaged;
	So I can get real-time feedback
Real quotes:	"My previous boss asked me to help him exit his company and then start a private equity firm together with a focus on the cement industry. I knew that the learning I would get by partnering with him would be priceless."
	"My previous colleague at [my old company], who was now the CEO of [a major restaurant company], pulled me out of my comfort zone. His belief in marketing and in me made the transition to [the new company] make sense."
	"Many senior leaders at [the company] had long tenures there. The head of restaurant and head of sales both started as front-line workers over forty years ago and rose to the executive team. I wanted to be surrounded by experienced people who knew the business inside out."
	"Throughout the interview process, my new boss was transparent, supportive, and committed to my development."
	"[The consulting firm] was a beacon—it promised an environment where my ambitions would be nurtured and realized."

So I can be part of a tight-knit team or community that I can count on:

Sentiments underlying this force:	So I can work with a small team;
	So I can work with people I trust and who trust me;
	So I can work with people I know;
	So I can work with a small team;
	So I can be part of a small, cohesive team;
	So I can work in a smaller organization;
	So I can work on a team with people I like
Real quotes:	"I already knew many of the executives I would be working with at [the company], which was especially important because the job called for thought partners."
	"I found that a higher salary didn't make up for a lack of community and culture. I would rather be at [the new company]; even though my growth would be slower, I feel like I belong there."
	"At [the new company], the team really moved me. I felt with my people again."
	"I had a friend at [the company], which drew me to work there, too."
	"My friend was general counsel at [the company] when I was thinking about joining. It's good to have someone supportive at the senior level when moving to a new place."
	"I was drawn to the tight-knit community at the [company]."
	"I interviewed with other firms in the second year of my MBA, but found myself drawn back to where I worked pre-MBA because of the camaraderie built through the social aspect."

So I can be challenged, grow, and learn on the job:

Sentiments underlying this force:	So I can be part of a fast-paced environment;
	So I can be challenged but don't have to start from scratch;
	So I can do something that I know I can do as well as be challenged and learn something new;
	So I can be challenged and do high-level problem-solving;
	So I can be pushed to grow;
	So I can grow and learn;
	So I can have a broader area of responsibility and opportunity;
	So I don't let an opportunity pass me by
Real quotes:	"The chief of staff role would allow me to skip a level up to leadership and get a higher-level view of the company without having to work my way up the typical product manager ladders. I wanted to be in the room where decisions were made."
	"I would be the first marketing person at [the company], in a period of extreme growth, so I knew I would have to reinvent my role often, problem-solve, and learn new skills, all of which appealed to me."
	"I wanted an opportunity that put a pit in my stomach."
	"I love the feeling of 'I think I'm in over my head' but then learning through the process."
	"If I was going to put my jersey back on and go back to work [after a two-year break with my family in Italy], I wanted it to be a challenge. I was ready to be intellectually stimulated again."
	"I felt a pull to work for the Steve Jobs–like founder, who had taken the business from nothing to $4 billion in revenue. While he was a difficult, and even toxic, person, I knew he would challenge me and give me as much responsibility as I was ready for."

So I will be in a job that I know I can do and not feel at risk:

Sentiments underlying this force:	So I can continue to excel—I'm proud of my achievements and work ethic;
	So I don't have to worry about losing my job;
	So I don't have to keep changing jobs;
	So I don't have to search for a job during a global economic shutdown;
	So I don't have to look for another job again in a few months;
	So I can have security in what I'm doing—my job's not going to disappear;
	So I can get back to be involved in all aspects of the sales cycle;
	So I know I can contribute and be a big fish in a small pond;
	So I can stay at the same level and not take a demotion
Real quotes:	"I wanted to explore private equity, but with a baby on the way, I chose to stick with what I know best: investment banking."
	"I chose to work at [the company] in part because it's a big company, but not as public facing as a FAANG company, which I wasn't ready for."
	"I graduated during the 2008 financial crisis, so I was looking for stability, and I was an international student from Canada, so I needed a company that would sponsor me until I got permanent residency."
	"After I had kids, I moved from my own company to working at a large technology company that was less financially risky."
	"With two young kids at home, one company offered me a safer option to build internally while also working from home. I was fine being a middle manager and not trying to be more. I couldn't 'lean in' more than I already was."

So I can support my growing personal responsibilities:

Sentiments underlying this force:	So I can prove to my family and my significant other's family that we're worthy of being together;
	So I can make more money;
	So I can have an income to support a family

Real quotes:	"I was getting divorced and needed a job that enabled me to support my two young children financially."
	"I had been laid off a few months into my second pregnancy and needed a job that was flexible enough to balance my at-home responsibilities."
	"I got laid off but needed to find a new job quickly to provide for my family [so this job provided that]."
	"I needed to support both my kids and my spouse, so that he could pursue his start-up career dreams."

So I can have more time for me:

Sentiments underlying this force:	So I can create space to think more clearly about the future;
	So I can figure out what I want to do next;
	So I can have time to continue to be involved in an area apart from my next job that I remain passionate about;
	So I can get out of this toxic lifestyle;
	So I can have more free time;
	So I can get some time to pour into my education

Real quotes:	"I was worried that my business would become my life."
	"At the restructuring consulting firm I worked at, I was on a project for five years and was exhausted by the end of it. The project required 80-to-100-hour workweeks and a lot of travel, which took a toll on my mental health. I still enjoyed the work I was doing but wanted to take a sabbatical to give myself a break."
	"Work had been all-consuming at times, and it had really taken a toll on my health, [so this job promised a welcome break]."

NOTES FROM CLARA'S INTERVIEW

When we interviewed Clara, we learned that before she started working in Ireland, she had gone to college on the East Coast of the United States and majored in neuroscience. After college, she took her first job working in the health and wellness industry in communications. She soon realized she wanted to get more experience "doing" science rather than reading and communicating other people's results. This motivated her to take a job in Ireland working in a neuroscience lab. After two and a half years as a lab manager, she became a research assistant while earning a master's degree in neuroscience.

She initially loved her work in the lab. She was learning a lot—and even got to do incredible things like perform brain surgery on a mouse. She also loved creating systems and processes for the brand-new lab. As she earned her master's degree and spent more time with researchers who had PhDs, the first thoughts crept in that she might want to do something different. She was growing bored by the research side. The moments where she learned something new were fewer and farther between. She began looking at the PhDs with skepticism as she witnessed the detrimental effect that the constant need to chase funding and publish results had on both the science and the researchers. On top of that, she had started rock climbing and began resenting her long hours at work when they got in the way of her hobby.

This threw her into a phase of passive looking, where she began brainstorming other fields she could work in—and wondering what credentials she would need to get into them. She ruled out a PhD and began thinking about different kinds of health-care roles. But she also started realizing her limitations in that field without a health-care degree.

The event that triggered her to begin actively looking for a new job was when she moved back home in the middle of COVID. She had dozens of informational interviews. Once she realized that she could be a physical therapy assistant without an additional credential, she applied for several roles in physical therapy clinics in different settings—and soon had five job offers. She selected the one that would allow her to move to Colorado and continue rock climbing.

Here is a simplified set of notes we took during that conversation:

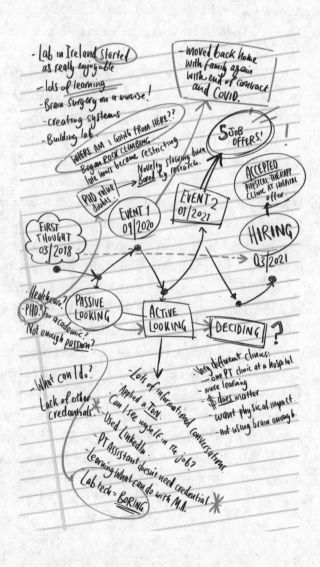

JOB PROTOTYPE TEMPLATE

Job Prototype: [Insert Job Title]	
What is it?	**What will I do?**
• X	• X
• Y	• Y
• Z	• Z
[Be as specific as you can about what the role would entail, whom you would work for and with (if anyone), what your daily environment might be like, etc.]	[List as many details as you can here, and be sure to refine following your informational interviews.]
How well will it align with my energy drivers?	
[Write thoughts relevant to each energy driver]	
How well will it align with my assets?	
[Write thoughts relevant to each asset]	

TEMPLATES FOR REQUESTING AN INTRODUCTION AND CONVERSATION

Template for Requesting an Introduction

Dear [Name of Mentor/Colleague/Friend],

I hope you're well.

As you know, I've been thinking through the next steps of my career journey. In doing so, I've identified several types of jobs I want to explore. One of those is [insert brief description of prototype of job].

As a next step, I'm hoping to speak with people who are currently doing a similar job so that I can learn whether my thinking lines up with their actual experiences. After these conversations, my plan is to refine my list of potential jobs.

Would you mind forwarding this note to [insert name of person you'd like to contact], as I believe you know them? It looks as though they are currently the [job title] of [insert organization], which I think is similar to what I'm interested in learning more about.

I'm not looking for an "in" at the company or anything like that. I'd just like to chat briefly—phone or video is fine—to learn more about what they do on a day-to-day and week-to-week basis. There won't be an ask beyond that.

Thanks so much.

Yours,

[Your name]

P.S. If [name of person you'd like to contact] would like more detail about the process I'm following for these conversations, they can find it here: jobmoves.com.

Template for Requesting a
Conversation/Informational Interview

Dear [Name of Loose Connection],

I hope you're well.

For the past [# of weeks/months], I've been working through a process focused on defining the next steps of my career. In doing so, I've identified some of the factors driving my job search at this point in my career, the sorts of activities that give me energy at work, and the capabilities in which I want to invest. These and other reflections helped me develop prototypes of several roles I want to explore. One of those is [insert brief description of prototype of job].

As a next step, I'm hoping to speak with people who do work that is similar to what I now think I want to do. If you're willing to chat briefly with me, I'd love to learn [insert either: "what you're seeing in this space" OR "how my thinking lines up with your actual experience"]. I'm also happy to share what I've learned in my journey so far that might be helpful to your interest in [insert mutual interest].

I know your time is valuable. That's why I've invested so much of my own in preparing for these conversations. My plan is to further refine my job search based on what I learn. To be clear, I'm not looking for an "in" at the company or anything like that. I'd just like to chat briefly—phone or video is fine.

Thanks so much.

Yours,

[Your name]

P.S. If you or [name of person you'd like to contact] would like more detail about the process I'm following for these conversations, you can find it here: jobmoves.com.

TEN COMMON INTERVIEW QUESTIONS

1. Tell me about yourself.

2. Why are you a good fit for this job?

3. What is your greatest strength?

4. What is your greatest weakness?

5. Why do you want to leave your current job? (Or, why did you leave your last job?)

6. What are your salary expectations?

7. What are your goals for the future?

8. What questions do you have for us?

9. Describe a difficult situation at work and how you handled it.

10. Tell me about a time when you had to do [something related to the job for which you're applying]. How did you approach it, what steps did you take, and what was the outcome?

PERSONAL CHEAT SHEET TEMPLATE

What drives my energy	What drains my energy
• This is the type of work that puts me in a state of flow (and makes me more productive):	• This is the type of work that takes me out of flow (and makes me less productive):
• What circumstances or conditions drive my energy?	• What circumstances or conditions drain my energy?

My current capabilities	Capabilities I'm working on

Some values I hold dear when I work are:

To build trust with me, colleagues can:

NOTES

Introduction: A New Approach to Your Career

ix switch jobs worldwide: This is the authors' estimate.

Roughly 3.4 billion people were employed worldwide in 2022. Einar H. Dyvik, "Number of Employees Worldwide 1991–2023," Statista, Nov. 1, 2023, https://www.statista.com/statistics/1258612/global-employment-figures/, accessed Jan. 23, 2024. Each year, roughly 30 percent of the US workforce changes jobs. Rakesh Kochhar, Kim Parker, and Ruth Igielnik, "Majority of U.S. Workers Changing Jobs Are Seeing Real Wage Gains," Pew Research Center, July 28, 2022, https://www.pewresearch.org/social-trends/2022/07/28/majority-of-u-s -workers-changing-jobs-are-seeing-real-wage-gains/.

Although many job markets are less dynamic than that of the United States, a percentage less than 30 percent would still yield close to 1 billion people. In Europe, for example, 18 percent changed employers in 2020, which means many more individuals actually changed jobs, as some of these individuals undoubtedly changed jobs but stayed with their current employer. Given that 2020 saw fewer job changes because of COVID further suggests that our rough calculation is reasonable. See also: Maria Gourtsilidou, "How Often Europeans Change Employer and for Which Reasons," CEO Advisory, June 1, 2021, https://ceoworld.biz/2021/06/01/how-often-europeans-change-employer -and-for-which-reasons/#:~:text=According%20to%20data%2C%2018%25 %20of,to%20achieve%20better%20career%20progression.

Also see: Katharina Buchholz, "Where People Stick with Their Jobs," Statista, Dec. 7, 2020, https://www.statista.com/chart/20571/average-time-spend-with -one-employer-in-selected-oecd-countries/.

ix rate in US history: Greg Iacurci, "2022 Was the 'Real Year of the Great Resignation,' Says Economist," CNBC.com, Feb. 1, 2023, https://www.cnbc .com/2023/02/01/why-2022-was-the-real-year-of-the-great-resignation.html #:~:text=About%2050.5%20million%20people%20quit,to%20leave%20 the%20workforce%20altogether.

ix they "quietly quit": "The majority [59%] of the world's employees are quiet quitting"—disengaging from work. "They don't know what to do or why it matters. They also don't have any supportive bonds with their coworkers, boss or their organization." "State of the Global Workforce 2023 Report: The Voice of the World's Employees," Gallup, p. 4.

To be clear, some have artfully pushed back on the notion that quiet quitting is the correct phrase to describe what many employees are doing when they scale back their work. See Jim Detert, "Let's Call Quiet Quitting What It Often Is: Calibrated Contributing," *MIT Sloan Management Review*, Jan. 9, 2023, https://sloanreview.mit.edu/article/lets-call-quiet-quitting-what-it-often-is -calibrated-contributing/. We will return to this notion of calibrated contributing, in spirit although not in terminology, when we introduce the pushes and pulls in Chapter Two.

x whirlpools of discontent: For more advice for those who are "career piloting" through challenge, uncertainty, and discomfort—rather than climbing a clear and comfortable ladder—see chap. 4 of Jay Conger and Allan Church, *The High Potential's Advantage: Get Noticed, Impress Your Bosses, and Become a Top Leader* (Boston: Harvard Business Review Press, 2017); see also Whitney Johnson, *Disrupt Yourself, With a New Introduction: Master Relentless Change and Speed Up Your Learning Curve* (Boston: Harvard Business Review Press, 2019) and Todd Rose, *Dark Horse: Achieving Success Through the Pursuit of Fulfillment* (San Francisco: HarperOne, 2018).

x seeking a new job: "Fifty-one percent of currently employed workers said they are watching for or actively seeking a new job," Gallup, p. 7.

xi jobs every year: Kochhar, Parker, and Igielnik, "Majority of U.S. Workers Changing Jobs Are Seeing Real Wage Gains."

xi every 4.1 years: "Employee Tenure Summary," U.S. Bureau of Labor Statistics, Sept. 22, 2022, https://www.bls.gov/news.release/tenure.nr0.htm.

xi where to work: Labor force participation has declined significantly in the United States compared to prior decades, which is making talent that much scarcer. Labor Force Participation Rate (CIVPART), FRED Economic Data, St. Louis Fed, https://fred.stlouisfed.org/series/CIVPART, accessed July 5, 2023.

xi 85 million people: Yannick Binvel, Michael Franzino, Jean-Marc Laouchez, and Werner Penk, "The Global Talent Crunch," Korn Ferry, 2018, https://www .kornferry.com/content/dam/kornferry/docs/pdfs/KF-Future-of-Work-Talent -Crunch-Report.pdf.

xi to unemployed individuals: The number of unemployed individuals doesn't include those who are out of the labor force and not actively searching for work.

xi per unemployed worker: "Number of Unemployed Persons per Job Opening, Seasonally Adjusted," U.S. Bureau of Labor Statistics, https://www.bls .gov/charts/job-openings-and-labor-turnover/unemp-per-job-opening.htm.

xi artificial intelligence, and robots: Among the many research studies ongoing on how technology, artificial intelligence, and robots are likely to change the nature of work, see: Fabrizio Dell'Acqua et al., "Navigating the Jagged Technological Frontier: Field Experimental Evidence of the Effects of AI on Knowledge Worker Productivity and Quality," Harvard Business School Technology & Operations Mgt. Unit Working Paper, 24-013 (2023); Katherine Kellogg, Melissa Valentine, and Angèle Christin, "Algorithms at Work: The New Contested Terrain of Control," *Academy of Management Annals* 14, no. 1 (2020): 366–410; Lindsey Cameron, "The Making of the 'Good Bad' Job: How Algorithmic Management Manufactures Consent Through Constant and Confined Choices," *Administrative Science Quarterly* (forthcoming 2024); Paul Leonardi and Tsedal Neeley, *The Digital Mindset: What It Really Takes to Thrive in the Age of Data, Algorithms, and AI* (Boston: Harvard Business Review Press, 2022); and work by William Kerr, Raffaella Sadun, and Joseph Fuller at the Managing the Future of Work project at Harvard Business School (https://www.hbs.edu /managing-the-future-of-work/).

xii "displaced by automation": James Manyika and Kevin Sneader, "AI, Automation, and the Future of Work: Ten Things to Solve for," McKinsey Global Institute, June 1, 2018, https://www.mckinsey.com/featured-insights/future-of -work/ai-automation-and-the-future-of-work-ten-things-to-solve-for.

xii artificial intelligence can be: Krystal Hu, "ChatGPT Sets Record for Fastest-Growing User Base—Analyst Note," Reuters, February 2, 2023, https:// www.reuters.com/technology/chatgpt-sets-record-fastest-growing-user-base -analyst-note-2023-02-01/.

xii means to them: Just as individuals are trying to adapt to and get ahead of change, so too are companies. For a review of how organizations are continuously innovating in the face of change, such as through making smarter use of their talent, see Ikujiro Nonaka and Hirotaka Takeuchi, *The Wise Company: How Companies Create Continuous Innovation* (Oxford: Oxford University Press, 2019) and Howard Yu, *Leap: How to Thrive in a World Where Everything Can Be Copied* (New York: PublicAffairs, 2018).

xii has defined it: Some have talked about a "lattice" structure to careers, as opposed to the "ladder" structure mentioned in the prior paragraph. For more on this topic, see Cathy Benko, Molly Anderson, and Suzanne Vickberg, "The Corporate Lattice: A Strategic Response to the Changing World of Work," *Deloitte Review* 8 (2011): 91–107.

xii needs and desires: Scholars and practitioners are increasingly advocating this broader approach to increase happiness and reduce burnout. See, for example, Christina Wallace, *The Portfolio Life: How to Future-Proof Your Career, Avoid Burnout, and Build a Life Bigger Than Your Business Card* (New York: Balance, 2024) and Arthur Brooks and Oprah Winfrey, *Build the Life You Want: The Art and Science of Getting Happier* (London: Portfolio, 2023). For tips on how to restore your physical and mental well-being at work, see Elaine Chin, *Welcome Back! How to Reboot Your Physical and Mental Well-Being for a Post-Pandemic World* (Toronto: Sutherland House, 2021).

xii more purposeful work: Put differently, individuals are looking for organizations whose purposes align with their own individual senses of purpose given their pushes and pulls. For more information on how to align individual and organizational purpose, see Ranjay Gulati, *Deep Purpose: The Heart and Soul of High-Performance Companies* (New York: Harper Business, 2022); Matt Spielman, *Inflection Points: How to Work and Live with Purpose* (Hoboken, NJ: John Wiley & Sons, 2022); Gerald Davis and Christopher White, *Changing*

Your Company from the Inside Out: A Field Guide for Social Entrepreneurs (Boston: Harvard Business Review Press, 2015); Michael Beer et al., *Higher Ambition: How Great Leaders Create Economic and Social Value* (Boston: Harvard Business Review Press, 2011); and Tony Hsieh, *Delivering Happiness* (New York: Grand Central Publishing, 2013).

xii *gives their lives meaning*: For a discussion of the importance of purpose and living a life of meaning, see Viktor Frankl, *Man's Search for Meaning* (Boston: Beacon Press, 2006). Research is increasingly revealing the divergence between the progression organizations are offering to their employees and the progress their employees actually want to make. For example, an in-depth research program on why women remain underrepresented in leadership roles has shown that the way those "leadership" roles have been designed may be partially at fault because they are relatively unattractive to those the organization is seeking to fill them with. For an example, see Sebastian C. Schuh, Alina S. Hernandez Bark, Niels Van Quaquebeke, Rüdiger Hossiep, Philip Frieg, and Rolf Van Dick, "Gender Differences in Leadership Role Occupancy: The Mediating Role of Power Motivation," *Journal of Business Ethics*, 120 (2014): 363–79.

xiii progress in their careers: "State of the Global Workforce 2023 Report: The Voice of the World's Employees," Gallup, p. 3.

xiv quarter-inch holes: This analogy is from legendary Harvard Business School marketing professor Theodore Levitt. Clayton M. Christensen, Scott Cook, and Taddy Hall, "What Customers Want from Your Products," Harvard Business School Working Knowledge, Jan 16. 2006, https://hbswk.hbs.edu/item/what-customers-want-from-your-products.

xiv Jobs to Be Done theory: Clayton M. Christensen, Taddy Hall, Karen Dillon, and David S. Duncan, "Know Your Customers' 'Jobs to Be Done,'" *Harvard Business Review*, Sept. 2016, https://hbr.org/2016/09/know-your-customers-jobs-to-be-done.

xiv new approach to innovation: The big change was a focus on causality—what causes someone to buy a certain product or service. What is the situation they are in, and what is the progress they seek? This focus on causality undergirds our use of the Jobs to Be Done theory in the context of job moves.

xiv thousands of participants worldwide: Since the course's inception, 47 percent of participants have been from North America; 20 percent from Europe; 12 percent from Asia Pacific; 11 percent from the Middle East; 6 percent from Africa; and 4 percent from Latin America. "Developing Yourself as a Leader—Virtual," Harvard Business School, https://www.exed.hbs.edu/developing-yourself-leader-virtual/statistics, accessed Dec. 4, 2023.

xiv after time away: The group we studied and coached crossed all levels of income, race, and gender.

xv really special here: Other books have laid a foundation for the job search process, from figuring out what you want—such as Jenny Blake, *Pivot: The*

Only Move That Matters Is Your Next One (New York: Portfolio, 2017); Reynold Levy, *Start Now: Because That Meaningful Job Is Out There, Just Waiting for You* (New York: Rosetta Books, 2020); and Timothy Butler, *Getting Unstuck: A Guide to Discovering Your Next Career Path* (Boston: Harvard Business Review Press, 2009)—to actually getting it, like Richard N. Bolles, *What Color Is Your Parachute? A Practical Manual for Job-Hunters and Career-Changers* (Berkeley, CA: Ten Speed Press, 1972); and Dawn Graham, *Switchers: How Smart Professionals Change Careers—and Seize Success* (New York: AMACOM, 2018).

xviii up until now: This could also be called a form of "metacognition"—awareness of your own thought processes.

xx "we can quit": David Epstein, "Here's How Quitting Can Be Your Competitive Advantage," Range Widely, Nov. 17, 2022, https://davidepstein.substack.com/p/annie-duke-quit.

xx other major trends: For more on how talent-oriented strategies are redefining workplaces (hybrid, remote, and in-office workplaces alike) and organizational success, see Peter Capelli, *The Future of the Office: Work from Home, Remote Work, and the Hard Choices We All Face* (Philadelphia: Wharton School Press, 2021); Tsedal Neeley, *Remote Work Revolution: Succeeding from Anywhere* (New York: Harper Business, 2021); and Joost Minnaar and Pim de Morree, *Corporate Rebels: Make Work More Fun* (North Brabant, NL: Corporate Rebels Nederland B.V., 2020).

xx have in the past: Fritz J. Roethlisberger and William J. Dickson, *Management and the Worker: An Account of a Research Program Conducted by the Western Electric Company* (Cambridge, MA: Harvard University Press, 1939); Alfred D. Chandler Jr., *Strategy and Structure: Chapters in the History of the American Industrial Enterprise*, vol. 120 (Cambridge, MA: MIT Press, 1969); Alfred D. Chandler Jr. and Richard S. Tedlow, *The Coming of Managerial Capitalism: A Casebook on the History of American Economic Institutions* (Homewood, IL: Richard D. Irwin, 1985); and R. Khurana, *From Higher Aims to Hired Hands: The Social Transformation of American Business Schools and the Unfulfilled Promise of Management as a Profession* (Princeton, NJ: Princeton University Press, 2010).

It's important to also acknowledge that there have been some glimmers of hope. For instance, many companies have increased their investments in educating and upskilling their employees. Forty-two percent of companies focused more on upskilling employees after the pandemic began. See Aris Apostolopoulos, "Employee Upskilling and Reskilling Statistics: Casting Light on the Trend," TalentLMS, June 25, 2020, https://www.talentlms.com/blog/reskilling-upskilling-training-statistics/, for example. And 75 percent of human resource managers said they were either maintaining or increasing their training budgets. See Kathy Gurchiek, "SHRM: Some Industries Boost Training in New Technology, Equipment During Pandemic," SHRM, June 11, 2020, https://www.shrm.org/topics-tools/news/shrm-industries-boost-training-new

-technology-equipment-pandemic#:~:text=%E2%80%8BThe%20knowledge
%20and%20service,Human%20Resource%20Management%20(SHRM).

But we wrote this chapter knowing that individuals could use far more support as they drive their own destiny and navigate the growth of the gig economy, the proliferation and normalization of flexible work arrangements, and the rise of time and purpose as valued forms of capital. In most workplaces, people are still forced to shoulder increased uncertainty, anxiety, change, and opportunity in their careers without much scaffolding.

xxi colleagues or friends: Those who want to offer advice and support to career seekers would benefit from first taking a look at David A. Garvin and Joshua D. Margolis, "The Art of Giving and Receiving Advice," *Harvard Business Review* 93, no. 1 (2015).

xxi and really *should* be: Phyl Terry advocated for job seekers to form a group of others in the same position in his book *Never Search Alone: The Job Seeker's Playbook* (New York: Collaborative Gain, 2022).

xxi never otherwise know: See, for example, Peter Dizikes, "The Power of Weak Ties in Gaining New Employment," MIT News Office, Sept. 15, 2022, https://news.mit.edu/2022/weak-ties-linkedin-employment-0915.

xxii position of power: If you don't feel like you have enough power to execute our steps in any given situation, you will find advice on how to draw on additional sources of power in Julie Battilana and Tiziana Casciaro, *Power, for All: How It Really Works and Why It's Everyone's Business* (New York: Simon and Schuster, 2021).

Chapter One: Learn What Causes People to Change Jobs

6 seeking to optimize: Scott Sonenshein cautions about not always trying to get "more" of everything and instead being targeted in what you want. See Scott Sonenshein, *Stretch: Unlock the Power of Less—and Achieve More Than You Ever Imagined* (New York: Harper Business, 2017).

6 challenges and priorities: As those challenges and priorities change over time, so too will the quest you're on. In order to effectively move from one quest to another, people need to be able to not just recognize the new quest but also be willing to leave the old quest behind. Doing so requires getting unstuck. For more on how to do so, see Frank Barrett, *Yes to the Mess: Surprising Leadership Lessons from Jazz* (Boston: Harvard Business Review Press, 2012). To unlearn past ways of thinking and being, see Adam Grant, *Think Again: The Power of Knowing What You Don't Know* (New York: Viking, 2021).

7 what you should do next: Our findings overlap in some interesting ways with former BYU management professor C. Brooklyn Derr's findings about "career orientations," in his book *Managing the New Careerists*. These orientations "tend to shift over time, depending on life circumstances," as Boris Groysberg and Robin Abrahams wrote. Derr wrote about five of these "orien-

tations": "Getting Ahead," "Getting Secure," "Getting Free," "Getting High," and "Getting Balanced." Although we look at individuals' quests for progress in particular circumstances, there are some similarities between our "Get Out" and Derr's "Getting Free"; our "Regain Control" and Derr's "Getting Secure"; our "Regain Alignment" and Derr's "Getting High"; and our "Take the Next Step" and Derr's "Getting Ahead." Boris Groysberg and Robin Abrahams, "Know What Kind of Careerist You Are," *Harvard Business Review*, March 25, 2014, https://hbr.org/2014/03/know-what-kind-of-careerist-you-are.

9   to work effectively: For reviews of work on flexible alternative work arrangements, even before the COVID-19 pandemic, see Gretchen Spreitzer, Lindsey Cameron, and Lyndon Garrett, "Alternative Work Arrangements: Two Images of the New World of Work," *Annual Review of Organizational Psychology and Organizational Behavior* 4 (2017): 473–99; and a decade before that, Susan Ashford, Elizabeth George, and Ruth Blatt, "2 Old Assumptions, New Work: The Opportunities and Challenges of Research on Nonstandard Employment," *Academy of Management Annals* 1, no. 1 (2007): 65–117. For an overview of pandemic-related changes, see Kevin Kniffin et al., "COVID-19 and the Workplace: Implications, Issues, and Insights for Future Research and Action," *American Psychologist* 76, no. 1 (2021): 63–77, https://ink.library.smu.edu.sg/lkcsb_research/6594.

9   offers more predictability: For great insights on the value of predictability at work (and the cost of not having it), see Leslie Perlow's research on predictable time off (https://hbr.org/2009/10/making-time-off-predictable-and-required) and her book, *Sleeping with Your Smartphone: How to Break the 24/7 Habit and Change the Way You Work* (Boston: Harvard Business Press, 2012).

13   at least at first: This could be the equivalent of the notion of an emergent strategy overtaking a deliberate one, as in the famous story of Intel moving out of memory chips in the 1980s. See Clayton M. Christensen and Michael E. Raynor, *The Innovator's Solution: Creating and Sustaining Successful Growth* (Boston: Harvard Business School, 2003), chap. 8. Also see the discussion of this idea in Clayton M. Christensen, James Allworth, and Karen Dillon, *How Will You Measure Your Life?* (New York: Harper Business, 2012), chap. 3.

Chapter Two: Step 1: Identify What Jump-Started Your Latest Quest

18   her latest move: This sort of "push-pull analysis" is common in psychology. It's used to understand what's motivating someone to take a specific action. The notion of forces that are pushing and pulling someone to make a change plays a big role in our framework.

21   "before switching again": Kathryn Dill, "These People Who Quit Jobs During the Pandemic Say They Have Regrets," *Wall Street Journal*, April 25, 2022, https://www.wsj.com/articles/some-job-switchers-are-having-second-thoughts-great-resignation-11650663370.

According to a survey by Paychex of 825 employees who left their job during the Great Resignation, an even higher 80 percent said they regretted the move. "Employee Regret After the Great Resignation," Paychex, Jan. 16, 2023, https://www.paychex.com/articles/human-resources/exploring-the-great-regret.

23   "bad is stronger than good": Roy F. Baumeister et al., "Bad Is Stronger Than Good," *Review of General Psychology* 5, no. 4 (2001): 323–70.

23   than positive ones: The absence of interaction can also be a push, as research on employee voice and how managers respond to it has shown. For example, see Elizabeth McClean, Ethan Burris, and James Detert, "When Does Voice Lead to Exit? It Depends on Leadership," *Academy of Management Journal* 56, no. 2 (2013): 525–48; James Detert and Ethan Burris, "Can Your Employees Really Speak Freely?" *Harvard Business Review* 94, no. 1 (2016): 80–87; Elizabeth Morrison and Frances J. Milliken, "Organizational Silence: A Barrier to Change and Development in a Pluralistic World," *Academy of Management Review* 25, no. 4 (2000): 706–25; and Jim Detert, *Choosing Courage: The Everyday Guide to Being Brave at Work* (Boston: Harvard Business Press, 2021).

24   not working for them: Katy Milkman, *How to Change: The Science of Getting from Where You Are to Where You Want to Be* (New York: Portfolio, 2021).

28   as you naturally recall it: The goal is to share not just the steps you took but also to verbalize the voice in your head—what Ethan Kross calls Chatter—so that your interviewer can be privy to those thoughts, too. For more on that inner voice, see Ethan Kross, *Chatter: The Voice in Our Head, Why It Matters, and How to Harness It* (New York: Crown, 2022).

28   people often think it is: Amanda Ripley, *High Conflict: Why We Get Trapped and How We Get Out* (New York: Simon and Schuster, 2021), chaps. 1 and 2.

30   "How many [product managers] do we really need?": Harvard Business School MBA student interview with Managing Human Capital course alumnus, December 2023.

30   turn the league around: Harvard Business School MBA student interview with Managing Human Capital course alumnus, December 2023.

30   he said: Harvard Business School MBA student interview with Managing Human Capital course alumnus, December 2023.

32   they might acquire: Daniel Kahneman and Amos Tversky, "Prospect Theory: An Analysis of Decision Under Risk," *Econometrica* 47, no. 2 (March 1979).

This human condition is not new. In Act III of Shakespeare's *Hamlet*, we are told:

The undiscover'd country from whose bourn
No traveller returns, puzzles the will
And makes us rather bear those ills we have
Than fly to others that we know not of.

35   make a change: To do this, we utilized the Pareto principle—the idea that roughly 80 percent of outcomes are caused by approximately 20 percent

of inputs. In other words, we've codified the most prevalent sources of change rather than cataloging every single one.

35   insights to the surface: Asking tough questions—in a respectful way, of course—to help someone grow is expanded on in Kim Scott's two popular books *Radical Candor: Be a Kick-Ass Boss Without Losing Your Humanity* (New York: St. Martin's Press, 2017) and *Radical Respect: How to Work Together Better* (New York: St. Martin's Griffin, 2024).

39   name their feelings: Naming your emotions is a powerful known technique in psychology, as it "tends to diffuse their charge and lessen the burden they create." See, for example, Tony Schwartz, "The Importance of Naming Your Emotions," *New York Times*, April 3, 2015, https://www.nytimes.com/2015/04/04/business/dealbook/the-importance-of-naming-your-emotions.html.

40   the demand side: Economists typically view employers as the "demand side" of the labor market, as they search for talent to fill human capital needs. They view employees as the "supply side" of that market. In this book, we've reversed those labels because we're writing from the perspective of individuals who have choices over where they work and which job to "hire." Just as consumers represent the demand side as they figure out which products to buy to make progress, so, too, do workers express demand as they seek progress through a job move. And employers provide a "supply" of jobs they can hire, whether full-time roles, part-time jobs, or gig or contract work.

Chapter Three: Think "Experiences" Before "Features"

46   near at hand: Studies show that focusing purely on compensation doesn't lead to lasting satisfaction. For example, research by University of Illinois professor Amit Kramer shows that the happiness bump from a pay raise is short-lived. See Devasheesh P. Bhave, Amit Kramer, and Theresa M. Glomb, "Pay Satisfaction and Work-Family Conflict Across Time," *Journal of Organizational Behavior* 34, no. 5 (2013): 698–713 Instead, there are numerous other ways to sustainably increase happiness; see, for example, Tal Ben-Shahar, *Happier: Learn the Secrets to Daily Joy and Lasting Fulfillment* (New York: McGraw Hill, 2007) and Marie Kondo and Scott Sonenshein, *Joy at Work: Organizing Your Professional Life* (New York: Little, Brown Spark, 2020).

47   originally from Europe: To continue our example of money: research suggests that how you spend it (an experience) is more important for happiness than how much of it you receive (a feature). See Elizabeth Dunn and Michael Norton, *Happy Money: The Science of Happier Spending* (New York: Simon and Schuster, 2013).

47   charting her quest for progress: This approach—focusing on experiences before features—has its roots in design thinking, which innovators use to conceive and develop new products. In that world, when designers and marketers explore the

reasons a customer might "hire" a product, their first step is to put aside all their data and analyses showing correlations in behavior and their preconceptions about what people want. After all, customers may be looking to satisfy a new priority that is not predicted by old habits, perhaps without fully realizing it yet.

47   rest of your life: In this case, we define fit as researchers Charles O'Reilly, Jennifer Chatman, and David Caldwell do via their Organizational Culture Profile instrument for measuring person-organization fit. For more detail, see Charles O'Reilly III, Jennifer Chatman, and David Caldwell, "People and Organizational Culture: A Profile Comparison Approach to Assessing Person-Organization Fit," *Academy of Management Journal* 34, no. 3 (1991): 487–516.

47   when you do it: In an interview with *Wired* magazine, Csikszentmihalyi described "flow" as "being completely involved in an activity for its own sake. The ego falls away. Time flies. Every action, movement, and thought follows inevitably from the previous one, like playing jazz. Your whole being is involved, and you're using your skills to the utmost." John Geirland, "Go with the Flow," *Wired*, Sept. 1, 1996, https://www.wired.com/1996/09/czik/.

48   "people stood up for each other": Harvard Business School MBA student interview with Managing Human Capital course alumnus, December 2023.

48   enhance their credibility: In some cases, this propels individuals through four distinct stages of their career: from learning and assisting colleagues to contributing independently to managing others to shaping organizational direction, as outlined by Harvard Business School professors Gene Dalton and Paul Thompson. They observed that high achievers who progressed through them let go of behaviors that had served them well in previous roles and picked up new skills and perspectives as they transitioned to the adjacent stage. For a summary of their research on the four stages of careers, see Dave Ulrich, Norm Smallwood, and Kate Sweetman, *The Leadership Code: Five Rules to Lead By* (Boston: Harvard Business Review Press, 2009): 116–19, which in turn builds on Gene W. Dalton and Paul H. Thompson, *Novations: Strategies for Career Development* (Glenview, IL: Scott, Foresman, 1986).

48   early in your career: Linda A. Hill, *Organizational Behavior Reading: Developing Your Managerial Career* (Boston: Harvard Business Publishing, 2016), https://hbsp.harvard.edu/product/8330-PDF-ENG.

48   the same organization: Harvard Business School MBA student interview with Managing Human Capital course alumnus, December 2023.

49   "[a high-ranking officer] one day": Harvard Business School MBA student interview with Managing Human Capital course alumnus, December 2023.

Chapter Four: Step 2: Know What You Want Driving Your Energy

54   offered such exercises: In addition to the examples that follow, many coaching practices involve energy drivers and drains exercises. See, for example, "How

to Find Fulfillment in Your Job Using the Drainers & Drivers Exercise," Seer Interactive, Sept. 14, 2021, https://www.seerinteractive.com/insights/how-to -find-fulfillment-in-your-job-using-the-drainers-drivers-exercise.

Some personality inventories also use this. See Christina Bowser, *How DISC Prevents Your Energy Drain*, Extended DISC Blog, May 13, 2021, https://blog .extendeddisc.org/05.20-how-disc-prevents-your-energy-drain.

54 what drains you: Bill Burnett and Dave Evans, *Designing Your Life: How to Build a Well-Lived, Joyful Life* (New York: Knopf, 2016), chap. 3.

54 want to say aloud: For more on the power of this approach, see Stefanie P. Spera, Eric D. Buhrfeind, and James W. Pennebaker, "Expressive Writing and Coping with Job Loss," *Academy of Management Journal* 37, no. 3 (1994): 722–33, https://doi.org/10.2307/256708. See also Duncan Mathison and Martha I. Finney, *Unlock the Hidden Job Market: 6 Steps to a Successful Job Search When Times Are Tough* (Upper Saddle River, NJ: Pearson Education, 2010), 44–47.

55 drove and drained your energy: The theoretical foundation for looking at energy drives and drains comes, at least in part, from research on thriving at work. For more background, see Christine Porath, Gretchen Spreitzer, Cristina Gibson, and Flannery Garnett, "Thriving at Work: Toward Its Measurement, Construct Validation, and Theoretical Refinement," *Journal of Organizational Behavior* 33, no. 2 (2012): 250–75; and Gretchen Spreitzer et al., "A Socially Embedded Model of Thriving at Work," *Organization Science* 16, no. 5 (2005): 537–49.

55 experiences felt like: Kevin S. LaBar and Roberto Cabeza, "Cognitive Neuroscience of Emotional Memory," *Nature Reviews Neuroscience* 7, no. 1 (2006): 54–64; James L. McGaugh, *Memory and Emotion: The Making of Lasting Memories* (New York: Columbia University Press, 2003).

56 passion for the job: Passion at work is well defined and explored by Jon M. Jachimowicz in "3 Reasons It's So Hard to 'Follow Your Passion,'" *Harvard Business Review*, Oct. 2019, https://hbr.org/2019/10/3-reasons-its-so-hard-to -follow-your-passion; Joy Bredehorst, Kai Krautter, Jirs Meuris, and Jon M. Jachimowicz, "The Challenge of Maintaining Passion for Work over Time: A Daily Perspective on Passion and Emotional Exhaustion," *Organization Science* 35, no. 1 (2024): 364–86; and Kai Krautter, Anabel Büchner, and Jon M. Jachimowicz, "Extraverts Reap Greater Social Rewards from Passion Because They Express Passion More Frequently and More Diversely," *Personality and Social Psychology Bulletin* (2023). In terms of energy drains and drivers, passion can also be separate from one's job, as explained in Zachariah Berry and Jon M. Jachimowicz, "When Following Your Passion Turns Toxic," *Harvard Business Review*, Nov. 2021, https://hbr.org/2021/11/when-following-your-passion-turns -toxic; and Lauren C. Howe, Jon M. Jachimowicz, and Jochen I. Menges, "Your Job Doesn't Have to Be Your Passion," *Harvard Business Review*, June 2021, https://hbr.org/2021/06/your-job-doesnt-have-to-be-your-passion.

61 best self to work: If applicable to you, to further explore your personal drivers and drains in the context of a dual-career couple or as a working

parent, see Jennifer Petriglieri, *Couples That Work: How Dual-Career Couples Can Thrive in Love and Work* (Boston: Harvard Business Review Press, 2019); Christine M. Beckman and Melissa Mazmanian, *Dreams of the Overworked: Living, Working, and Parenting in the Digital Age* (Redwood City, CA: Stanford University Press, 2020); and Daisy Dowling, *Workparent: The Complete Guide to Succeeding on the Job, Staying True to Yourself, and Raising Happy Kids* (Boston: Harvard Business Review Press, 2021).

62   yourself "five whys": For more on the origins of this technique devised by Taiichi Ohno at Toyota, see, for example, Bradley Staats and David M. Upton, "Lean Knowledge Work," *Harvard Business Review*, Oct. 2011, https://hbr.org /2011/10/lean-knowledge-work.

63   them more accurately: Emily Singer, "The Neuroscience Behind Bad Decisions," *Quanta Magazine*, Aug. 23, 2016, https://www.quantamagazine.org/the -neuroscience-behind-bad-decisions-20160823/. See also the Decision Lab, https://thedecisionlab.com/.

65   such as performance evaluations: Peter Cappelli and Anna Tavis, "The Performance Management Revolution," *Harvard Business Review* 94, no. 10 (2016): 58–67.

65   Lake Wobegon effect: This phrase is derived from Garrison Keillor's work—both in his novel *Lake Wobegon Days*, which was published in 1985, and from his earlier radio show. The radio segment always ended with a phrase about how "all the women are strong, all the men are good-looking, and all the children are above average." This in turn spawned the social psychology term the Lake Wobegon Effect, which is "the human tendency to overestimate one's capabilities." Here we use the phrase to refer to how each job one has held seems above average along each energy driver. See, for example, Russell N. Carney, "The 'Lake Wobegon Effect': Implications for the Assessment of Exceptional Children," *Journal of School Psychology* 29, no. 2 (1991): 183–86.

66   *helps create meaning*: Linda J. Kray et al., "From What Might Have Been to What Must Have Been: Counterfactual Thinking Creates Meaning," *Journal of Personality and Social Psychology* 98, no. 1 (2010): 106–18; Karl E. Weick, *Sensemaking in Organizations* (New York: Sage, 1995).

Chapter Five: Step 3: Catalog Your Capabilities

73   with different environments: "The Ball Aptitude Battery," Ball Foundation, http://www.ballfoundation.org/ball-aptitude-battery/.

73   their strong points: Gallup, *StrengthsFinder 2.0* (Washington, DC: Gallup Press, 2007).

73   our strengths are: People often focus too much on their innate talents and underestimate their ability to learn and develop (through building character skills and motivational structures), leaving untapped potential, as Adam Grant

argues in *Hidden Potential: The Science of Achieving Greater Things* (New York: Viking, 2023).

74   you are interdependent?: Indeed, in the field of education, motivation is thought to be pegged to two factors: the desirability of an activity or goal (its value) and the belief or expectation that you can successfully do that activity or accomplish the goal. See, for example, Susan A. Ambrose, Michael W. Bridges, Michele DiPietro, Marsha C. Lovett, and Marie K. Norman, *How Learning Works: Seven Research-Based Principles for Smart Teaching* (San Francisco: Jossey-Bass, 2010), chap. 3.

74   career balance sheet: We gratefully acknowledge HBS professor Boris Groysberg, who originally introduced us to the idea of an individual's balance sheet, and HBS professor Luis Viceira, whose Harvard doctoral dissertation, "Optimal Consumption and Portfolio Choice for Long-Horizon Investors," touches on the notion of an individual's balance sheet shifting over different periods in their career and who helped us advance our thinking about how this should be conceptualized.

76   static and restrictive: Such a focus on static traits also ignores the evidence from Stanford professor Carol Dweck about the benefits of having a growth mindset. Carol Dweck, *Mindset: The New Psychology of Success* (New York: Ballantine Books, 2007).

76   or switching occupations: James Manyika et al., "Jobs Lost, Jobs Gained: What the Future of Work Will Mean for Jobs, Skills, and Wages," McKinsey Global Institute, Nov. 28, 2017, https://www.mckinsey.com/featured-insights /future-of-work/jobs-lost-jobs-gained-what-the-future-of-work-will-mean-for -jobs-skills-and-wages.

For a wealth of resources on upskilling, see Paul Fain's articles on the website WorkShift, https://workshift.opencampusmedia.org/author/pfain/. As Robert Putnam and Glen Loury remind us, though, "social capital" plays a critical role in enabling individuals to upskill and move into new jobs. Writes Loury in "What Is Social Capital? With Larry Kotlikoff," *The Glenn Show* (2022), https://glennloury.substack.com/p/what-is-social-capital, "The acquisition of knowledge and skills can help an individual acquire wealth, but the social environment into which that individual is born and within which they mature will have consequences for their ability to acquire that knowledge and those skills in the first place, and then to put them to work in a productive fashion."

76   so-called Peter Principle: Laurence J. Peter and Raymond Hull, *The Peter Principle: Why Things Always Go Wrong* (New York: William Morrow, 1969).

78   practice and exposure: We provide other examples of career balance sheets at http://www.jobmoves.com.

80   jobs in the future: Note that, like any balance sheet, it may be that the combination or *portfolio* of assets on a career balance sheet is more important than any one asset on its own. The value of your assets may come in pairs,

for example, just as some exquisite research on leaders has shown that excellent leaders succeed by having "dual power modes" or "two leadership gears" (Lindy Greer, Francesca Gino, and Robert Sutton, "You Need Two Leadership Gears," *Harvard Business Review* 101, nos. 3–4 [2023]: 76–85).

81   and so on: For a recent review of the behaviors often involved in the process of leading, see Andrew Carton's review of the science of leadership: Andrew Carton, "The Science of Leadership: A Theoretical Model and Research Agenda," *Annual Review of Organizational Psychology and Organizational Behavior* 9 (2022): 61–93.

Chapter Seven: Step 5: Prototype and Design Your Future

89   what actually will: Rita McGrath and Ian MacMillan, "Discovery-Driven Planning," *Harvard Business Review*, July–Aug. 1995, https://hbr.org/1995/07/discovery-driven-planning.

89   after they launch: Sadly, this statistic rings as true today as it did in this article published two decades ago: Clayton M. Christensen, Scott Cook, and Taddy Hall, "Marketing Malpractice: The Cause and the Cure," *Harvard Business Review*, Dec. 2005, https://hbr.org/2005/12/marketing-malpractice-the-cause-and-the-cure.

89   from experimentation, too: For more information on using experiments to grow and make progress, not only for career choices but also more broadly throughout daily life, see Susan Ashford, *The Power of Flexing: How to Use Small Daily Experiments to Create Big Life-Changing Growth* (New York: Harper Business, 2021).

89   because of "anchoring": Deepak Malhotra and Max Bazerman, *Negotiation Genius: How to Overcome Obstacles and Achieve Brilliant Results at the Bargaining Table and Beyond* (New York: Bantam, 2007).

89   to obvious choices: Abhijit V. Banerjee, "A Simple Model of Herd Behavior," *Quarterly Journal of Economics* 107, no. 3 (1992): 797–817.

89   from exploring alternatives: James G. March, "Exploration and Exploitation in Organizational Learning," *Organization Science* 2, no. 1 (1991): 71–87.

90   A/B testing in marketing: For more detail on choice architecture, see Katy Milkman, *How to Change: The Science of Getting from Where You Are to Where You Want to Be* (New York: Portfolio, 2021).

92   a couple weeks: To help stay committed, keep in mind that a little focused time each day can have big results. If you're interested in learning more about the power of focus and attention, see Amishi P. Jha, *Peak Mind: Find Your Focus, Own Your Attention, Invest 12 Minutes a Day* (San Francisco: HarperOne, 2021).

92   some possible jobs: Check out the Innovator app built on ChatGPT in OpenAI's GPT store: https://chat.openai.com/g/g-JaiQEuHRU-innovator, accessed Jan. 24, 2024.

93   to new opportunities: For more advice on how to successfully network, see resources such as Keith Ferrazzi and Tahl Raz, *Never Eat Alone: And Other Secrets to Success, One Relationship at a Time* (New York: Crown Currency, 2014) and Orville Pierson, *Highly Effective Networking: Meet the Right People and Get a Great Job* (Newburyport, MA: Weiser, 2009).

93   hold these roles: Online communities like that at CareerVillage.org, which has connected over 7 million people to free career advice from over 130,000 professionals, can also help you in this process.

101 "betting the farm": Recent research of independent workers (i.e., those who are not affiliated with an organization or established profession) has shown the stark emotional tensions encompassing both the anxiety and fulfillment of working under precarious and personal conditions for these gig workers, suggesting how valuable it can be to initially explore side hustles while still in an organization rather than giving up membership in an organization entirely to do gig work. See Gianpiero Petriglieri, Susan J. Ashford, and Amy Wrzesniewski, "Agony and Ecstasy in the Gig Economy: Cultivating Holding Environments for Precarious and Personalized Work Identities," *Administrative Science Quarterly* 64, no. 1 (2018).

102 "making a commitment": Herminia Ibarra, *Working Identity: Unconventional Strategies for Reinventing Your Career* (Boston: Harvard Business School Press, 2004) and Ibarra, "Provisional Selves: Experimenting with Image and Identity in Professional Adaptation," *Administrative Science Quarterly* 44, no. 4 (1999): 764–91.

102 It's to act: As our friends at IDEO who started the Purpose Project (https://www.purposeproject.org/) shared with us, action, not talk, clarifies one's purpose. What are you doing today? What do you like doing? What can you do so that you can get more clarity around what drives you, what you like, and what you don't?

Chapter Eight: Step 6: Converge on Your Path

108 of the book: Keep in mind that the middle of a process can often feel the most challenging, so stick with it. As Rosabeth Moss Kanter writes in "Change Is Hardest in the Middle," *Harvard Business Review* 12 (2009): "Everything looks like a failure in the middle. Everyone loves inspiring beginnings and happy endings; it is just the middles that involve hard work."

Part III: Getting to Where You Want to Go

109 test and learn: We're not advising you to just translate one of your prototypes into your next job. Rather, you'll engage with the marketplace and continue to learn before switching, just as innovators are advised to learn before

launching in: Rita Gunther McGrath and Ian C. MacMillan, *Discovery-Driven Growth: A Breakthrough Process to Reduce Risk and Seize Opportunity* (Boston: Harvard Business Review Press, 2009) and Eric Ries, *The Lean Startup: How Today's Entrepreneurs Use Continuous Innovation to Create Radically Successful Businesses* (New York: Currency, 2011).

Chapter Nine: Step 7: Embrace Trade-offs in the Job Market

112 through personal connections: "Eighty-Percent of Professionals Consider Networking Important to Career Success," LinkedIn, June 22, 2017, https://news .linkedin.com/2017/6/eighty-percent-of-professionals-consider-networking -important-to-career-success.

Whereas the above article suggests that 70 percent of jobs are filled through personal connections, other estimates suggest the number is as high as 80 percent. Julia Freeland Fisher, "How to Get a Job Often Comes Down to One Elite Personal Asset, and Many People Still Don't Realize It," CNBC.com, Dec. 27, 2019, https://www.cnbc.com/2019/12/27/how-to-get-a-job-often-comes-down -to-one-elite-personal-asset.html.

112 web-based job boards: Although there are disputes around this number, estimates suggest that somewhere between 60 to 70 percent of jobs aren't published on job boards. For example, see Wendy Kaufman, "A Successful Job Search: It's All About Networking," *All Things Considered*, NPR, Feb. 3, 2011, https://www.npr.org/2011/02/08/133474431/a-successful-job-search-its -all-about-networking, and Jo Green, "80% Nonsense—Busting the 'Hidden' Job Market Myth," LinkedIn, March 20, 2018, https://www.linkedin.com /pulse/80-nonsense-busting-hidden-job-market-myth-jo-green-1c/.

113 has long shown: Mark S. Granovetter, "The Strength of Weak Ties," *American Journal of Sociology* 78, no. 6 (1973): 1360–80, http://www.jstor.org/ stable/2776392.

113 "supports, and opportunities": Julia Freeland Fisher, "Don't Discount the Power of Students' Acquaintances to Expand Supports and Horizons," Clayton Christensen Institute, Feb. 19, 2020, https://www.christenseninstitute .org/blog/dont-discount-the-power-of-students-acquaintances-to-expand -supports-and-horizons/.

114 network of relationships: Linda A. Hill, *Becoming a Manager: How New Managers Master the Challenges of Leadership*, 2nd edition (Cambridge, MA: Harvard Business School Press, 2003).

114 or loved ones: Mario Luis Small, *Someone to Talk to: How Networks Matter in Practice* (Oxford: Oxford University Press, 2019).

115 out of hiding: This is how you engage in what's called the pursuit of an "intelligent career." Linda Hill, "Organizational Behavior Reading: Developing Your Managerial Career," (Boston: Harvard Business Publishing, 2016, https://hbsp.harvard.edu/product/8330-PDF-ENG.

115 researchers phrased it: Tiziana Casciaro, Francesca Gino, and Maryam Kouchaki, "The Contaminating Effects of Building Instrumental Ties: How Networking Can Make Us Feel Dirty," *Administrative Science Quarterly* 59, no. 4 (2014): 705–35.

115 the other person: Tiziana Casciaro, Francesca Gino, and Maryam Kouchaki, "Managing Yourself: Learn to Love Networking," *Harvard Business Review* 94, no. 5 (2016): 104–7.

121 one "perfect" mentor: Note that your "personal board of directors" does not need to be one fixed group of individuals, but rather it can be a "team of teams"—as General McChrystal et al. describe in *Team of Teams: New Rules of Engagement for a Complex World* (New York: Portfolio, 2015)—comprised of different sets of people to aid in different aspects of your development. For more information on how to develop one's career, see Hill, "Organizational Behavior Reading."

Chapter Ten: Step 8: Craft Your Career Story

126 of this chapter: For more on this topic, see resources on positioning yourself to employers, such as Dorie Clark, *Reinventing You: Define Your Brand, Imagine Your Future* (Boston: Harvard Business Review Press, 2013) and Kerri Twigg, *The Career Stories Method: 11 Steps to Find Your Ideal Career—and Discover Your Awesome Self in the Process* (Vancouver: Page Two Books, 2021).

128 loved without moving: You may have noticed that the language around "crafting" your career narrative bears similarities to "job crafting"—a concept that management scholars Jane E. Dutton and Amy Wrzesniewski introduced in 2001. In their research, they describe how employees can shape their roles—and increase satisfaction at work—by changing the cognitive, task, and/or relational boundaries that govern their interactions and relationships with others at work. Although our narrative-crafting concept differs from job crafting, it can overlap in two ways. First, as Alex's example shows, a manager who hears your career story may be able to change your role to match what you want. Second, people who effectively craft their narrative often build a sense of purpose into the arc of their story, just as those who "job craft" often reframe their role to fit their purpose. See Amy Wrzesniewski and Jane E. Dutton, "Crafting a Job: Revisioning Employees as Active Crafters of Their Work," *Academy of Management Review* 26, no. 2 (April 2001): 179–201, https://www.jstor.org/stable/259118?origin=crossref. Also see Jane E. Dutton and Amy Wrzesniewski, "What Job Crafting Looks Like," *Harvard Business Review*, March 12, 2020, https://hbr.org/2020/03/what-job-crafting-looks-like.

129 creating a "story spine": Pixar actually borrowed this concept from playwright Kenn Adams's book about the art of improvisation. Kenn Adams, *How to Improvise a Full-Length Play: The Art of Spontaneous Theater* (New York: Simon and Schuster, 2010).

129 information through stories: See, for example, Daniel Willingham, *Why Don't Students Like School?* (San Francisco: Jossey-Bass, 2010), chap. 3.

133 of course, isn't new: Graham Wilson, "The History of the Elevator Speech," Nov. 25, 2012, https://www.the-confidant.info/2012/the-history-of-the-elevator -speech/.

133 "for just 1 minute": Philip B. Crosby, *The Art of Getting Your Own Sweet Way* (United Kingdom: McGraw-Hill, 1972). Others also give credit for pop- ularizing the elevator pitch to journalist Ilene Rosenzweig, who described how a *Vanity Fair* editor she was dating in the 1990s, Michael Caruso, would liter- ally jump into the elevator when then-editor in chief Tina Brown was riding the four floors down from her office to the lobby in order to pitch his latest 15,000-word story idea. Presenting: Rob, "Elevator Pitches: A Brief History," Jan. 14, 2016, https://presentingrob.blogspot.com/2016/01/elevator-pitches -brief-history.html.

134 good at simulating: AI isn't good at everything. But it can work well here because of what you've done in the first seven steps of this process to create something unique that is tailored to your past and your current quest. That work isn't generic. With those unique elements in place, now we're just trying to help you market it. The function of the AI is to help make your unique story sound like something that employers have selected before.

Chapter Eleven: Step 9: Apply for Jobs You'd Like to Hire

137 is well established: Kerri Anne Renzulli, "75% of Resumes Are Never Read by a Human—Here's How to Make Sure Your Resume Beats the Bots," CNBC, Feb. 28, 2019, https://www.cnbc.com/2019/02/28/resume-how-yours-can-beat -the-applicant-tracking-system.html.

137 ATS will screen: Interview with Tom Dowd, Nov. 17, 2022. See also Bill Burnett and Dave Evans, *Designing Your Life* (New York: Knopf, 2016), 136–37. Burnett and Evans suggest going as far as "rewrit[ing] your résumé using the same words used in the job posting." They add: "If you have a specific skill that is posted as required, put it in your résumé exactly the way it is written in the Internet posting. If you don't have that skill, find a way to describe your skill set that uses the same words that will be found in a keyword search."

141 for a list: For more on this topic, see resources on interviewing well, such as James Storey, *The Art of the Interview: The Perfect Answers to Every Interview Question* (Scotts Valley, CA: CreateSpace Independent Publishing, 2016).

141 the open position: Using the story spine structure to answer a question aligns well with the common STAR interview framework, which advises dis- cussing the specific situation (S), the task at hand (T), the action you then took (A), and the result (R).

143 personal user manual: Adam Bryant, "Want to Know Me? Just Read My User Manual," *New York Times*, March 20, 2013, https://www.nytimes

.com/2013/03/31/business/questbacks-lead-strategist-on-his-user-manual
.html. See also Chelsea Greenwood, "Managers Are Starting to Make Personal
'User Manuals' That Explain to Their Coworkers What Makes Them Tick,"
Business Insider, Apr. 11, 2019; and Marko Saric, "Why You Should Write a
'How to Work with Me' User Manual," *The Startup*, Oct. 17, 2018, https://
medium.com/swlh/user-manual-to-me-92c8ce68f960.

143 traction in recent years: We gratefully acknowledge a number of faculty
members at HBS, including Tony Mayo, Sandra Sucher, and Tom Delong,
who cocreated a version of this exercise to use in the FIELD and Interpersonal
Skills Development Lab courses in the MBA program.

143 and group performance: Creating this sort of manual can also help in your
personal life. For example, Daisy Dowling observed in her book *Workparent*
that we each have a template for how to raise children, but until we make it
explicit, it is very hard for others—including our coparent—to understand why
we do the things we do. Daisy Dowling, *Workparent: The Complete Guide to
Succeeding on the Job, Staying True to Yourself, and Raising Happy Kids* (Boston:
Harvard Business Review Press, 2021).

143 how you share it is important, too: In her research on positive and negative connections in people's experience at work, Jane Dutton describes how to
use these kinds of exercises to build positive connections. For more detail, see
Jane Dutton, *Energize Your Workplace: How to Create and Sustain High-Quality
Connections at Work* (San Francisco: Jossey-Bass, 2003).

145 good manager knows this: Peter Drucker, *The Effective Executive: The
Definitive Guide to Getting the Right Things Done* (New York: Harper Business, 2017).

146 be your best self: For more on this idea, see the Reflected Best Self exercise. A summary is here: Laura Morgan Roberts, Gretchen M. Spreitzer, Jane
E. Dutton, Robert E. Quinn, Emily D. Heaphy, and Brianna Barker, "How
to Play to Your Strengths," *Harvard Business Review*, Jan. 2005, https://hbr
.org/2005/01/how-to-play-to-your-strengths.

146 earn your trust: There are several forms of trust within organizations that
can shape an individual's answer to how trust is earned at work. For a comprehensive view into what trust is and the ways it can be earned, see Denise M.
Rousseau, Sim B. Sitkin, Ronald S. Burt, and Colin Camerer, "Not So Different
After All: A Cross-Discipline View of Trust," *Academy of Management Review*
23, no. 3 (1998): 393–404.

148 what matters most: As Laura Huang advocates in *Edge: Turning Adversity
into Advantage* (New York: Portfolio, 2020), it is critical to translate what is
uniquely "you" (both your strengths and your shortcomings) into your "edge"
that others can appreciate.

149 if they show interest: If not, and you find yourself struggling to work with
a colleague, take a look at Robert I. Sutton, *The Asshole Survival Guide: How to
Deal with People Who Treat You Like Dirt* (Boston: Mariner Books, 2017).

Chapter Twelve: Build a Team Your Employees Want to Rehire Each Day

155 quests for progress: For more advice on how leaders can help their teams navigate their quests for progress, see J. Richard Hackman's classic management book *Leading Teams: Setting the State for Great Performances* (Boston: Harvard Business Review Press, 2002).

155 be mutually reinforcing: Conceptual foundations for this can be found in, among other resources, Michael Beer, *High Commitment High Performance: How to Build a Resilient Organization for Sustained Advantage* (San Francisco: Jossey-Bass, 2009); John J. Gabarro, *The Dynamics of Taking Charge* (Boston: Harvard Business Review Press, 1987); Zeynep Ton, *The Good Jobs Strategy: How the Smartest Companies Invest in Employees to Lower Costs and Boost Profits* (Grand Haven, MI: Brilliance Audio, 2014); and the resources offered by the Good Jobs Institute, https://goodjobsinstitute.org/what-is-the-good-jobs-strategy/.

156 a new direction: Sometimes, having members of the team venture out in a new direction can actually be good for team performance too, as it can spur new connections that bring previously unavailable information and opportunities back to the team. For example, see Deborah Ancona and Henrik Bresman, "Turn Your Teams Inside Out," *MIT Sloan Management Review* 64, no. 2 (2023): 24–29 or, for more detail, Deborah Ancona and Henrik Bresman, *X-Teams: How to Build Teams That Lead, Innovate, and Succeed* (Boston: Harvard Business Review Press, 2023).

156 and service economy: This is the continuation of a trend that extends at least as far back as when Michael Beer decided to title his classic management book *Managing Human Assets* (New York: The Free Press, 1984).

156 keeping good people: "Almost Half of U.S. Companies Can't Fill Open Positions," Cision PRWeb, March 8, 2023, https://www.prweb.com/releases/almost-half-of-u-s-companies-can-t-fill-open-positions-814091777.html. And yet employees still struggle to find employment, per Peter Capelli, *Why Good People Can't Get Jobs: The Skills Gap and What Companies Can Do About It* (Philadelphia: Wharton School Press, 2012). This challenge of matching talent to open roles rather remarkably echoes other supply-demand challenges, such as that of online dating: even though there is a wide funnel of potential matches, singles frequently struggle to find the right match, as summarized in Emily A. Vogels and Colleen McClain, "Key Findings About Online Dating in the U.S.," Pew Research Center, Feb. 2023, https://www.pewresearch.org/short-reads/2023/02/02/key-findings-about-online-dating-in-the-u-s/.

156 over their lifetimes: "One Third of Your Life Is Spent at Work," Gettysburg College, https://www.gettysburg.edu/news/stories?id=79db7b34-630c-4f49-ad32-4ab9ea48e72b, accessed July 20, 2023.

157 evolve in their careers: "More Than Skills: How to Put Purpose Back into Work and Learning," ASU+GSV Summit, Apr. 19, 2023, https://www.youtube.com/watch?v=pfKfBiE6k58.

158 the job market: Remember, in this book we're focusing on the "demand side" of the market—the perspective of individuals "hiring" new jobs.

159 "diagnose an issue early": Email from Mark Stephens to Bob Moesta, April 4, 2023.

159 dynamic as well: Interview with Joseph Carver, May 30, 2023.

160 that employee's context: For more on deep listening, see Amanda Ripley, *High Conflict: Why We Get Trapped and How We Get Out* (New York: Simon and Schuster, 2021).

160 energy and productivity: This matches insights from the book *The Expertise Economy*, which suggests that individuals shouldn't be put in jobs where their skills perfectly map to what the role will ask of them. Instead, they should have room for growth. The moment an employee's skills quotient exceeds 90 (on a 100-point scale), they should be flagged for a review "because these high performers will likely look for their next growth opportunity elsewhere if they aren't given one within the company." Kelly Palmer and David Blake, *The Expertise Economy: How the Smartest Companies Use Learning to Engage, Compete, and Succeed* (Boston: Nicholas Brealey, 2018), chap. 8. For additional tips on how to engage employees, see Daniel M. Cable, *Alive at Work: The Neuroscience of Helping Your People Love What They Do* (Boston: Harvard Business Review Press, 2018).

164 an elevator pitch: Having a common language built upon research-based ideas and established exercises for constructing career narratives increases the quality and frequency of dialogue about how employees can make the progress they seek. And more progress for individuals within an organization typically translates into more progress for the organization.

164 what they recommend: https://www.gallup.com/cliftonstrengths/en/254033/strengthsfinder.aspx.

164 offset the weaknesses: Peter Drucker, *The Effective Executive: The Definitive Guide to Getting the Right Things Done* (New York: Harper Business, 2017), chap. 4.

166 you want to fill: This speaks again to the concept of job crafting. See Amy Wrzesniewski and Jane E. Dutton, "Crafting a Job: Revisioning Employees as Active Crafters of Their Work," *Academy of Management Review* 26, no. 2 (April 2001): 179–201, https://www.jstor.org/stable/259118?origin=crossref. Also see Jane E. Dutton and Amy Wrzesniewski, "What Job Crafting Looks Like," *Harvard Business Review*, March 12, 2020, https://hbr.org/2020/03/what-job-crafting-looks-like.

166 pay people fairly: That's because the combination of 7.4 roles didn't necessarily track to an external benchmark.

166 our research shows: Ethan Bernstein, John Bunch, Niko Canner, and Michael Lee, "Beyond the Holacracy Hype," *Harvard Business Review* 94, no. 7 (2016): 38–49.

167 1960s and 1970s?: Frederick Herzberg, "One More Time: How Do You Motivate Employees?," *Harvard Business Review*, January 2023, https://hbr.org

/2003/01/one-more-time-how-do-you-motivate-employees, accessed Aug. 30, 2023; William J. Paul Jr., Keith B. Robertson, and Frederick Herzberg, "Job Enrichment Pays Off," *Harvard Business Review*, March 1969, https://hbr.org/1969/03/job-enrichment-pays-off, accessed Aug. 30, 2023; J. Richard Hackman and Greg R. Oldham, "Motivation Through the Design of Work: Test of a Theory," *Organizational Behavior and Human Performance* 16 (1976): 250–79; and Douglas McGregor, *Leadership and Motivation* (Cambridge, MA: MIT Press, 1968).

168 "and they stay?": Marc Ramos, chief learning officer of Cornerstone, made this comment in response to a famous line from Sir Richard Branson, who said in 2014, "Train people well enough so that they can leave. Treat them well enough so they don't want to." See "Turning a Corner in Learning on the Job," *Future of Education*, July 31, 2023, https://www.youtube.com/watch?v=obulfA-W3n4.

169 good for business: For a much more detailed and historical perspective on how leaders can enable both employee and business success (i.e., how leaders can lead well), see Nitin Nohria and Rakesh Khurana, *Handbook of Leadership Theory and Practice* (Boston: Harvard Business Review Press, 2010) and Anthony J. Mayo and Nitin Nohria, *In Their Time: The Greatest Business Leaders of the Twentieth Century* (Boston: Harvard Business Review Press, 2005).

169 the customer side: "Why firms should treat their employees well," *The Economist*, Aug. 28, 2019, https://www.economist.com/graphic-detail/2019/08/28/why-firms-should-treat-their-employees-well?utm_medium=cpc.adword.pd&utm_source=google&ppccampaignID=17210591673&ppcadID=&utm_campaign=a.22brand_pmax&utm_content=conversion.direct-response.anonymous&gclid=CjwKCAjw_MqgBhAGEiwAnYOAeib6gIfxDN1XzTz0zxtSahGCvrotDaYyzwPxAT3sQZq2MeBzTSdjDxoC0yMQAvD_BwE&gclsrc=aw.ds.

169 to happier customers: Carolyn Cutrone, "Danny Meyer to 'Treps: Put Your Employees First, Customers Will Follow," *Inc.*, Jan. 28, 2014, https://www.inc.com/carolyn-cutrone/danny-meyer-speaks-at-inc-business-owners-council.html.

169 customers-second strategy: Linda Hill, Tarun Khanna, and Emily S. Stecker, "HCL Technologies," Harvard Business School Case 408004, 2007. See also V. Nayar, *Employees First, Customers Second: Turning Conventional Management Upside Down* (Boston: Harvard Business Press, 2010).

169 form, isn't news: Shep Hyken, "How Happy Employees Make Happy Customers," *Forbes*, May 17, 2017, https://www.forbes.com/sites/shephyken/2017/05/27/how-happy-employees-make-happy-customers/?sh=182e84585c35.

169 "for his studies": "How AT&T, the Index's Top Performer, Extends the Ladder of Opportunity," American Opportunity Index, Oct. 13, 2022, https://americanopportunityindex.com/newsroom/2.

170 employees enroll nationwide: Lou Pugliese and Bobby Babbrah, "The Workforce Intermediary Market: How Must Education Intermediaries Evolve

with Shifts in a Turbulent Labor Market Environment?," Flipp.ED Ventures, Jan. 2023, p. 2.

170 would be more uptake: See also Michael B. Horn and Bob Moesta, *Choosing College: How to Make Better Learning Decisions Throughout Your Life* (San Francisco: Jossey-Bass, 2019).

171 for employers and employees alike: Regardless of whether a job move failure results in a boomerang hire or not, managers and organizations almost always benefit from treating these job moves out of their teams and organizations as the kind of productive failure that Amy Edmondson describes in her book *The Right Kind of Wrong: The Science of Failing Well* (New York: Simon and Schuster, 2023). Like many other things in work and life, success in a career necessitates failure along the way—it is often how we learn—and thus, as she writes, "If you're not failing, you're not journeying into new territory." So long as you are using all the knowledge in this book to avoid preventable failures.

171 you might think: Anthony C. Klotz, Andrea Derler, Carlina Kim, and Manda Winlaw, "The Promise (and Risk) of Boomerang Employees," *Harvard Business Review*, March 15, 2023, https://hbr.org/2023/03/the-promise-and -risk-of-boomerang-employees.

171 a job offer: Ryan Craig, "Stop Ranking Skills," *Forbes*, June 16, 2023.

172 roles lack them: Joseph B. Fuller and Manjari Raman, "Dismissed by Degrees: How Degree Inflation Is Undermining U.S. Competitiveness and Hurting America's Middle Class," Accenture, Grads of Life, and Harvard Business School, Dec. 13, 2017, https://www.hbs.edu/ris/Publication%20 Files/dismissed-by-degrees_707b3f0e-a772-40b7-8f77-aed4a16016cc.pdf.

    Also, although many employers and state governments have dropped degree requirements from job postings—paid posts not requiring a degree rose from roughly 20 percent to almost 30 percent on LinkedIn by 2022, for example— the early evidence suggests that, outside of a few industries like consumer services, entertainment, and government, most employers are still hiring workers who have degrees. See Greg Lewis, "Fewer Job Posts Now Require Degrees. How Has That Changed Hiring?," LinkedIn *Talent Blog*, Aug. 29, 2023, https://www.linkedin.com/business/talent/blog/talent-acquisition/fewer-jobs -require-degrees-impact-on-hiring.

172 ensure a good match: With the emergence of generative AI, there's some evidence that these dynamics could accelerate. According to the Neuron, a newsletter about AI, "recruiters now have the tools to draft job postings that only attract the right candidates. All it takes is a quick prompt to ChatGPT (how-to) or LinkedIn's AI-powered job description generator." As a result, it's never been easier to sift through endless numbers of potential hires. But on the flip side, there are now platforms like WonsultingAI that will tweak a candidate's résumé and cover letter "to make them a perfect match for that dream job." See Noah Edelman and Pete Huang, "Zoom Controversy," The Neuron, Aug. 8,

2023, https://www.theneurondaily.com/p/zoom-recording?utm_source=www
.theneurondaily.com&utm_medium=newsletter&utm_campaign=zoom-is
-recording-you. In other words, AI is turbocharging the game of unicorns and
superheroes.

172 and its requirements: "The History of the Job Description," Tailored Thinking,
Aug. 10, 2021, https://tailoredthinking.co.uk/blog/2021/8/10/job-descriptions
#:~:text=It%20all%20started%20with%20Job%20Analysis&text=They%20
were%20originally%20produced%20as,necessary%20to%20perform%20
those%20activities.

172 to find workers: Christine Overby, "Why Job Descriptions Need to Go,"
Post*Shift, Jan. 19, 2017, https://postshift.com/job-descriptions-need-go/.

173 "the mortgage documents": Maury Hanigan, "The Evolution of Job Postings,"
SparcStart, Feb. 24, 2016, https://www.sparcstart.com/the-evolution-of-job
-postings/.

Chapter Thirteen: Pay It Forward

178 the "messy middle": Rosabeth Moss Kanter, "Change Is Hardest in the
Middle," *Harvard Business Review*, Aug. 12, 2009, https://hbr.org/2009/08/
change-is-hardest-in-the-middl.

178 pay it forward: Not only will you be paying it forward but you will also
be improving your collaboration skills. Getting "smarter" about collaboration
is an increasingly important skill in the workplace, not just for career development but for problem-solving and getting work done. For tips on how to do so,
see Heidi Gardner and Ivan Matviak, *Smarter Collaboration: A New Approach
to Breaking Down Barriers and Transforming Work* (Boston: Harvard Business
Review Press, 2022). In addition, you might very well learn valuable insights
for yourself by mentoring another person lower in the organizational hierarchy
than you; valuing the knowledge that such people have increases your engagement and effectiveness as a mentor—as shown in Ting Zhang, Dan Wong, and
Adam Galinsky, "Learning Down to Train Up: Mentors Are More Effective
When They Value Insights from Below," *Academy of Management Journal* 66,
no. 2 (2023): 604–37—not to mention makes the experience richer for both of
you. See additional works by Ting Zhang for more on how, ideally, good advice
travels in all directions.

179 about "sparking relationships": Michael Horn, "Using AI to Drive Alumni
Engagement," March 6, 2023, https://www.youtube.com/watch?v=PfSa
WyuzJ6Q.

179 connection to the mentee: See Bob Moesta's contribution to: Whitney
Johnson, "Get the Mentoring Equation Right," *Harvard Business Review*,
Oct. 25, 2011, https://hbr.org/2011/10/get-the-mentoring-equation-rig.

180 "barely even autobiography": Derek Thompson, "Your Career Is Just One-

Eighth of Your Life," *The Atlantic*, Sept. 9, 2022, https://www.theatlantic.com /newsletters/archive/2022/09/career-ambition-advice-data/671374/.

181 needs, like money: Putting employees first by focusing on the progress *they* want to make—rather than the progress *you* want to make—is key to effective leadership. As Frances Frei and Anne Morriss write in *Unleashed: The Unapologetic Leader's Guide to Empowering Everyone Around You* (Boston: Harvard Business Review Press, 2020), "Leadership, at its core, isn't about you. Instead, it's about how effective you are at empowering *other* people and unleashing *their* full potential."

182 may not exist: Not only does asking questions create space for solutions to fall into but it is also a key component of "conversation-powered leadership" (involving leaders asking questions, listening well, and talking straight with their employees), as expanded on in Boris Groysberg and Michael Slind, *Talk, Inc.: How Trusted Leaders Use Conversation to Power Their Organizations* (Boston: Harvard Business Review Press, 2012).

186 listening deeply here: Research from multiple fields suggests the value of active listening in building empathy. For example, see Carl Rogers, "The Necessary and Sufficient Conditions of Therapeutic Personality Change," *Journal of Consulting Psychology* 21, no. 2 (1957): 95–103; Chris C. Gearhart and Graham D. Bodie, "Active-Empathic Listening and Its Association with Conversational Induction," *Communication Reports* 24, no. 2 (2011): 79–89; and Greg J. Stephens, Lauren J. Silbert, and Uri Hasson, "Speaker-Listener Neural Coupling Underlies Successful Communication," *Proceedings of the National Academy of Sciences* 107, no. 32 (2010): 14425–30. Niels Van Quaquebeke and Will Felps have termed this "respectful inquiry" in their review of leading through asking questions and listening; see Niels Van Quaquebeke and Will Felps, "Respectful Inquiry: A Motivational Account of Leading Through Asking Questions and Listening," *Academy of Management Review* 43, no. 1 (2018): 5–27.

191 best in them: After all, as Peter Drucker observed, a good manager lets employees work in the ways that are best for their productivity. Peter Drucker, *The Effective Executive: The Definitive Guide to Getting the Right Things Done* (New York: Harper Business, 2017), chap. 3. See also Ethan S. Bernstein, "Making Transparency Transparent: The Evolution of Observation in Management Theory," *Academy of Management Annals* 11, no. 1 (2017): 217–66 and Bernstein, "The Smart Way to Create a Transparent Workplace," *Wall Street Journal*, Feb. 22, 2015.

Conclusion: Where Are They—and You—Now?

196 congruence with those: The rise in focus on building resilience has occurred in many quarters, including Greg Lukianoff and Jonathan Haidt, *The Coddling*

of the American Mind: How Good Intentions and Bad Ideas Are Setting Up a Generation for Failure (New York: Penguin, 2019). For a summary of some of the advice on how to build resilience, Boise State University offers a condensed overview. See Boise State University, https://www.boisestate.edu/broncofit/resilience/, accessed Aug. 31, 2023.

197 other life circumstances: As a process built primarily in the United States, of course it may need to be translated for the culture in which a person is working.

Appendix A: Glossary of Pushes and Pulls

207 the force's meaning: Harvard Business School MBA student interviews with Managing Human Capital course alumnus, December 2022 and December 2023.

Appendix E: Ten Common Interview Questions

246 Ten Common Interview Questions: This tool is based largely on the document "What to Say: Answering Common Interview Questions," Guild, https://pages.guildeducation.com/rs/139-BSA-643/images/guild-Answering%20Common%20Interview%20Questions%20%281%29.pdf, accessed Sept. 21, 2023. We also consulted Ethan Bernstein and Amy Ross, "Note on Structured Interviewing," Harvard Business School Publishing, Aug. 20, 2019 (N9-420-032).

INDEX

ABOUT THE AUTHORS

Ethan Bernstein is the Edward W. Conard Associate Professor of Business Administration in the Organizational Behavior unit at the Harvard Business School. He spent five years at the Boston Consulting Group and two years in executive positions at the Consumer Financial Protection Bureau. Bernstein earned a doctorate in management and JD/MBA from Harvard.

Michael B. Horn is the author of *From Reopen to Reinvent* and coauthor of *Disrupting Class*, *Blended*, and *Choosing College*. He is the cofounder of the Clayton Christensen Institute and teaches at the Harvard Graduate School of Education. Cohost of the podcast *Future U.*, he also writes the Substack newsletter The Future of Education and contributes regularly to Forbes.com.

Bob Moesta is a founder, maker, innovator, speaker, and professor. He is the president and founder of the Re-Wired Group, as well as an adjunct lecturer at the Kellogg School of Management at Northwestern and a research fellow at the Clayton Christensen Institute. He is the coauthor of *Choosing College*, *Demand-Side Sales 101*, and *Learning to Build*.

Make Your Move.

Find the tools, templates, and examples mentioned throughout the book at JobMoves.com, including:

- Job Moves Assessment (to Help Determine Your Quest)
- Job Prototypes Template
- Letter Templates (to Ask for an Informational Interview)
- Rank Your Prototypes Tool
- Personal Cheat Sheet Templates
- Career Balance Sheet Examples

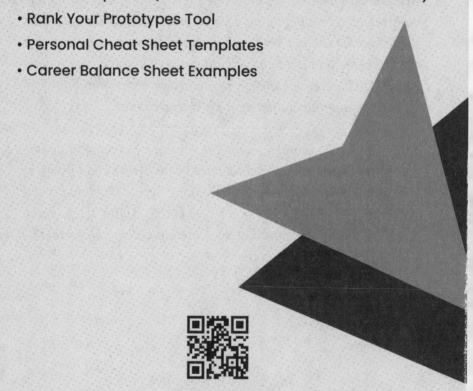

JOBMOVES.COM